NOTHING BUT THE BEST

The Struggle for Perfection

NOTHING BUT THE BEST

at The Juilliard School

JUDITH KOGAN

RANDOM HOUSE NEW YORK

Copyright © 1987 by Judith Kogan
All rights reserved under International and Pan-American
Copyright Conventions. Published in the United States
by Random House, Inc., New York and simultaneously
in Canada by Random House of Canada Limited,
Toronto.

Library of Congress Cataloging-in-Publication Data
Kogan, Judith.
Nothing but the best.
1. Juilliard School.   2. Conservatories of music—
New York (N.Y.)   I. Title.
ML200.8.N52J8   1987   780'.7'297471   86-21965
ISBN 0-394-55514-7

Manufactured in the United States of America
Typography and binding design by J. K. Lambert
98765432
First Edition

TO MY MOTHER

ACKNOWLEDGMENTS

I want to thank all of the people who shared
their stories with me and gave me permission to
use them.

This book covers a period of years. Some of
the stories belong to my days as a student, some
to the present. The book spans the
administration of two Juilliard presidents. The
second brought with him a new administration
and policies. The spirit of Juilliard, however,
remains the same.

JUDITH KOGAN
New York, May 1987

CONTENTS

NOTHING BUT THE BEST

INTRODUCTION

Juilliard is the most famous music school in the world. There, in one building in the heart of New York City, the most promising musical talent converges. The roster of people who have studied there is staggering. Itzhak Perlman went there, and so did Pinchas Zukerman, Leontyne Price, Yo-Yo Ma, James Levine, Emanuel Ax, Philip Glass, Wynton Marsalis and Van Cliburn. Richard Rodgers went there, and so did Miles Davis, Chick Corea, Marvin Hamlisch and Neil Sedaka.

Juilliard is a shrine to young musicians. One calls it his Mount Sinai. Another calls it her Vatican. Juilliard is *the* place to go—for some, the only place. Juilliard is where toddlers trot across concert stages before they can dress themselves and where impresarios scout the greats of tomorrow. Some people call it "the" Juilliard, as if there were impostors.

This was not always the case. For a long time America had no place to train serious musicians. Young American musicians, like young musicians from all over the world, flocked to the conservatories of Europe. At the turn of the century, a man named Frank Damrosch set out to change that. He was a member of New York's most famous musical family. His father, Leopold, a violinist and conductor, had founded the New York Oratorio Society and the New York Symphony, an orchestra that eventually merged with the New York Philharmonic. His brother Walter was also a conductor. Frank, named after his godfather, Franz Liszt, was not as musically gifted as they were, but he shared with them a love for music. He wanted to create a musical life in America as rich as the one in Europe.

He decided to establish a music school that would rival—or improve on —the conservatories of Europe. His school would teach scales but also inspire the students to think of music as a step toward a better life. His music education would involve mind, body and spirit, and produce great performers and great teachers.

He needed money. He approached his friend Andrew Carnegie, whose millions had built the concert hall in the center of New York City. Carnegie refused him. He thought that Damrosch would do more for music by spreading the love of music among "the people" than by establishing an expensive school for those who would become professionals. He wrote to Damrosch's wife, who, along with her husband, pleaded for the endowment, "There can be music so finished as to rob it of feeling. The Great Musician, intense and wrought up in his calling, is very apt to miss what is really uplifting in music. There must be such character, but it is not such I wish to help." Carnegie went so far as to say that he hoped Damrosch would fail in the venture. "I must not have anything to do with this venture because I doubt very much its success, and I don't consider it the best work he can do for the spread of music in this country."

Damrosch persevered. He ultimately persuaded another friend, James Loeb—a pauper compared with Carnegie, but an amateur musician and a member of a wealthy family—to donate five hundred thousand dollars to found the school. He then went to Europe to study the conservatories. Luring teachers from London, Vienna, Berlin and Paris, as well as Boston and Philadelphia, he lined up a renowned faculty. The teachers came partly because he offered huge salaries and partly because his work as a musical patron was well known in both Europe and America.

The Institute of Musical Art, known informally as the Damrosch School, opened in 1905. Its faculty made it the preeminent conservatory in the country. Woodrow Wilson, president of Princeton University and later president of the United States, predicted that the Institute would create an American musical culture. He prophesied that the Institute would soon establish American music and American musicians. "We have not yet any national word to say in the form of music, for America is not yet ready to express itself. It is not sure of itself," he said. "In the United States the springs of sentiment are covered up. If you will but unseal these springs, you will see the real sentiment beneath. Unseal them!"

The Institute was indeed an immediate success. The training offered was unparalleled in America. The standards were high. The students were required to take a core of courses as well as private lessons. They were told how to behave, how to dress and what to do with their free time.

In 1919 a textile merchant named Augustus Juilliard died, leaving a large part of his $20 million estate to the enhancement of musical life in America. A portion of the money was used to establish the Juilliard Graduate School, a new conservatory, to train gifted American musicians tuition-free. The school had a distinguished faculty but was poorly administered. There was no core curriculum, the building used was unsuitable and the head of the school argued with the trustees of the estate over the use of funds.

The Institute proposed a merger with the Graduate School. Each saw the advantage of combining the vision of the one with the wealth of the other. They merged to become the Juilliard School of Music. The doors were opened to people of all nationalities.

The political unrest in Europe fed the school. The Russian Revolution and the rise of fascism brought some of the finest European musicians to America. Refugees from Russia, Vienna and Paris joined the Germans who had dominated musical life in New York. They came from cultures where music was a rich part of the heritage and were willing to work hard. Asian musicians joined them after World War II. Juilliard had become Mecca to musicians from all over the world.

The Institute was first housed in the old Lenox mansion, a three-story brownstone at Fifth Avenue and Twelfth Street, but soon moved to a building at Broadway and 122nd Street, on the edge of Columbia University. The Juilliard Graduate School started in the former Vanderbilt mansion on East Fifty-second Street off Fifth Avenue, then moved next door to the Institute. They became part of the same complex when they merged.

Then, in 1969, Juilliard moved to Lincoln Center. The move was symbolic as well as practical. Lincoln Center was the magnificent new performing arts center on Broadway near the center of town. Juilliard joined the Metropolitan Opera, the New York Philharmonic, the New York City Opera and the New York City Ballet there. It was to train the musicians who would perform on the stages of the halls beside it, as well as on the stages of the great halls of the world.

Juilliard underwent a metamorphosis. It added a drama department, headed by John Houseman. It invigorated its dance department, headed by Martha Hill, and established the American Opera Center. It refined its Pre-College division. It took the preeminent School of American Ballet, headed by George Balanchine, into its home. It cut enrollment, pared the faculty to a uniformly impressive list and shortened its name to The Juilliard School. The Juilliard president announced that the new school would not train musicians who would teach—it would train performers only. Demands for applications soared. Competition stiffened.

The Juilliard president announced that as a music conservatory Juilliard was without peer in the United States and Europe.

Juilliard now has nine hundred students. Seven hundred and fifty of them are music students. They are the subject of this book.

1   THE ATMOSPHERE

"Excuse me," she says. "This is my room."

He doesn't answer.

"Excuse me," she says again.

"I'm sorry," he says. "I've been here forty-five minutes. You can't have it."

He is a pianist. She is a violinist, half his size.

They are on the fourth floor of The Juilliard School. The fourth floor contains the practice rooms. There are rows and rows of them, all nearly uniform cubicles. Most of them house Steinway grands. Heavy velvet curtains cover the walls. Narrow windows on the doors reveal who is practicing in them, but some people prop music stands against them to prevent interruptions and protect anonymity. A reputation is always on the line. Without the scarves and music stands, one "performs" for people in the halls. One sinks into a piece and throws hands from the keys, only to hear a neighbor in the next cubicle echo the passage, two notches faster. The fluorescent lights buzz. The gold carpet dizzies. The air stands still. Some of the rooms have windows to the world outside, but they do not open. The rooms suggest prison cells.

Juilliard students would kill to get one.

"It's mine," she says.

"Come on," he replies, articulating each word as if speaking to a deaf person. "I've been here forty-five minutes."

Empty rooms are hard to find. Some students need the rooms for all their work. Some students who could practice at home refuse to, unable to tune out the distractions that keep them from focused work. One pianist uses a practice room ten hours a day. Another has been known to sleep under a practice-room piano. Some rooms are never vacant because teams of friends monopolize them. The team member who prefers morning practice claims the room the moment the building opens. He joins the early morning crowd in the lobby. At eight the guard nods to tell him he can go up, and he and the others squeeze into the first elevator to open. The doors open at the fourth floor like the starting gate at a horserace. The students break out and dash to their preferred rooms. When a team member wants a break, he turns the room over to another. The first in the lineup may try to reserve a number of rooms by spreading music and clothing around them. The tactic fails, however, unless he runs back and forth between the rooms, practicing a few minutes in each. A practice room vacant for fifteen minutes is up for grabs.

"You've been gone at *least* forty-five minutes," he says.

She looks him dead in the eye. "I refuse to leave."

He lifts his right hand, presses the music back where the pages meet, runs his hand down the page and continues to practice.

"I was only gone five minutes," she says. The edges of her mouth turn down and start to quiver.

He doesn't look up.

Her eyebrows arch. "Are you a student here?"

"As a matter of fact, I'm a teacher."

She walks over to the corner of the room, takes her violin out of the open case, puts it under her chin and starts to practice. He continues to practice as well. She walks back to the corner of the room, returns the violin to the case, strides over to the pianist and starts to push him. She presses lightly at first, and he doesn't budge. So she gives him a full-bodied two-handed shove, as if she were pushing a stubborn bookcase across the floor.

He gets up and leaves. If he were to lay a hand on her, he would hurt her.

"I bet your mother would be proud of this," he shouts from the hall before the door slams shut.

Everything at Juilliard seems to happen in a big way. The building is as stately as a mausoleum. Grand and spacious, it covers more than half a city block and spans the Broadway side lengthwise. It is top-heavy and covered with white Italian marble. It is set at an angle and envelops Alice Tully Hall, a full-size concert hall.

The interior is as imposing as the exterior. One enters Juilliard through a double set of heavy glass doors. Floor-to-ceiling display cases on either side tell the story of what goes on upstairs and down. There are intricate miniature stage sets from theatrical productions. There is a pair of stiff pink ballet slippers suspended from long ribbons and arranged in first position. There are jumbo-sized black-and-white photos of musicians at work. There are manuscripts of faculty composers, some closed, with the composers' names shooting across them like banner headlines, others open to pages that look like Rorschach blots in their flurry of notes cutting up and down the staff. Hardly anyone stops to look at the displays, but they leave the indelible impression that something magnificent and vital is brewing nearby.

Another set of glass doors heralds the lobby itself. The lobby is an uncarpeted cavernous expanse, half of it virtually never used. The space seems to exist for its own sake.

Juilliard extends five stories above ground and four below. It houses three theaters and two rehearsal rooms the size of basketball courts. There are fifteen two-story studios for dance and drama rehearsals, three organ studios, eighty-four practice rooms, twenty-seven classrooms, thirty-five private teaching studios, a recording studio and scenery and costume workshops. The library has 45,000 scores and 18,000 books, 12,000 LP's, twenty-eight phonographs, four cassette machines and four tape decks. The lounge, cafeteria and administrative offices consume an entire floor. The walls are barren. Bright fluorescent lights illuminate the workplaces, and dimmed lights the hallways. Gold, green, red or orange wall-to-wall carpets cover most of the floors. Everything is square corners and wide unused spaces. Those who like the barrenness call this the blank canvas for the creation of art. Those who don't say that the barrenness reflects the coldness of the institution. A hermetic seal wraps the building. No one in the halls seems to speak above a whisper. The sound in the halls is so dead that any who actually do seem to be whispering.

Two middle-aged Jamaican security guards are the only signs of life in the lobby. They sit, with a plump pink-cheeked Irishwoman whose smile warms her corner, at a wood-paneled security desk. A sign beside the desk says:

ID CARDS MUST BE SHOWN TO   GUARD
WHEN ENTERING BUILDING.

The sign does not inhibit those who walk with purpose and avoid eye contact with the guards. The individuals at Juilliard are larger than the institution. Artists live by their own rules.

The visitor is stopped only if there is ample ground for suspicion. An unshaven ponytailed man in soiled white overalls is stopped. He is carrying a guitar case. Juilliard offers no guitar instruction.

He takes a step past the security desk. "Where are you going?" the guard shouts.

"I'm going to the second floor to meet my girlfriend."

"Why are you carrying that instrument?" the guard asks. One wonders whether he is most concerned with what the intruder has carried in, what he might carry out or whether the man is planning to make a practice room his for the afternoon.

The man shrugs.

"This is the last time you get in without a pass," the guard says. He waves the man through, his vacant gaze already fixed back at the doorway.

The lobby is noisiest each hour on the hour. Streams of people click through, en route to and from classes and lessons. The lithe leotard-clad ten-year-old ballerinas cross paths with frail octogenarian professors, the vibrant actors with the sun-starved pianists, the backpack and blue-jean-clad brass players with the poised and painted divas. People convene and cluck away, some in English, others in French or Russian or Korean. There are the chance encounters in the lobby, too: the affectionate embraces between old friends and sweethearts and the dreaded confrontations with jilted lovers and archrivals.

Everyone seems to be in a hurry. There is no time to waste at Juilliard, no opportunity to be missed, no edge to be lost. "Too young" and "too early" are meaningless concepts. Juilliard does not care how old its students are.

Juilliard does not care whether they can tie their shoes, crack an egg or boil a pot of water. Juilliard does not care whether they can screw in a light bulb, mend a fence or feed a cat. Juilliard does not seem to care whether they can put an English sentence together either. Juilliard cares about whether they can do one thing: perform.

One must perform to get in, and one must perform to make the grade there. Anxiety grabs hold and doesn't let go. All day there, one feels one should be practicing, at least to keep the level of playing up. One buries oneself in a practice room for days, unraveling intricate passagework. Snippet by snippet, phrase by phrase. Right hand alone, then left hand alone. In distorted rhythms and distorted phrasing. With a featherlike touch, then a medium touch, then a bulletlike touch. Slow, then a little faster, then a little faster. Some of the practice is mindless. A practicer, cigarette in one hand, slogs through tortuous arpeggios with the other while reclining as if lounging on his living-room sofa. Another moans to a friend about the sorry state of his love life while working his scales up and down the fingerboard. Some of the practice is downright harmful, the relentless hammering away to strengthen the fingers merely hastening the onset of tendinitis. No matter. Time is passing, and the next guy is getting ahead.

The practice bug eats away at students, inside the practice room and out. The chorus rehearsal is no exception. Chorus is a required course for pianists. The first rehearsal is abuzz with restless students. Four bulky Russians in the back of the room pore over tiny little books on piano technique. Three chic Korean girls study a hot new issue of *Musical America*. Six unkempt boys slouch and stretch out, limbs extended in every direction. The conductor goes to the front of the room and claps his hands. The room falls silent. Everyone must sign up for auditions, he says. The auditions are five-minute ordeals to identify them as sopranos, altos, tenors and basses. He says there is a sign-up sheet on the piano behind him, and leaves the room. There are six seconds of deafening quiet. Then there is a lunge for the sheet. A hundred hands zoom like meteors through space, all aiming for the first slot. The one who gets the first slot gets the audition out of the way, leaving uninterrupted time to practice. The sheet, within seconds, is ripped to crumpled shreds.

The student signs an attendance sheet at every chorus rehearsal. The student who plans to cut gets someone to sign him in. (Sometimes he scribbles his name on a piece of paper and forces his cover to practice the signature, but sometimes the cover just prints it to be safe.) The attendance sheet once indicated that 80 percent of the chorus was present, when only 20 percent of the seats were filled. The conductor was forced to crack down. He called out the names of those signed in and sent the registrar a list of those not responding. She sent them notes telling them to show up at a special meeting or risk failing chorus. A failure could lead to repetition of the course, revocation of a scholarship or probation or—in an extreme case—expulsion.

The registrar officiated. "Go to chorus," she said. She didn't slap their wrists. There were too many wrists to slap. And chorus, after all, is only chorus. Rules about chorus attendance—like most rules at Juilliard—are not to be taken too seriously. The rules at Juilliard are made to be bent and broken. Where the exceptional are trained, exceptions must be made.

One student went to chorus only three times. She had good cover, so she got an A. But she regrets that she did not go more often. The chorus sings music she loves and performs in Alice Tully Hall. But mostly she regrets that she failed to take advantage of the forced vacation from practicing. She says chorus was kind of fun. When she was there, her mind could wander.

The level of playing must be kept up not just for artistic and professional reasons but for social reasons, too. Those worth knowing are those on top. The hallways are full of gossip about who is playing what and where and how. The information spawns friendships. The good players are never without friends. "Who do you study with?" and "What are you working on?" probe for clues to proficiency. Some hype their wares at every opportunity. "How are you?" one asks in the hall and gets an update on the strides of the other's career. "Oh, I just played for—don't say anything to anybody, of course—but I just played for some really important managements and they asked me to come back, and this is all very exciting." *The New York Times* reported that one violinist played a piece "with panache." The morning the review appeared, the violinist asked ten people what panache meant.

People know who is who and what is what:

"He's a jerk."

"How do you know?"

"He can't play."

"Did you ever hear him?"

"Well, no, but . . . everyone says that . . ."

The student ambles down the fourth floor. If he hears someone whipping up and down the keyboard, he walks by the practice room nonchalantly. He peeks inside, pretending to be looking for an empty room. If he wants to listen for more than a few seconds, he stands beside the door, out of sight. His first couple of years at Juilliard, he wouldn't dare be seen spying. After that, some confidence gained, he stares in, fixing his gaze right on the target.

"I hate audition time at Juilliard.
The whole building shakes."

Juror walking colleagues to elevator at lunch break

2   THE AUDITION

The audition is the hardest hurdle to jump at Juilliard. It is like
nothing anyone has experienced until then, except for the candidate who is making a second or third attempt to get in.

Auditions are sometimes called "entrance exams" and sometimes
"entrance juries." The jurors are Juilliard faculty members. They
sit in panels of three to five and decide who shall get in and who
shall not. The cello department hears cello auditions, the piano
department hears piano auditions, and so on.

Auditions are held in the fifth-floor studios. The admissions
committee advises each candidate to check in an hour early. A
monitor near the fifth-floor elevators marks him present. The monitor this time around is a first-year student. She is a violinist, a
romantic-looking girl in a pale pink sweatshirt and black spandex
leggings with a pink Madonna bow harnessing her thick brown hair.
She remembers her audition and wants to see how the other side

of the table feels. She asks each candidate to fill out a beige four-by-six card. The card requests a name and mailing address. The pens shake. One candidate notices his trembling hand and grimaces. His teacher has warned him, as a final bit of advice, "Whatever you do, don't let the jury see you're nervous." This wisdom has him shaking even more.

Nearly every candidate wants to know where the bathroom is. Some pay four or five visits. Some complete bathroom business, then decide to run through the audition program there. (Everyone within twenty yards hears the program. The bathroom's acoustics are as live as the inside of a hollow tin drum.) The monitor invites candidates who show up extra early to warm up in a fourth-floor practice room. Some seize the opportunity but later regret that they did. Walking down the fourth-floor corridors often induces an unwelcome psychological setback.

The candidate who heads straight for the audition room returns within minutes to ask where the room is. The fifth floor is a maze of corridors with fire-engine-red studio doors. There are white numbers on the studio doors, but there are studios on the interior and exterior corridors, so the numbers jump as one winds around the maze. The candidate spends five minutes in search of Room 542. With both comfort and trepidation, he comes upon Room 533, sensing at last his proximity to his target. 535, 536, 537. His heartbeat quickens. 539, 540, 541. Pause. 541, and then . . . 576! He returns to the monitor in despair. She pulls a map of the floor from her audition-material packet. If she's running low, she shows him, with a map and freshly sharpened pencil, the route to take.

There are rows of chairs near each audition room. There are folding bridge chairs, cushioned lounge chairs and metal classroom chairs with depressed seats and writing surfaces attached. When the jury runs behind, the row of candidates grows long. They tense up and smile when a grown-up walks by. They do not know what the judges look like. They are extra polite to anyone who might qualify.

Some candidates are auditioning in secret. They want to leave their teachers and schools and have made excuses to slip away for the audition. Some have had to learn the audition program in secret, on top of repertoire already under study.

There are high school students, college students and graduate students. Some come with a teacher, some with a parent. Some come with friends —current Juilliard students—to make them feel part of the family. Their clothes reflect the range of their ages and backgrounds. Some of the boys are in Shetland sweaters, cords and tennis shoes. Others are in dark custom-tailored suits. Some of the girls are in rainbow-colored hair ribbons, frilly white blouses, tartan kilts and shiny flat pumps. Others come bejeweled in silk and satin evening dresses, fingers and toes manicured and painted to match, hair inventively twisted and turned and planted at seductive angles. There is always someone who bucks convention, too. One delicate girl shows up in threadbare jeans, mud-stained basketball sneakers and her boyfriend's lumpy alpaca ski sweater, chewing gum like a cow. Her accompanist, a prim Rumanian girl, is horrified. She offers the candidate her skirt. It is big, but a safety pin could disguise that. The candidate is not the least bit interested. She has dressed this way on purpose. She wants to make herself feel as if there were nothing special about the day.

The candidates eye one another tentatively. Each sizes up the next, like junior high schoolers at their first dance. The first time eyes lock, both look away, embarrassed. When their eyes meet again, inquiry begins.

"You auditioning?" the assertive one asks.

"If I make it through the next half hour," the tentative one replies.

"Yeah, I know what you mean." There is a deathly silence. Half a minute later, the assertive one picks up where he left off. "Where're you from?"

"The West Coast."

"Really?" he says with such animation one might think the entire West Coast had just been swallowed by the Pacific. The intermittent chatter continues. Neither listens to the other. The one who started the conversation talks only to calm his nerves. Anything to distract himself. He feels a mixture of excitement and dread, as if he were at once going to the gallows and the gates of heaven. The tentative one flips through his music, running his hand down the pages as if reading them in braille. At one break in the conversation, virtuosic sounds from behind a heavy red door draw the attention of the candidates. One of them raises his eyebrows. The two who have been conversing chuckle nervously. By now, two others have joined the convention. They, too, smile.

"What're you playing?" the assertive one asks.

"Schumann *Carnaval*, Prokofiev sonata, Beethoven sonata, Bach prelude and fugue."

"Oh yeah?" he says. He too is prepared to play a prelude and fugue. "Which one?"

"I haven't decided yet."

This response casts a pall. One of the candidates not party to the conversation smirks. The one who asked the question doesn't know what to make of the answer. Instead of dwelling on it, he decides to concentrate on his music. He pulls from his briefcase the Urtext edition of the Beethoven sonatas, Volume II.

The handle on the heavy red door clicks and a candidate emerges. All heads in the row of chairs turn.

"Next victim," says the ashen candidate, instructed by the jury to send the next in.

"How'd it go?" someone asks.

"It went."

"How was it? Were they nice?"

"They looked noncommittal." He reflects for a second, slipping into his coat. "They looked like they were on drugs." So does he.

Auditions are mostly cold and businesslike. They are like military trials. The jurors are elderly and distinguished-looking. They sit shoulder to shoulder at long tables. Some look dead from the neck up. Candidate after candidate comes in to plead his case. The jurors scribble on evaluation sheets. Sometimes they whisper to each other. The bored ones rustle papers. The jurors do not address the candidates unless they know them or adore them. The juror who knows a candidate jokes to relax the atmosphere. The juror who adores a candidate asks whom he studies with. But for the most part, silence prevails. One candidate who had flown in from

Vienna auditioned earlier in the day at the Manhattan School of Music, the conservatory in Juilliard's old home. "Oh, my darling," the Manhattan juror had said, scanning his application and trying to put him at ease, "I have cousins from Vienna." (She told the next candidate, a Texan, that she had cousins from Texas.) The candidate broke into tears at his Juilliard audition. The jury sat expressionless while the tears streamed down his cheeks.

Auditions are a mixed bag for the faculty. On the upside, they get to scout new talent. Some candidates come claimed, and some are available only to the three teachers they've listed (in order of preference) on the application, but there is room for bidding. On the downside, they have to sit there three times a year, three days at a time, all morning and all afternoon. And they hear their share of mediocre candidates. (Juilliard does *some* screening: if an application suggests that a candidate is not up to Juilliard standards, the admissions committee recommends "further preparatory study," but most who submit the completed application with the sixty-dollar application fee get to audition.) There is another downside to the auditions. The faculty members must sit with their colleagues, some of them bitter adversaries. Rivalries between faculty members are legion; feuds between some of them, decades old. Some teachers make no secret of their antipathy for others. They disparage them whenever and wherever possible. (That, some say, is why the fifth-floor carpets are red.) Adversaries behave cordially at the auditions, though. Some sit at opposite ends of the room, a buffer between them.

Auditions are short. Candidates are slated fifteen minutes apart, but get no more than ten in the room. (Juries need time to usher them in and out and evaluate them.) The ten minutes include the hello (optional), the tuning of the instrument or adjusting of the bench and the waiting for the jury to decide what to hear. To the candidate, ten minutes feels barely enough time to warm up. To the jury, ten minutes more than suffices to size up a candidate. Some juries are shorter than ten minutes. The duration depends partly on how quickly the candidate impresses or repels the jurors.

Candidates must prepare a whole program of music from choices listed in the catalog. The candidate hands each juror a slip with his chosen program. Each candidate begins with the piece of his choice. One recent Soviet émigré began with a scale. (His Moscow Conservatory juries had always begun with a scale.) The jurors were amused and they started to chuckle and whisper to one another. The candidate was shaken. All these knowledgeable people were laughing at him and jabbering in a foreign language. (The candidate knew one English word: hamburger.) A juror who happened to know some Russian calmed him down, at least enough to finish the audition.

The jury wants to hear what the candidate does with pieces of different styles and periods. In the middle of one piece, he is asked to jump to another. The chairman of the jury does the honors.

"O.K.," he says. Or "O.K., thank you, now may we hear the Beethoven?"

When he has heard enough of the Beethoven, he taps on the table. Edgy candidates warned about the tapping falter at every noise, wondering whether it was a cue to stop. Others ignore even the unmistakable stop signals. The brazen candidate pretends he hasn't heard the tapping and plows ahead. He may just be getting started. He may just have reached the part he thinks will knock the socks off the jury. He may want to impress the jury with his intensity. He may be trying to stall on one piece to avoid getting asked to play another, not half so solidly prepared.

Auditions, to some extent, test a candidate's chops. Chops are technique. Chops are the raw material artists are made from. Chops enable one to play fluently and accurately. Without them, even the most poetic soul sounds like a bumbler. For pianists and string players, chops are sometimes called fingers, as in "He's got great fingers." For wind and brass players, chops are chops, as in "He's got great chops." Those without chops often belittle those with them. They accuse them of having nothing but, of being inferior musicians. Much of this is sour grapes. Chops are merely a means to an end, but they are the sine qua non for those with ambition. They are also among the few things a jury will agree are or are not up to snuff.

———

There are two rounds to voice auditions. In Round One the candidate sings to half the voice faculty in a fifth-floor studio. The other half of the faculty sits in another room, listening to other candidates.

Two things distinguish the voice candidates from the others: how they look and how they act. Singers look and act different from instrumentalists because (some say) they are vulnerable in a way that instrumentalists are not. The singer is his instrument. The singer is judged not only on what he does with his instrument but on the quality of the instrument itself. The voice faculty looks for exceptional voices, exceptional natural endowment. The voice faculty that rejects a candidate seems to say there is a structural defect. Singers are more touchy, more flamboyant, more exuberant than instrumentalists because, in a way, there seems to be more at stake.

The voice auditions are running behind, and the candidates crowd outside the audition room. They look older than the instrumental candidates. They look ultraprofessional. Their faces are broad. Some of them are overweight. The women are in their finest evening attire. They wear dramatic jewelry. They tweeze their eyebrows to oblivion. They paint their faces. They have hairdos. One of them has two very yellow streaks running through salmon-pink hair. Another has a nest of midnight blue on top of her head. They wear decorative pieces—scarves and shawls and sheer jackets—and tinted stockings and suede shoes. The men look professional, too, but less dramatic. Their hair is short and well-groomed. They wear professional suits in conservative colors, mostly grey or charcoal. They wear white shirts and soft ties, cuff links that match their belts, and loafers or wingtips, shoes that spell success.

The jury chairman opens the door. "Next?"

The candidate follows the chairman into the room and waits for him to sit down.

"Hello," the candidate says. He is all neck and barrel chest, too much for even his jacket to contain. He introduces himself, walks down the table and shakes hands with each juror, then returns to where he started and walks down again, handing each juror his audition program. He goes over to the accompanist, shakes his hand and introduces himself again. He believes he must establish rapport with everyone in the room. He has no instrument to hide behind. He has spent years polishing his poise and presentation for just such a moment as this.

He walks to the crook of the piano.

He knows he gets to choose his first piece. He has decided on something upbeat, to get things going. "I would like—if it pleases you—I would like to begin with "Ich Grolle Nicht" from the Schumann *Dichterliebe.*" He bows slightly from the neck.

The jury chairman smiles. The candidate takes this to mean he should begin.

He belts out the first phrase as if he were singing in Carnegie Hall, but he feels as if he were in his aunt's sewing room. He is not loud, he is downright bombastic. On that first note, he flicks his fingers against his palm and thrusts his arm to the heavens to express the intensity of the song. He feels stupid. The jury is two yards in front of him and can see down his throat. A couple of jurors scribble like mad. A couple appear completely unmoved. Those he tries to block out.

He finishes the song. The jurors whisper to one another. One of the old ones doesn't whisper as softly as he thinks he does. "His bottom is very good," he says to the juror on his left, "but his top is very shaky." The candidate pretends he hasn't heard, but all of him starts to shake.

The chairman chooses another song on the audition program. The candidate sings this one to a nick in the plaster above the heads of the jurors. That feels uncomfortable too. So he sings the next song to the EXIT sign, and the one after that to a bouquet of forsythia in a baby-blue ceramic urn on the window seat. The forsythia inspires him more than the EXIT sign and plaster crack combined.

The chairman of the jury checks his watch. "Thank you, thank you very much." The candidate nods. The juror at the left of the chairman elbows him.

"Oh, yes, yes," the chairman whispers apologetically. He looks back at the candidate. "Without telling us with whom," he says, "please tell the jury how long and where you have studied." The singing world is partisan. The voice faculty acknowledges this by asking the candidates to conceal the names of their teachers. The nervous candidate sometimes blurts out the name anyway. The jury pretends it hasn't heard.

One of the jurors writes the information down. "Thank you again," the chairman says. "Go to the registrar at the end of the day to find out whether you have been invited to callbacks."

"Thank *you,*" the candidate says. He collects his music and leaves.

Three minutes pass. The chairman goes to the door to collect another candidate.

A woman with the bearing of the Queen of England follows him in. She is a lyric soprano. She curses God for not making her a tenor, a rare commodity in comparison. She takes one graceful step per second. Her chin is up. There is a 120-degree angle between her chin and collarbone. She stops two feet from the juror nearest the door and smiles the smile she rehearsed at home. She hands each juror a cream colored card with a delicate double blue border framing the engraved audition program. She glides across the room and hands the accompanist her music, then glides to the crook of the piano, concentrating on control over her body.

"You may begin with anything you like," the chairman says.

She nods to the accompanist. The accompanist shrugs. She has forgotten to name the piece.

"Oh, yes," she says, embarrassed, and touches her lips with the three middle fingers of her right hand. She makes the motion at the same speed as she walks. It looks almost deliberate. "I would like to begin with my French song," she says, showing off her diction lessons. She grabs the closed lid of the piano. The pianist feels the vibrations from her hand. He plays the plaintive opening.

Relax, she tells herself. The jury will hear the teeniest bit of tension in my voice. It's just me now, just me on my two little feet. O.K., I need control now from my feet up. She places one foot slightly in front of the other so she doesn't look like a wooden soldier, and shifts her weight to it. The other knee starts to shake. God, she thinks, they're looking at my shaking knee.

She begins the song. She falls short of breath. There is not enough oxygen for the long notes. She gets to *"fleurer,"* a word held two bars— one syllable per bar—but runs out of breath at the end of the first. She breathes so she can finish the word. The moment she inhales, every juror lifts his pencil and starts to scribble.

The breathing lapse aside, things are going well. The French nasals are resonating in the proper part of her head. Her legato is extra smooth. Her sound is floating from the center of her voice in little round circles, the way her teacher says it should. Then, panic. She forgets the words. She doesn't know *exactly* what they mean, so she can't approximate them. She can't stop either. That'll give her away. So she fakes it. Get those French vowel sounds on the long notes, she thinks. She patters up the short running notes with little indistinct syllables, then gets to a long note. She puckers, her lips extended like the bell of a small horn. *"Teux,"* she sings, to rhyme with the *"yeux"* of the previous line. That is the most French sound she knows. She uses it on every long note after that, always hooking a different consonant in front.

The juror near the door asks for her Italian song. The candidate sighs inaudibly. The Italian song is her old standby, the song she has sung for every audition since she was fifteen. But this time something new happens in the middle. Her throat goes as dry as the Mojave Desert. She glances toward the windowsill, fantasizing about a pitcher of ice water behind the baby-blue urn. Nothing there. She considers running out for a sip from the water fountain, but that would draw attention to her dry throat. She doesn't want to keep them waiting either. She rasps through to the end, then smiles broadly.

The chairman thanks her, asks about her training and gives her the registrar spiel. She smiles again, collects her music and leaves, gliding out of the room at the same tempo that she glided in.

The jury recognizes the next candidate. He auditioned last year—and the one before—and sang each time as if his tongue were wrapped around his larynx. That, however, is not why they remember him. They remember him because of the speeches he delivered at the end of each audition.

"I'm training for the Olympic swimming team and haven't had time to practice," he said two years ago to explain why things had not gone well.

"A tornado has just wiped my family out," he said the next.

The chairman thanks the candidate, who wriggles his nose and collects his music from the pianist. It seems for a moment that he will let his performance speak for itself this time. But, one hand on the door, he turns to the jury. "An armed bandit on the subway stole my music. I had to buy new music and that left me no time to warm up."

"I see," the jury chairman says and forgets to tell him about checking in with the registrar at the end of the day.

The registrar refuses to give callback results over the phone. Candidates must meet their fate in the flesh. No one is sure what "end of the day" means, but the first candidates show up around three. By four-thirty there is a small congregation of singers outside the registrar's office. They talk to one another. They tell where they are from, where they study and how much flying to the audition cost them. They look at their watches. They talk about how nervous they are. Everything boils down to one moment, one moment away.

The registrar comes out of her office. She is a stout lady in a pale yellow cashmere sweater, sensible brown tweed skirt and sensible shoes. She is holding an Eberhard Faber No. 1 pencil with a blackened and nearly obliterated eraser.

"I am ready to see people," she announces and returns to her office.

There is a pregnant silence outside the door. One brave soul steps forward. She takes a deep breath and grabs the door handle. The crowd outside stands quiet. She emerges a minute and a half later with damp eyes.

The lambs go in one by one. Some come out flushed. Some come out smiling. Some come out bouncing, as if they've been shot up with speed. Some come out numb. They walk past the people they chatted with for the last hour as if they were invisible.

The candidate who sang to the EXIT sign and baby-blue urn goes in. He tells the registrar his name. She checks her list.

"We don't see your name on the list," she says.

"What does that mean?"

"That means we're no longer considering your application. Thank you very much for coming. I'm sure they enjoyed your singing."

His music starts to slide from his grip. He grabs it just before it falls and leaves the office.

Twenty seconds later the office door whips open and the registrar shoots past the crowd. She gallops down two short hallways, recklessly turning the corners, then reaches the long corridor with the elevator at the other end.

She spots the candidate down at the elevator. "Excuse me, excuse me," she calls down the corridor. The burnt-orange corridor, lit by buried spotlights, is large enough for an army flank twenty men wide and a hundred men deep. The candidate doesn't hear her. He touches the heat-activated down button. The orange ring around it lights up.

"Wait a minute, wait a minute," she calls to him, running, her left hand clutching her glasses against her chest, her right hand waving a piece of paper, her nylons swishing against each other like sandpaper.

"There has been an error, there has been an error," she cries, breathless. He turns. He realizes she is calling him. He takes two steps away from the elevator toward her.

She catches her breath and walks quickly to him. "So sorry, so sorry," she says. "I was looking at the *morning* audition sheet. You were on the *afternoon.* Come back to my office. We'll find you a slot for tomorrow." Callbacks are tomorrow.

He goes with her. There is only one slot left open.

"I'll take it," he says, although it is the undesirable first slot of the day.

In the morning he takes the elevator down to Level B, three floors below street level. That gets him to the backstage of the Juilliard Theater, where Round Two is held. The Juilliard Theater is wide and deep, with red carpets, nearly a thousand shiny black seats and a balcony that starts far back. Juilliard stages opera, drama and dance productions there. When he arrives, the house lights are dim, the stage lights are on. *La Bohème* closed last night, and the stage crew is dismantling the Parisian café set, patisserie and all. Hammers and drills and blocks of falling wood echo backstage. It smells like sawdust. The candidate pulls his audition letter out of the front flap of his *Don Giovanni* score to make sure he's in the right place.

The chairman of the jury, a different one from yesterday's, comes backstage. He tells the candidate the voice faculty is in the house, ready to hear him. "Are you nervous?" he asks.

"Yes. I think I have every right to be, don't you?" The candidate is referring in part to yesterdays' emotional roller coaster. The chairman, of course, knows nothing about it.

"There's no reason to be nervous," he says blithely and taps the candidate's elbow.

The candidate points to a doughy man in military green overalls with a power tool drilling at ninety decibels.

The chairman looks for the stage manager. "Joe," he yells to the wings, stage left. Joe peeks from behind a curtain. The chairman motions for him to come over.

Joe ambles over. The chairman wraps an arm around his shoulders. They talk for half a minute before Joe returns to the other side of the stage. Two workmen wheel a grand piano out on a Y-shaped metal contraption two inches off the ground. They stop right under the center spotlight and take the piano off.

The chairman grabs the banister, descends the steps along the right side of the stage and walks toward his seat. Halfway down the aisle he pivots toward the stage. "Joe, tell the workmen to quiet down. We're going to do auditions." In fifteen seconds there is utter silence. The candidate backstage, who is nearsighted, takes off his glasses so he can't see the jurors from the stage. Head up, shoulders back, he breathes deep and heads across the stage, his accompanist three steps behind. He stops dead under the spot.

"Joe," the chairman calls from the resonant back of the house, "do you think we can drop a curtain to match this young man's blazer?"

Three seconds later a blue velour curtain drops.

———————

Auditions for conductors pose problems beyond those of instrumental and voice auditions. Most of the conducting candidates have never before stood in front of a full-sized orchestra. They tend to be older than the instrumental candidates but far less experienced at their "instrument." Some of them have waved batons in high school and some at music camps, but the experience for most is new. Preparation is a problem. Despite the hours spent standing before the stereo conducting Herbert von Karajan and the Vienna Philharmonic, the conductor is largely helpless without an assembly of live bodies. And his awesome task first begins when the bodies assemble. The conductor's instrument has hearts and minds of its own, as many as there are players. He must unify them, then sculpt to his taste. He must know how to work with people, and he must be able to withstand the scrutiny of one hundred colleagues at a time. The career of a conductor paralyzed by the harsh gaze of an orchestra will end before it begins.

There are two rounds to conducting auditions. In Round One each candidate gets five minutes to conduct a piece of chamber music: the Schubert octet for strings and winds. Chamber music is rarely conducted in concert, but this exercise gives the judge (the head of the conducting department) a sense of what each candidate can do. An octet of students paid five dollars an hour plays snippets of the piece for each candidate. The candidates show up in clusters and sit in a vestibule near the audition room, each waiting his turn to go in. The judge periodically comes into the vestibule. He tells the candidates he is more interested in how they work with the group—whether they can hear problems and make constructive suggestions—than in whether they can run straight through the piece. He is looking for potential: candidates with acute ears, expressive gestures and something to say.

There are always some Juilliard students who want to switch to the conducting department. They know what to expect at the audition. They know the judge plants wrong notes in the score to test the candidate's ear. They know what the audition room feels like. If nothing else, they know that the level of playing will be high. Uninitiated candidates leave the first round stunned by the quality of the playing they have just heard. "They're so good!" one candidate exclaimed, retrieving his bags from the vestibule, "I didn't have to tell them *anything!*"

Of all the conducting candidates, under ten make the finals. Each one who does gets fifteen minutes to show what he can do with a real orchestra: the Juilliard Orchestra.

An entire rehearsal is set aside for the auditions. Each candidate comes prepared to conduct Brahms's First Symphony, Copland's *Appalachian Spring* and Haydn's Ninety-third Symphony.

The judge once again looks for potential. But in this round, potential seems as difficult to detect as the likelihood that an infant chosen at random from a nursery will one day be president of the United States. Candidates are nervous beyond terror. The conducting auditions make those upstairs look like homey little parlor run-throughs.

The unathletic candidate up on the podium feels as if he is simultaneously up at bat and out in left field. He starts the last movement of the Brahms by cuing the trombones, one of the only instruments that don't play at the start. When the trombones miss their entrance minutes later, he can't find them in the sea of faces to tell them so. He calls the cellos the violins. They look at him blankly. He blanches. "What are you?" he asks. He looks back at the score and sees that he has read "violoncello," but not past the third syllable. His mouth dries up. He is so tense his hands don't shake, but they don't move either. His senses overload. The candidate with perfect pitch often can't hear note mistakes. One of them who didn't trust his ears decided before the audition what was likely to go wrong. "You'd be surprised," he says, packing his bags to leave. "It sometimes doesn't."

The atmosphere is tense. The orchestra is attentive and respectful. The players have all been through the Juilliard audition. They know these are fifteen of the most decisive minutes in each candidate's life. As each candidate takes his turn on the Room 309 podium, the others sit outside. A monitor makes sure they do not eavesdrop on the audition in progress and tries to put them at ease.

"Yes, they put traps in," the monitor tells a candidate, "but they're very obvious."

One waiting candidate, cradling a fancy German score under his arm, sits and mutters to himself in some exotic accent while fiddling with his shiny Tiffany cuff links. This intimidates the daylights out of a skinny young candidate from down South, a beanpole with braces who wonders to himself what he's doing there. Not just where he got the gall to apply, but whether he should head for the exit. Before he decides what move to make, the heavy black back door to 309 pops open. One candidate out. The door slams shut behind him. The orchestra bursts into gales of laughter over the nervous tic that had him flicking his head back, like a punctuation mark, at the end of every sentence. Next candidate in. He passes through the narrow aisle between the violas and cellos. His heart thumps thunderously. He hops onto the podium. His bouncy confident manner belies the terror beneath.

He starts with the piece of his choice and gets five minutes of that, uninterrupted. (Two if he's doing poorly.) Then the judge asks him to jump to another piece or another spot.

He does. There is a wrong note planted in the second clarinet. He misses it.

"Did you hear a wrong note?" the judge asks.

If he hasn't, the moment is scary. As scary as running through a room full of furniture in total darkness. He knows something is wrong but doesn't know what. A guessing game begins. Over one hundred musicians are witness.

He takes a stab. "Second trumpet, you're sharp."

"No," the judge says politely.

"First trumpet, you're flat."

"No," the judge says politely again. The candidate fantasizes about a switch to a trapdoor that will enable him to disappear into the podium.

The questions come flying. "Excuse me, did you hear a wrong entrance?" "Excuse me, can you go back and tune the winds?" The candidate tries to, but his neck muscles are so tense he cannot hear. The intonation problems are painfully obvious.

"Deaf," the judge writes on his evaluation sheet.

The next candidate has prepared an interpretation of the first move-ment of the Brahms where the volume drops dramatically at the eighth bar so the orchestra can make a big crescendo—a huge swell in volume —into the ninth. The first time through, the orchestra fails to drop the volume. He motions for them to stop.

"On the eighth bar," he says with dramatic authority when the room falls silent, "it has to come down a bit so we can make a smell." He realizes the faux pas even before the word has left his lips. The atmosphere is tense. The orchestra has played seven auditions. But a split second after the word "smell" fills the air, the orchestra breaks up. The judge breaks up. The candidate breaks up. "I didn't say that on purpose," he assures the orches-tra.

The incident defuses the tension. Everyone relaxes, even the candidate.

Composition candidates don't have auditions, they have "interviews." Each candidate must submit, as part of his application, every piece he has written in the previous two years. (The faculty is not interested in tapes of the pieces, but they, too, are sent in.) The faculty invites each of the most promising candidates for "an interview." A member of the Juilliard composition department—the elder statesman of American composers— ushers him in. The rest of the clan is sitting there, informally spread around.

One of them is at the piano.

The interview turns out to be neither an interview nor an audition, but a test. First, an ear-training test. The composer at the piano plays a note and tells the candidate what it is. Then he plays a series of others for the candidate to identify. After that he plays intervals. After that, chords.

Next, a repertoire test. The composer at the piano plays a few bars from the slow movement of a classical concerto.

"Beethoven Third Piano Concerto, second movement," says the candi-date, a pianist himself.

Correct. The clues get tougher. The composer plays a single chord.

" 'Pathétique'!" he blurts out, pleased as punch.

Correct again. Next, a four-bar phrase from a baroque work.

"Saint Matthew Passion." He is batting a thousand. He tries to resist it, but is overcome by the sudden sensation that he might possibly have the entire store of Western music literature at his fingertips.

Next, a symphony. Eight bars.

The candidate squints, as if his ocular muscles will jog the appropriate gear in his musical memory bank. "Sounds like Schubert," he says, unable to identify the piece.

There is no response. Just another eight bars, from another piece.

"Sounds like mid-to-late Tchaikovsky."

"Good guess," the composer says. "It's Sibelius, but I can see why you'd guess Tchaikovsky."

This is not a game of "Name That Tune." The players don't accumulate points for right answers and suffer penalties for wrong ones. One of the composers, his elbow propped on the right arm of the tweed sofa and his head resting on the knuckles of his right fist, tells the candidate that his wrong answers may be as satisfactory as his right for revealing that he understands music literature.

This candidate is prepared. He has spent an entire month listening to recordings of the standard literature. A friend who took the exam last year warned him what to expect. His friend came to the so-called interview prepared to discuss his scores and hold forth on his theories about composition. He had a flawless ear and knew music literature cold. But he walked into the room, looked around, and, recognizing the faces of his jurors from books and music and newspapers, got completely flustered. He recognized every interval, chord and excerpt but couldn't name a single one.

The prepared candidate thinks the composers behave like a chummy bunch of Ivy League professors. He feels as if they want to get to know him.

The composer at the piano plays an eight-bar phrase from the first movement of a classical string quartet. The candidate knows the quartet but can't remember whether it's Mozart or Haydn.

"Perfect fourth," he says haltingly to himself but audibly, referring to the interval the main theme is built on.

The men laugh.

The composer plays eight bars of "Smoke Gets in Your Eyes," in French Impressionist style, accompanied by parallel dominant ninth and half-diminished chords.

The candidate knows "Smoke" no better than he knows the Purdue University fight song.

"Debussy," he says.

The composer plays a final eight bars.

The candidate stares at his freshly polished oxfords in silence, as if the answer were faintly scrawled between the creases. He rewinds the mental tape and replays the phrase in his memory twice. "Sounds like good Tchaikovsky or terrible Brahms," he says, so relaxed by now that he feels like an old chum of the jurors.

The composer identifies the excerpt as an obscure moment from the third act of *Tristan and Isolde*. The candidate snaps his fingers in dismay. *Tristan* was the one opera he thought he could identify in his sleep.

The candidate is thanked and ushered from the room.

The candidate passes the monitor on his way to the elevator. He wants to know when he'll hear the results. He asks whom he can call. She, as instructed by the administration, tells him not to call, please. The verdict, she says, will be in the mail within the week.

What goes on inside the audition room is sometimes less important than what goes on outside. Before the formal audition some candidates audition for a faculty member privately. If the teacher and the candidate get on, the candidate is at an advantage when he comes to the formal audition. Acceptance by some teachers in a private audition virtually guarantees admission to the school. One teacher auditions candidates when he is on the road and writes to Juilliard naming those he wants. Virtually any teacher can advise the candidate as to the dos and don'ts of auditioning at Juilliard. He can create a warm atmosphere at the audition and barter for his candidate. If his candidate does poorly, he can tell the jury that the candidate's mother has been ill.

The alliance eases the aftermath too. The endorsed candidate need not sweat over the verdict for two weeks. His teacher can follow him out of the audition—or call that evening—to let him know how he has done.

There is sometimes a price to be paid. Teachers often want to run a trial lesson or lessons before committing themselves to a student. The teachers charge up to two hundred dollars an hour. Some charge impoverished students less than the regular rate, but no fee is too high. The value of artistic advice (or edge) is impossible to pinpoint. The law of supply and demand controls. In the case of Juilliard teachers, the supply is small and the demand is big.

The real challenge is not getting a commitment from a teacher. The real challenge is getting a commitment from the *right* teacher.

Alexander was one of the best young pianists in South Africa. He had won virtually every prize available to a young South African musician. Alexander thought of South Africa as the tip of the world and longed to be where the action was. He had heard about Juilliard as a child. If he could get in and cut it there, he thought, a world-class career would be his on a golden platter. The prominent musicians he knew in South Africa had cushy lives. They had servants and estates and concerts whenever and wherever they liked. A world-class career, he thought, would be that, ten times over.

Alexander's father worked for a diamond export company. The summer Alexander finished high school, the company transferred his father to New York. Alexander applied to Juilliard his first week in the United States.

The application asked for preferred teachers. Alexander didn't recognize the names of any of the piano teachers in the catalog. He was afraid of getting a teacher he didn't like, so he called a South African friend who had studied in New York. His friend didn't know any Juilliard teachers either, but he gave Alexander the name of someone he thought did, someone, he said, who knew the New York piano scene inside out. Alexander called the man, who recommended two teachers. One of the names suddenly rang a bell. He remembered the horror stories he had heard. He didn't remember where or when he had heard them, but her name evoked a vivid image. Alexander pictured a giant luna moth flying around a student whose hands were tied behind his back. The moth was spitting rope, constructing a tight elaborate case no light could penetrate. Yes, he remembered. She was said to manipulate her students. She was said to keep them in cocoons, so they would always have to rely on her. The intensity of the slander piqued his interest.

He called her. Her line was busy, so he called the other teacher. Alexander introduced himself, then stammered. "I'm calling because I would like to study with you," he said. He had wanted to say something more original. He felt very clumsy. He blushed.

"Who told you to call me?" the teacher asked.

Alexander felt she was trying to unnerve him. He wasn't going to let her put him on the defensive. He mentioned the name of the man.

She didn't recognize the name. "So you don't know any of my students, and you don't know my teaching," she said.

"True," Alexander replied, "but I'd like to meet you and play for you."

She was not yet ready to set up an appointment. "I have a very good friend in South Africa named Hedda Markov," she said. Hedda Markov had been a childhood neighbor of her late husband.

Alexander said he didn't know a Hedda Markov.

"What?" she responded, incredulous. "You don't know her? You don't know Hedda Markov? But *everyone* in music in South Africa knows Hedda Markov!"

"Well, I don't," Alexander said.

Hedda Markov *is* a powerful figure in musical circles in South Africa —but in Johannesburg, not Capetown, where he is from. The two cities are a thousand miles apart.

"Well, you can come play for me," the teacher said finally, "but I'm completely full." Teachers often claim to be full, then invite people to audition for them. Some want to appear desirable. Some want a graceful means to reject a candidate who turns out to be a dud. The teacher who loses interest during the audition sometimes tells the candidate that he will be kept in mind should an opening arise. If the candidate is a real prize, the teacher always seems to find room immediately.

"And if you come play for me," the teacher added, "that'll be fifty dollars."

Alexander was irritated by the tenor of the conversation, and outraged at the fee. He had never paid more than five dollars for a lesson in South Africa. This was merely an audition.

"Well, if you're completely full, there seems no reason to play for you," Alexander said.

"Well, uh . . ."

"Thank you very much," he said. "Good-bye."

Alexander left the application spaces asking for desired teachers blank. He was admitted to Juilliard and didn't like the teacher he was assigned to, so in the middle of the year he once again called the teacher he had spoken with and asked whether he could schedule an audition. This time he was prepared to hear that her class was full and knew what to say. A friend of his, someone he thought knew the ropes, had prepped him. "If she starts to talk about her class being full," he had said, "tell her you'd slit your wrists to study with her."

The teacher remembered Alexander's earlier call and agreed to hear him. She didn't say anything about a full class. He said he'd remember to bring the fifty-dollar check. She didn't say anything about that, either.

Alexander walked into her apartment. There were toy pianos all over the place, as small as thimbles and as large as telephones. Some were so flimsy they looked as if they had come from Cracker Jack boxes. Some were so delicate and exquisite they looked as if they had been hand-carved and painted with dyes from exotic berries. Alexander dropped his sheepskin coat and Danish book bag on the sofa and sat down at the piano. There were two Steinway grands, side by side. Alexander sat at the slightly larger of the two, the one nearer the door. The teacher was in the kitchen fiddling with an electronic gadget that made a gravelly noise, a Cuisinart or an automatic garbage disposal. Eventually she came out and sat down at the other piano.

"So," she said and sighed and reviewed what she knew about him.

Two minutes later the doorbell rang.

"This is what happens when I try to be nice," she said, exasperated. Alexander imagined that there must be something missing in her life, something perpetually eating away at the lining of her stomach, like an acid.

"I could come back another time," he said. She told him to wait a moment.

A perky little black-haired girl was at the door. The teacher talked to her mostly in whispers, then ushered her into the sitting room.

Her attention returned to Alexander, who was sitting at the piano. His hands were resting in his lap awkwardly. His fingers were clenched in loose fists, as if each held a piece of chalk. The backs of his hands were parallel to the ceiling. He was sitting so straight, his back looked like a board. He had wanted to doodle at the keyboard while she was at the door but decided that would be bad form.

"She has a concert in three days," the teacher explained, walking back to the piano, "but I'm going to hear you anyway." Alexander felt as if she had just said, "The world is about to blow up, but I will hear you until it does."

The teacher heard him for ten minutes, then talked with him for ten more about his pianistic strengths and weaknesses. She finished her exposition neatly, then segued into the coda, the subject of taking him on as a student. She said she never took students from other teachers, but she would make an exception in his case, if he could wait until the fall.

"Fine," Alexander said and handed her the check. She handed it back.

Johanna had studied privately with a man on the Juilliard faculty. She auditioned for Juilliard, intending, if she got in, to continue with him there.

Her teacher followed her out of the audition and called her aside. "The audition went extremely well, very solid," he whispered, adding that he was pretty sure she would get in. Johanna was beaming. Then he told her he had just decided to take a sabbatical from Juilliard.

Johanna was crestfallen.

He recommended that she study with another man on the jury.

"I don't know anything about him," she said.

Her teacher said he would talk to him.

Johanna left Juilliard dizzy with mixed feelings. She ambled across Broadway to John's Coffee Shop. She had sat dazed on the red-cushioned swivel counter stool for no more than five minutes when the man her teacher had recommended wandered in and sat down beside her. Johanna tried to ignore him. It was very uncomfortable. He ordered a hamburger with onions. The hamburger came, and he opened his mouth as if to say "Aaaaah" for a dentist and took a big bite. He turned to Johanna, the sautéed onions all over his chin.

"So, I hear you want to study with me," he said.

"I really don't know," Johanna responded. "I don't know anything about you. I wanted to continue with my teacher."

Boris wanted the violin teacher with a big reputation back home in the Soviet Union. Her students compete in the Tchaikovsky Competition in Moscow. Bootleg tapes of some of her former students circulate through the Soviet music underground.

Boris and his family arrived in New York in late August. His father worried that if he didn't act quickly, Boris would lose an entire school year, so he immediately got in touch with another family of émigré musicians. One of his most valuable possessions was a list of telephone numbers of Soviet émigrés in New York, a list he kept in his passport. He had opened and closed the passport so often, the paper was stained and crumpled, but the numbers were still legible. A teenage girl answered the phone. She said the Juilliard application deadline had passed but that auditions were being held the next week. Boris's father thanked her quickly but kindly. "Send my love to the family," he said.

Boris wasn't ready for an audition. He and his family didn't have a home yet. They were living in a run-down Brooklyn hotel, courtesy of the United States Immigration and Naturalization Agency. Boris didn't have proper audition clothes either. There happened to be a white shirt in the hotel closet—something to replace the blue T-shirt he had worn for three solid months—but its sleeves were too short to move his bow arm comfortably. Worst of all, his violin wasn't exactly fit for an audition. The Soviet Union forbids émigrés to take precious possessions out of the country. Boris left his good violin with relatives in Moscow and took one that sounded like a strung-up cigar box.

Boris and his father hopped a subway to Juilliard anyway. They spent the entire ride standing at the subway map, running their index fingers along the different-colored routes. When they got out at Broadway and Sixty-sixth Street, they spotted Juilliard and went straight to the office where applications were processed. A secretary managed to find a student who spoke Russian, a boy who happened to study with the teacher Boris wanted. He called his teacher to arrange an audition for Boris. The audition was that evening. The good feeling was mutual.

The Juilliard audition was the next week. The teacher followed Boris out of the room.

"Everything went fine," she said. "I'll see you when school starts."

*"Every hour spent doing something else
could be spent practicing."*

A Juilliard piano teacher

3 THE PRESSURES

*The raucous buzz of his alarm clock wakes him at seven-fifteen every
morning. He keeps it set to ring at seven-thirty, but he keeps the clock
fifteen minutes fast. That way he gets to at least some of his appointments on time. It takes him time to focus when he wakes up, and
when he's not focused, he forgets that the clock is set fast. He can
see, through the sliver of window the draped madras tablecloth has
not obscured, that it's foggy outside. The thick menacing fog that
hovered over the city yesterday hovers there still. His stomach and
headache remind him of the greasy fries and Miller High Life he ate
and drank last night. He shouldn't have been out so late. He's trying
to keep a curfew. If he's not strict with himself, his practice gets
off-schedule and unfocused. Unfocused practice is better than none,
he thinks, but not by much.*

*He remembers once when he was in high school he prepared for
an English exam in front of the TV set, watching a Yankee–Red Sox*

double header. He was studying Othello, *trying to memorize Othello's soliloquy that opens Act V, Scene II, the climactic bedroom scene where Othello murders Desdemona, mistakenly believing that she has been un-faithful to him. In the speech, Othello reveals his thoughts just before the murder. The violinist got the words to the soliloquy down, but when he tried to write the exam, his associations were all wrong. "It is the cause, it is the cause," referring to Desdemona's presumed infidelity, made him think of the ninth-inning clutch strikeout that stranded three Yankee base runners. "Put out the light, and then put out the light," referring to Desdemona's bedside light and life, made him think of the series of Red Sox batters who could have ended the game with one timely base hit, putting out the hundreds of floodlights illuminating Fenway Park.*

Whenever he wakes up in this shape, he curses himself.

"Goddammit," he mutters and tries to muster the strength to get out of bed and over to the medicine cabinet to grab a couple of aspirin.

Whether he struggles out of bed or lies there daydreaming depends on the day of the week, the demands of his schedule. Today is Monday. Tomorrow is his violin lesson. There is catching up to do, almost a week's worth. The weekend was full of distractions. A buddy from the Aspen Music Festival flew in to New York on Thursday for a Friday audition and stayed for the weekend, camping out on the living-room sofa. They went out drinking every night, talking shop and reminiscing about the summer, like two depressed old men recounting the glories of their high school varsity football championship season.

He is a first-year student at Juilliard. He gets a dull knotty stomach, a nervous but excited feeling, when he wakes up in the morning. He loves Juilliard. He feels he's at the center of the musical universe. Even Juilliard's telephone number puts it in the middle of things. 799-5000. 799, the Lincoln Center area exchange. 5000, the numerical center of four-digit numbers. He lives at Broadway and Seventy-first Street, five blocks north of the school, but thinks of Lincoln Center as his campus. He doesn't use Lincoln Center much (outside of Juilliard), but its presence in his backyard, as he calls it, suggests the possibilities. Lincoln Center is like the donkey's carrot. It gives him something to aspire to. Something that seems well within reach.

It's not just the buildings. It's the people, too, the stream of famous musicians coming to Juilliard: the composers coaching their works, the conductors conducting the works that made them famous, the students moving into the big leagues. He's starting to feel like a colleague of theirs. He can't call himself a full-fledged colleague yet, but he feels more like a colleague than a student. A colleague-in-embryo, perhaps. Itzhak Perlman comes to Juilliard and advises the crowd gathered to hear him talk, "If you have a Carnegie Hall concert on March third, it's not a good idea to play in Avery Fisher Hall on March second." The young violinist pictures himself on the Carnegie Hall stage, then on the Avery Fisher Hall stage. As Perlman talks, the youngster's violin sits at his side in its sturdy canvas-covered rectangular case. He is never without it. Except, that is, when he goes drinking at night.

He feels like a burning mass of latent brilliance. The possibilities seem limitless. He compares himself to a golf ball. When he was ten, he and a bunch of friends found a dirty golf ball, took it to his house, and peeled it open with a steak knife. Under the hard white rind was a long skinny elastic wrapped tight around a rock-hard center. The elastic and the nucleus give the ball momentum and keep it traveling after it bounces. Juilliard exists, he says, to peel the rind off him, tighten the elastic and rewrap the rind.

The feeling of distinction is nothing new, only more pronounced than it's been. His parents planted the seeds years ago. His teachers nourished it. His admission to Juilliard fortified it. He still considers himself only partly formed, but moving closer to completion every day. He can't describe the goal, but says he'll know when he is there. He brings a real sense of purpose into the practice room. He is free of financial and other mundane concerns, free to immerse himself in his work, just like a concert artist with managers and agents and lawyers looking after his bank accounts and recording contracts.

His life seems magic. His week revolves around his violin lesson, an hour with his teacher, a link with generations of artists. She keeps the tradition alive through her dedication to passing it on to him and his friends. He has chosen a few role models at school. He calls them "the kids who can play." He studies them from a distance: their style of playing and dressing, their manner of talking with teachers and friends. He has started to walk like one of them, a measured gait, shoulders back, fiddle case slung over the shoulder on a detachable belt. The gait is a little on the slow side, slow enough to feel the beat between the actual steps. It is the gait of one who won't be hurried, one who knows what he's about, one perhaps a little world-weary. The gait doesn't suit the nineteen-year-old. He is too slight. His shoulders are too narrow, and his eyes too nervous.

He should force himself out of bed, but he dallies, contemplating the day ahead. A three-hour orchestra rehearsal will kill the afternoon. An ear-training class at nine-thirty will break up the morning. He needs a solid block of time to do practice of any value.

"Goddammit," he says under his breath.

He considers cutting ear training. If he cuts, his grade drops a point. He's pissed off at the new grading system in ear training. He's allowed only two unexcused absences. Every absence beyond that, his grade drops a point. To get his absence excused, before class he'd have to turn in a teacher's note saying he's off playing a concert. Or turn in a note afterward from a doctor. He's in a dilemma. He can't tell his teacher he needs an excuse because he's behind in his practice. He can't afford a doctor. He can't cut ear training because his scholarship hinges on his passing the course. If he loses his scholarship, half of the $6,500 tuition, he'll have to leave school.

"Goddammit," he says, this time aloud. He'll go to ear training.

He remembers that he forgot to do his laundry. He has only two clean shirts left. The olive-green turtleneck has a half-dollar-sized hole in the right armpit. The blue oxford buttondown is missing a button on the left cuff. He decides to wear the turtleneck. It's more comfortable for practice than the button-down, and he can wear a sweater to hide the hole. He'll wear the button-down for his lesson tomorrow, rolling up the left sleeve. The next day he'll do his laundry.

He leaps out of bed. "Right," he says and nods, even though there's no one to nod to.

He saunters into school at eight-fifteen. He is early enough to find an empty practice room. He chooses Room 467, a room without a piano on the corridor farthest from the elevator. This way he minimizes interruptions. This way no pianist will barge into his room and ask if he'll trade that room for one without a piano. His room has a window facing Broadway. The window doesn't open, but he doesn't care. The sun has come out and is streaming through the shatterproof glass, embracing him in its wide soothing rays. It is a fine substitute for the morning coffee he had no time to stop for.

He puts his fiddle case on the handsome wooden chair in the corner, unzips the canvas cover, snaps the case open and lifts his fiddle from its soft velvet cranberry-colored resting place. With the middle finger of his left hand, the hand holding the violin, he strums the four strings lightly. He's learned this one-handed trick watching the older students. It's second nature by now.

He releases the bow from the upper stirrup of the case, tightens the bow hair, flops the bow on the fiddle and starts to tune. He walks around the room while he tunes. He can tune in his sleep. The perfect fifths are in his system. He decides the bow needs a fresh coat of rosin. He lays the fiddle at an angle on the partitions of the open case and rosins the bow. The excess rosin flies off the rosin cake and pollutes the air with a heavy acrid smell, like something from the woods. That sticky pine stuff. Not a pleasant smell, but not downright repellent either. The odor dissipates.

He stands erect facing the window, his back to the door. Practice begins. He is calm. Practicing calms him as nothing else does. Practicing keeps his fear at bay and fuels his fantasy.

A musician is the hardest thing in the world to be. If you want to do something easy, one musician says, become a brain surgeon.

A musician spends most of his life in a practice room. No one pays him to practice. No one talks to him while he practices. No one even hears him practice. If his practicing goes well, maybe someone will think him worthy to be heard one day. Maybe. If he's lucky.

Music isn't simply his work. It is his life. His personal and professional lives meld together. He lives from concert to concert. The buzz of the alarm clock at 7:30 A.M. and the mug of beer at 11:00 P.M. are bookends on his day, but there is no order to his weeks. There is no weekend. His is not a nine-to-five job, followed by playtime with family and friends. His workplace is his play place, his work clothes are his play clothes. Stress in his personal life shows in his playing. Stress in his professional life shows at home. Emotional jolts threaten his work, so that even if he finds time for relationships, he keeps them at arm's length. At curtain time, come hell or high water, he must go onstage and project cool confidence.

He must constantly consider what others think. He doesn't want to pander to his audience, but if he pleases only himself, there's no point playing outside his living room. If he doesn't reach his audience, he fails almost by definition.

If he's lucky, he gets to live in airports and out of suitcases. He goes onstage in strange cities to play his guts out for a thousand people he doesn't know, to return to an empty hotel room to rest up to catch a plane the next morning to another strange city to perform for another thousand people he doesn't know, to return to another empty hotel room. His relationships blossom and prosper or falter and die by mail or by phone. His family grows up in his absence. Between his arrival at the airport and the rehearsal, he practices. Between the practice session and rehearsal, he prays. He prays the concert goes well, so he can repeat the cycle the next season.

Nothing is certain. Any moment he could break a finger. When his fingers are in shape, his mind could fail. He walks onstage with no guarantee that he'll be able to summon a piece of music from the recesses of his memory, or that his nerves will be calm enough to allow him to play the intricate passagework. The sounds that enrapture him may bore or offend an audience. When things are going poorly, he's only as good as his last review. When things are going well, there's no guarantee for the future. As sure as day follows night, an ambitious talented upstart will be waiting in the wings. Audiences are fickle. Everyone loves a rising star. The star takes its place in the firmament, and the audience starts looking around for the next.

His faith and his doubt are in a constant tug-of-war. A good review or encouraging word strengthens his faith. A negative word or silence eats away at it. He needs both. The first gives him confidence to project total conviction. The second gives him critical distance. He must sustain the delicate balance between them. The fact of life in music is that the doubts are bound to outweigh the boosts. The musician's ego is huge but fragile. To protect it from constant assault, he builds a fortress, fortified by people and things that nourish the faith and deflect the assaults. If he does this successfully—and plays masterfully and has something special to say—he's got a shot at a career.

Juilliard is a training ground where the distinction between student and professional blurs.

At times Juilliard seems less a school than a collection of people who happen to do the same thing. The students don't live together and don't work together. Anonymity is easy to come by. In some ways, Juilliard students are like commuters who meet on a train platform at the same time each morning and disperse when the train pulls in at the final stop.

There are no movies, no clubs and no athletic facilities. Once upon a time there was a Ping-Pong table on the fourth floor, but throngs crowded the table from two o'clock every afternoon until the building closed at ten in the evening. The students demolished three tables in a row, and the administration stopped replacing them.

The student who knows what he's about and what he wants derives wonderful things from Juilliard. The student who doesn't may be in trouble. The dean told *The New York Times,* "Juilliard cannot perform its ordained function and be a center for musical therapy. It may seem brutal, but it behooves us to let students know when we don't think they are going to make it." The thing is, Juilliard never tells anyone directly. It lets them figure it out for themselves. Juilliard in fact leaves its students pretty much alone. It doesn't even require much of them, other than a fifteen-minute jury at the end of the year and a passing grade in courses that demand little more than attendance.

There is a frenzy of competitive activity and a plethora of big egos. In the shuffle, those without a strong identity or sense of purpose become invisible. The Big J, they call Juilliard. Big J, little you.

People at Juilliard seem to think that students at any other conservatory (except, maybe, the Curtis Institute of Music in Philadelphia) couldn't get into Juilliard and therefore can't play. The administration perpetuates the elitism. There was once a campaign to print Juilliard T-shirts and sweat-shirts. The administration repeatedly rejected the proposals. The Juilliard name was meant to be embossed on diplomas and carved and painted in gold leaf on the building facade, not printed on garments one sweats in. An administrator once summoned a student who noted in his concert-program biography that he studied "at Juilliard." The proper way to identify the school, the administrator said, is The Juilliard School. Capital T, capital J, capital S.

Juilliard is the universe where the world starts and stops. Its windows sealed, Juilliard is cut off from the world even physically. The tie that binds is music, and the force that creates order is ability. Some invisible hand ranks people. Ability loosely corresponds to technical proficiency. In some ways, the focus on ability blinds people to music itself. In some ways, music is appreciated not as something beautiful but as a tool of commerce. Professional motivation is more important than artistic, the glamour of personality more important than the art of music. Juilliard sometimes seems little more than a series of board games. On the basic board are axes for teachers and for students, each running the spectrum from best to worst:

The players are the students. The object is to reach the throne. Each instrument has a different grid. The "best" student on each grid—the best student of the "best" teacher—sits on the throne in the upper left-hand corner. The "best" teacher has students clustered on his left side. (His rank drops as his students drift to the right.) Student rank rests on proximity to the throne. The second best student of the best teacher (one step from the throne) is on a par with the best student of the second best teacher (also one step from the throne). The best student of the third best teacher (two steps from the throne) is on a par with the second best student of the second best teacher. (No diagonal moves allowed.) A competition victory, a big concert, a fancy endorsement, and the player moves a step (or more, depending on the luster of the achievement) closer to the throne.

The kings and queens of each grid compete at Championship Juilliard. Championship Juilliard is a glorified game of Giant Steps. Advancement again hinges on the luster of achievement. There is a schedule of points: more points for soloing with a major symphony orchestra than for getting onto the roster of a major manager, more points for winning a big competition than for soloing with a second-tier orchestra, more points for a live radio recital than for a chamber music concert in Carnegie Recital Hall. Nonsolo instruments are at something of a disadvantage at Championship

Juilliard: they have limited opportunity to excel in these domains. Well, that's the way of the world.

Under the pressure, a fair amount of denial goes on. Some of the denial prevents distraction. Most protects morale.

The Juilliard student excludes from his life anything that might detract from his work. "Tunnel vision" is the operative concept. He builds a shell around himself and his instrument. No books, no plays, no museums. Television only if mindless. Only classical music. Only classical music directly related to his. Violinists don't go to clarinet recitals, and flutists don't go to cello recitals. One tubist who goes to piano recitals always gets asked what she's doing there. Pianists and violinists don't even go to piano and violin recitals, unless the performer is a close friend or reputed superstar. Then they go to hear one piece and leave.

Those who play one of the big three—piano, violin and cello—focus practice on solo literature. They, at least at first, plan on solo careers. Anything less, they believe, represents failure. Those who play wind and brass instruments focus on solo repertoire and orchestral excerpts. They plan on careers in major symphony orchestras. Everyone practices to build facility and accumulate repertoire. Any other demands—even musical ones—are annoying distractions. Pianists fulfill the chamber music requirement with undemanding accompanying or soloistic sonata-playing. Theory and ear training are considered classes to be endured. Music history is considered worthwhile only when it deals with the pieces the students play. Little is expected in the classrooms. Teachers spoon-feed students and apologize for minimal demands. Tests insult the intelligence. Cheating is commonplace. Despite one teacher's warning to test-taking students that "this is not chamber music," cheating seems almost acceptable.

Social life is strange. On the one hand, students are drawn to one another by common goals and problems. They are like members of a fanatic sect. But these devotees are not equal in the eyes of the Juilliard god, so alliances yield tension as often as solace. Talk of success rankles friends who always consider the news in light of their own circumstance. Sensitivity and suspicion are heightened. Intimates one day don't acknowledge each other the next.

Social life is confined largely to those who do the same thing at the same level of proficiency. They are easy to identify. At Juilliard, one is known by (1) the instrument one plays, (2) how well one plays, and (3) who teaches one. Information beyond that is mere detail. Musicians are notoriously insular. A women's magazine once published an informal survey of "stand-out" parties, an article called "The Best (and Worst) of Times." At the top of the "worst" list:

A party with only classical musicians—and me. Everyone who talked to me began with: "And what do you play?" When I said I wasn't a musician, no one wanted to talk to me at all.

Identification with the instrument is strong. Some students refer to others by its name. They say Jimmy Piano goes out with Tanya Flute and Peter Cello lives with Mark Violin. For some, the instrument is a crutch. They can't function without it in hand.

The psychological denial protects morale. If nothing succeeds like success, nothing weakens like failure. Subjects that reveal vulnerability— anxiety over memory or physical problems, for example—are taboo. Some people refuse to admit that a performance went badly, or, if it clearly did, that they were responsible. To admit this would be to raise the question of whether they've got the goods. They justify their little failures to keep their doubts from paralyzing them:

"I'm not getting any breaks."

"I didn't have time to practice."

"She slept her way to the top."

"They didn't like the pieces I played."

"He sucks up like there's no tomorrow."

"The judge eliminated me because I was a threat to his student."

"The judge eliminated me because I play better than he does."

The explanations sometimes contain an element of truth. Even when they don't, the people who offer them often believe them. They latch onto people and ideas that support the theories, turning and returning to them in moments of doubt. When they don't believe them, they sometimes articulate them to convince themselves, or others. The public's perception is critical. The musician sells himself in street-corner conversation just as he sells himself across the footlights.

Negative press reviews are hard to take. They are public and seem to have an unimpeachable credibility. The review is the scorecard. Students take bad reviews personally, then explain them away. A *New York Times* critic panned the performance of one student. The morning the review appeared, the performer penned this ominous letter to the critic:

> Thank you for your constructive criticism.
> We will see you soon. Bye-bye.

He signed and sent the letter, then dwelled on the review nonstop. He discussed it with teachers and friends and concluded that it was negative because the critic was married to a woman who had been married to his teacher. He therefore could not *possibly* have listened objectively. He believes the critic may even have written the review before the concert.

One student has the whole thing figured out. "Face it," he says, "music is a business like any other. You start with your product: talent. After that, it's all capital and marketing. Some people would slit their grandmother's throat to get ahead, but that's not necessary." He has a formula. "There are three ingredients in building a career: talent, money and ass-kissing. You can go somewhere on one. You can go pretty far on two. On three, the sky's the limit."

"Talent you either do or don't have," he says, "but you can play concerts even without it. You get money from some nice person. It can buy an instrument to make an arthritic sound like a virtuoso. The New York

Philharmonic may not engage you, but you can rent halls for recitals. Enough money buys publicity to lure people to your concerts. The critics who can't be bought don't matter. Advertising can counteract any damage they do. Money comes from ass-kissing. I know it sounds gross, but it's not half as bad as it sounds. It just means putting yourself in the right place at the right time and relying on what you've relied on your whole life: your personality. With a forte on the charming side."

Some say that anyone at Juilliard who plays his cards right gets what he wants. One student told a friend about a series of successes that fell her way like dominoes.

"My God," the friend said, "what luck!"

"I don't believe in luck," she responded, "I believe in creating opportunities."

There is a student who says he lied and cheated his way into passing grades when necessary. He would scribble the "do-re-mi" syllables in his book before doing a "quiz performance" in front of his ear-training class.

The administration was looking for a pianist to tour Europe as soloist with the Juilliard Orchestra, and this student was recommended. The president's secretary called him to arrange an appointment. He walked into the president's office, shook his hand and sat down. The president came straight to the point. "We're looking for a pianist to tour Europe with the Juilliard Orchestra," he said. "Do you know the Rachmaninoff Third Piano Concerto?"

"Yes," the student lied. "In fact, I've performed it with four different orchestras in Europe." He left the office and headed for the library to take the piece out. The president called him a week later to say he had been chosen to do the tour.

There is a student who decided his name would be a stumbling block. John P. Jones, Jr., came to Juilliard straight from the backwaters of the sun belt. He had fallen in love with music reading *Reader's Digest* opera plots on his grandmother's front porch. He did his early performing playing the piano in funeral and pizza parlors. His first two years at Juilliard he was a piano major, buried in practice rooms eight hours a day. Then he took on a second major, conducting. Conducting brought him into contact with people. He became aware of the potential for influence and the importance of image. "This is a performance school," he says. "You perform from the moment you walk in, with what you wear and how you look and what you say. For me, the competition is eight A.M. to ten P.M. That may be sick, but that's how it is."

He lost thirty pounds. He traded in his Coke-bottle glasses for tinted contacts, his Levi jeans for designer pants. Then he traded in his name. John P. Jones, Jr., became Peter Jones. (Peter was his middle name.) But Peter Jones was satisfactory for only so long. Jones seemed too flaccid for a concert artist. His teacher agreed a change was in order.

She and John Peter Jones, Jr., sat down together one fateful afternoon. The scene was straight out of Hollywood. The sun was setting, the rays bouncing off the Hudson River into the living room of the teacher's Riverside Drive apartment. The walls were covered with signed photographs of legendary pianists. The cracked white paint on the decorative molding suggested that some of the pianists might once have inhabited that very room. The air was full of Chanel No. 5. Lilies and orchids adorned the windowsill. The elderly teacher settled into her armchair and lit her antique floor lamp. Then, in her inimitable style, she talked to her student. She talked about her childhood and former students, her concert career and torrid love affairs. Between anecdotes, they tried out names. "Peter," they decided, would become the surname. They looked for a resonant first name. They wrote each name on a strip of paper, then held the paper up to the light.

They started with John, his given name, the logical place to start. First they tried the French and German equivalents. They rejected the French Jean, afraid that people would pronounce it like an American girl's name. Johann was too closely associated with Bach. They tried Jaan, but worried people would opt for the J rather than the Y sound. They moved across the Continent. Juan, Janos, Ivan. *Gian!* They liked the ring, but Gian needed a smooth cadence. John Peter, they thought . . . Gianpietro. No, too bumpy. Gianluca, Giancarlo, Gianfranco, *Gianmarco!* Gianmarco Pietro. The scan was wrong again. Peter, *Petrarco. Gianmarco Petrarco.* It looked right and sounded right. Gianmarco Petrarco. Lyrical and exotic, dapper and dynamic. They smiled. The teacher hoisted herself up from her chair and walked her student to the door. She craned her neck and tilted her head, beckoning for a kiss. He gave her a peck on the right cheek. All the way home he rehearsed his new name.

The immediate forebears of Gianmarco Petrarco are Scotch-Irish. He thinks he may discover an obscure Italian relative, but even if not, no sweat. Changed names, he says, are the rule in Hollywood. Classical musicians change names, too. Van Cliburn, he says, changed his name. He thinks Vladimir Horowitz did, too.

"Higher, Faster, Louder" is the Juilliard Fight Song. It was written by a bass player on his commutes between Brooklyn and Juilliard on the Seventh Avenue subway. The song is set to the tune of "Sharp Dressed Man," written by ZZ Top and recorded on their best-selling album, *Eliminator.* ZZ Top is a heavy-metal rock group of three obese Texans with beards down to their bellies and perpetual who-stole-my-beer scowls on their foreheads. The composer of "Higher, Faster, Louder" thinks they are everything performing artists should be.

Juilliard has no football team. The song is to be sung where the Juilliard action is: in the hallways, the elevators and outside fifth-floor studios, before lessons.

Higher, Faster, Louder, or The Juilliard Fight Song
(To the tune of "Sharp Dressed Man," by ZZ Top.
Note: a steady quarter $\quarternote = 72$) beats throughout.
The beat is critical, the melody less so.)

First chair, Prix de Rome,
Critics said I had exquisite tone.

Sing "la," perfect pitch,
Always knows just where 440 hits.

(Chorus)
We play as loud and as fast as we can
'Cause the whole world's crazy for a Juilliard man.

(Guitar and drum riff, with rhythmic grunts)
Competition, second round,
Grinnin' as I put my colleagues down.

Quartet, Galimir,
Looks good on my transcript when I'm
gone from here.

(Chorus)
We play as loud and as fast as we can
'Cause the whole world's crazy for a Juilliard man.

(Guitar and drum riff with rhythmic grunts.
Fiddle solo, Tchaikovsky violin concerto cadenzas
ad libitum, with electric guitar vamping in.)

Solfège, Boulanger,
They all try to make us think their way.

Well I'm glad, God damn,
I started music in a ga-rage band.

(Chorus)
They don't know what kind of background
we've had,

Still the whole world hungers for the
Juilliard grad.

(Guitar and drum riff, with rhythmic grunts.)
Show your ID *(on the last shimmer of the
brush on the cymbals.)*

Time passes, and the practice-room scene gets bleaker and bleaker. The
new students catch on to the fourth-floor felonies and become conspirators
in them. Rooms become tighter and tighter as year-end juries approach.
There are eighty-four practice rooms for 750 students. Locating an empty
one becomes an awesome challenge. One student, frustrated by the absence of vacant rooms on the floor, begs his buddy to let him use his room's
second piano to run through the Liszt sonata just before his lesson. His
buddy says O.K., and the Liszt weaves a tight dissonant web with the Bach
Goldberg Variations already under surgery in there. Some students organ-
ize to petition the administration to extend the hours the building is open
during the week and to open the building on Sundays, sealing off all but
the fourth floor. The administration rejects the proposal on the ground
that heating and security costs would be prohibitive. One student suggests,
as an alternative, that Juilliard admit fewer pianists.
    The floors and walls and pianos, shampooed and painted and polished
during the summer, become soiled and finger-smudged, scrawled with
graffiti. Body odor and cigarette smoke pollute the unventilated rooms.
The curtains absorb the stench. Smokers use the three top and three
bottom piano keys as ashtrays for burning cigarettes and flick the butts into
the pianos or rub them into the carpets. Potato chips caught in cracks
between piano keys emit stale odors. Juice cartons and valve-oil tubes litter
the baseboards of the walls. Milky coffee rings on piano ledges loop in
interlocking ring patterns. The piano technician—a balding German who
always wears a bow tie—circles the floor several times a day, reminding
students that food and drink are not allowed in the practice rooms. They
discard the snacks only to return with replacements. The cleaning woman

who scrapes and vacuums the fourth-floor pigsties at the end of each day
calls the students a bunch of spoiled brats. The security guard says they
worry too much about their lessons. Half of the fluorescent lights in one
room go out. The soundproofing tiles in another room collapse, and a
cellist is mortified to learn that the entire floor has been audience to her
tortured double thirds. A pianist overhears the conversation and decides
to make the room his for the rest of the year. He practices with the lid
open to full stick.

The hours under the fluorescent lights in the airless rooms drive the
cloistered crazy. There is a rumor that someone has planted a razor blade
between the piano keys in one room. In another a near-violent argument
erupts over whether a certain trill in a Bach partita should start on the
upper note. The dispute evolves into one over the "tackiness" of playing
each section of the partita softer in the repeat. Someone comes in wailing
about how boring slow movements are. Some carve on the piano keyboard
lids. Others chip away at them. An unhinged student in a fit of anger kicks
a five-inch-deep hole in the plaster wall of a room. In other rooms, frustrated souls deface walls with declarations of love, illustrations of the
female anatomy and dirty limericks with musical angles or punch lines:

A handsome young fiddler from Rio
While seducing a girl in his trio
Went and slid down her panties,
When she squealed, "No andantes,
I want this allegro con brio."

The mystery word SKEET screams in black letters across entire practice-
room walls. Few know what it means, but most assume it is dirty. (One
guy who doesn't know what it means says he scribbled it for amusement.)
One wall covered with Russian profanity has a drawing entitled "Lenin's
Daughter," a picture of a bearded man with a beaky nose and receding
chin. Another wall says, "Drummer, a homosexual sado-masochism magazine, would like to do a spread on you," urging the interested to meet at
a stated date and time in the Juilliard lobby. Someone has responded to

the obscenities on that wall, "Why don't you all just concentrate on the love in the heart that was given to you and that you were meant to give to others"—and drawn an arrow to an addendum at an angle several inches below—"instead of acting like lunatics."

But they practice, mindless of the change of seasons, oblivious to the world beyond the practice-room walls. They call the institution "The Jailyard School," but they tuck themselves in the fourth-floor cells, convinced they must be there. Practicing is an integral part of living for them, different from eating and breathing only in that they ate and breathed before they walked. They practice because practice gives them security. A passage practiced thirty times feels more secure than one practiced twenty. The cost of not practicing can be enormous. If you don't practice one day, you lose a day. If you don't practice two, you lose a week. Or, as Heifetz said, if he doesn't practice one day, he knows it. If he doesn't practice two, the critics know it. If he doesn't practice three, the world knows it. At Juilliard there is additional incentive. Practicing enables the students to tune out the world: the hassles of life in New York City, the agony of adolescence and young adulthood, the pain of a shaky or battered ego, the unpredictability of a course in an unstable profession, where one can pick up the instrument and sound heavenly one day and hellish the next. And they practice because if they leave—even for a bathroom break—they never know whether the room will be empty when they return.

Not everyone makes it through. There are casualties, students who can't deal with life in New York, life without a built-in support system. Some who have spent their lives in practice rooms suddenly have to interact with people and can't tell a good person from a bad. Some can't deal with the scene in the hallways, where people guard their space and avert their eyes rather than say hello. Some are psyched out by the competition. Some would rather not bother with classwork, so with massive incompletes or failing grades on their records, they are asked to leave, or choose to leave, convinced that the lack of a Juilliard degree will not affect their careers. Some drop out, sensing that their rightful place is outside the classical-music mainstream. Miles Davis spent nights during his term at Juilliard in Harlem and midtown jazz clubs, listening to Charlie Parker, Thelonious

Monk and Dizzy Gillespie, and the next days in Juilliard practice rooms trying to reproduce the chord changes he had scribbled on matchbook covers. He told his father to save his money, that he wasn't going to join any symphony orchestra, and left. Neil Sedaka failed a keyboard harmony class, burned the scores he was forced to read in the class and took a six-month leave of absence. His mother said, "If nothing happens with your pop music in six months, you must return to school." Something did, and he didn't. Some grow disillusioned with a scene where technical polish seems to count more than anything. One girl left Juilliard because she believed that no one there valued her intellectual gifts. Some find that not even a magnetic personality compensates for lack of musical muscle. Some who leave are extremely talented but unable to adjust to the notion that they will not be the next Itzhak Perlman or Yo-Yo Ma. One left when a new young hotshot replaced him in his teacher's affection. Some play better when they enter than when they leave. Some ease out slowly. They stop practicing, stop going to classes, spend entire days eating ice cream or drinking beer and talking to friends. Some stop going to lessons, or go to them on one day's preparation. Most who leave, leave disenchanted, their dreams of stardom punctured early.

But for those who stay, the dream is somewhere kept alive.

It's ten-fifteen. The practice day is over. At ten every evening the security guard does the rounds. He knocks on the doors of practice rooms to signal the closing of the building. The tired practicers pack up. The desperate ones squeeze in an extra minute or two until the guard comes around on his final check.

The violinist who checked into Room 467 at eight-fifteen in the morning leaves at the first signal. He's done over seven hours up there, plus three in orchestra. Enough for one day.

He agrees to go out for coffee with a friend. She is another first-year student, another student of his teacher. He shouldn't go, really. He should go home, relax and go to sleep. His lesson tomorrow is at noon. He's wired from all the hours under the white lights. Caffeine will pump him up even more and keep him awake until two or three in the morning. He says he would like to go for a beer, but then remembers the weekend's indulgence. That was bad, but at least that was the weekend. Today is Monday. So they head off—he leads the way—to the Rhapsody Restaurant, a Greek diner at Broadway and Sixty-seventh Street. The waitresses know him. One of them, with jet-black teased hair, no (apparent) bottom teeth and a ketchup-stained white apron, brings two cups of coffee to the table and smiles.

"Hi, Marie," he says.

She winks. Her brusqueness and the clatter of coffee cups, salad bowls and utensils suggest there's no time for chit-chat. She disappears through the swinging saloon doors to the kitchen.

His friend across the wooden booth, her arms and legs twisted like a pretzel, is lost in her obsession of the week: life after Juilliard.

"If you don't become a world-class soloist," she asks him, "will it be a great letdown?"

He rips the aluminum-lined paper top off the hard plastic tub of nondairy creamer and dumps the contents in his cup. The coffee rises to the rim. "I don't think about it that way," he says. "I imagine myself standing in front of orchestras playing concerts. Everywhere." The fantasy is striking because he has never stood in front of an orchestra anywhere.

He takes a sip of coffee, returns the cup to the saucer and explains the way things have to be. "To be a world-class soloist, you can't walk around as a youngster thinking it might not happen. Otherwise, you can't go all the way. You have to walk around thinking, Of course!" He sits up, his eyes bright. He smiles.

"What happens when you're thirty, and things aren't going as you planned?" she asks.

He lifts the stainless-steel spoon from his saucer and balances the end between his thumb and index finger. He presses and releases with his thumb so the spoon rocks back and forth across the callused first knuckle of his index finger. "I would feel my time hadn't come."

"What when you're forty?" she asks.

His eyes shoot to the door, then back to her. "Rubinstein started when he was forty." There is a moment of silence. He returns the spoon to the saucer. "He did, didn't he?"

"To be the best, he must get the best."

A Juilliard mother

4 THE PRE-COLLEGE DIVISION

The woman is in a restaurant. She takes the last bite of her cheese-and-egg casserole, lays her fork on the edge of her plate and lifts her napkin to dab her lips. She leans forward to whisper.

"God commanded me to do it," she says, explaining why she started her child on the piano at age four. "God gave him the talent. God left it to me to take it from there."

The explanations run the gamut. A favorite is that the four-year-old asked for lessons. No four-year-old asks for piano lessons. He may show an affinity for the instrument, even some skill. In the crib, he may wiggle his fingers in sequence. At two, he may gallop to a Chopin polonaise. At three, he may pick out the notes to "Happy Birthday" on the piano. The parent at this point detects a Horowitz in the making. The parent who says the four-year-old asked for lessons has plans for him.

"Parent" at the Juilliard Pre-College Division means mother.

The mother sometimes comes with a father, sometimes even with grand-parents. Generally, though, it's a one-woman operation.

The Juilliard mother is a strange breed. She is not the classic stage mother who sells her kid to soap companies and carts him to every *Annie* and *Oliver!* audition around. Stage mothers are a dime a dozen. There are always roles for a child to fill and products for him to sell, a ready-made market awaiting a fresh face. The child star's career may be lucrative, even if brief.

Not so the young classical musician's. His career is never lucrative and rarely brief. He must postpone his childhood. He must start practicing his scales as soon as he can sit upright on the piano bench. No one can resist a nine-year-old tossing off Liszt's Mephisto Waltz, but only so many can marvel at him before he is nine no longer. The novelty wears thin. The critics are suspicious. They've seen the show before.

The Juilliard mother knows the obstacles but is determined. Her child will be the best. "I've never liked mediocrity," the woman in the restaurant confesses. She sacrifices her time and money, her energy and friends. Nothing worth having comes easy. He is sent to Juilliard, and she becomes a Juilliard mother.

She is actually not a bona fide Juilliard mother unless she accompanies him for the lessons and classes that consume most of Saturday. She does not sit at the wheel of the station wagon waiting for him to emerge. She, like him, works on his career. He works in the classrooms and practice rooms, she works in the lounge and lobby. She compares notes with the other mothers. One of them, fed up with another's boasting about her son, decided to silence the woman by demonstrating that her own son—also a pianist—had a thing or two to offer. She brought a tape of Horowitz playing some of his knuckle-breaking encores to the lounge the next week. In the middle of a friendly debate on the longevity of nylon stockings, she turned to the woman. "Would you like to hear some of a concert Michael played last week?" she asked, the play button sinking deeper with each word. The woman had no chance to remember that she had to run down to put a quarter in the parking meter, so they listened to the tape. The woman agreed that the boy, at the very least, had good fingers.

The Juilliard mother studies the competition. She knows the recitals to check out, the teachers that are hot and the competitions to go after. She knows because she can't help overhearing conversations between students and teachers, teachers and teachers, students and students, and the coat-room lady and the security guard. On Saturday there is no rest before sundown.

The glass-encased sign at the second-floor elevators says NO PARENTS ALLOWED ABOVE THE SECOND FLOOR. The mother slips past the sign and into an up elevator. She gets out on the fifth floor and winds around to the studio where her child takes his lessons. She waits outside, sitting cross-legged at the foot of the door, an ear to the door and an eye on her watch. Five minutes before the hour she stands up. On the hour the door opens. She smiles innocently.

Practice and promotion, promotion and practice. The schoolboy knows his three R's. The Juilliard mother knows her two P's.

The Juilliard mother knows that a proper day of practice requires her presence throughout. Her musical sophistication has little to do with her usefulness. Her presence comforts the child and helps his concentration.

The mother makes sure that the child does enough practice. (The Pre-College says a daily minimum of four hours.) An early morning start is critical for the development of iron fingers and an iron constitution. The first task of the day is to get the child out of bed and into the practice room. This requires no physical contact with the child, only a solid set of vocal cords.

The first round of reveille comes from the doorway to the child's bedroom. "David, it's time to practice." This is "Good morning" and "Get to work" in her argot. If David is not at the piano within five minutes (allowing toothbrush and travel time) the shouts come, like labor contractions, at shorter and shorter intervals.

"David, I don't hear you." She calls from far enough away that David cannot easily reply that he's halfway there or not feeling well. If David is not at the keyboard within five minutes after that, the next call punctures the air. Then, no matter how ill he feels, he scrambles out of bed just to avoid another call.

The mother often tries to get the child out of school early. If the school board is unsympathetic, she considers other options. One had her daughter practice during the lunch hour at the home of a friend who lived near the school. Every day at noon, the mother packed the car with a tuna sandwich and cello, picked her daughter up, practiced with her and returned her to school. The arrangement worked out for the best. The full day at school enabled the girl to compete academically, guaranteeing her admission to an elite college. This was insurance. The Juilliard mother knows that an injury or a failure to attract the right people can nip a promising career in the bud. She has faith, but understands the obstacles to building a concert career.

She knows that the artist gets nowhere on art alone. He must promote himself—or be promoted—to be recognized. Promotion, to the Juilliard mother, involves (a) knowing the right people and (b) getting them to see that her child is special. The first right person to know is the right teacher. Right teachers have connections. Connected Pre-College teachers tend to be connected to the administration. The contact never hurts.

The Juilliard mother devises schemes to set her child apart from the rest. The goal is to "out-prodigy" the competition. Two ingredients combine to make up a prodigy: skill and youth. The mother can do only so much about the skill, so she works on the youth. She keeps her child looking young. One dressed her two girls in nursery clothes. As the girls got older the dress hems rose and the knee socks fell. At sixteen the buxom girls performed in sausage curls, party dresses and Mary Janes. But even stranger than the get-up was what each birthday did to them: every birthday they grew a year younger.

The Juilliard mother reveres the private teacher but feels that he fails to push her child (and his career) sufficiently. She realizes that the teacher has many students and that the endorsement of one can preclude the endorsement of another. So she lends a hand. She watches her child develop and calls a conference when something looks amiss. She asks the teacher why her child is studying Beethoven's First Piano Concerto when another child in his stable—a year younger—is studying the Second.

Some Juilliard mothers believe that reverence for the teacher is misplaced. They believe that reverence, if appropriate at all, should flow from the teacher to the child. Leonard Bernstein reportedly called one Pre-College cellist who soloed with the New York Philharmonic "the next generation's Casals." The boy's mother, conveying this to his teacher, said she was pleased that her son had put him on the map. (The teacher himself had soloed with the Philharmonic a dozen times by then.)

The Juilliard mother protects her child from the evil that would undo him. Sports are discouraged. Sports devour practice time, threaten his hands, and expose him to seedy elements of society. Nonmusical friends are discouraged too. Nonmusical friends corrupt. The child is not to see how the other half lives.

The Pre-College girl has just done five hours of practice.

"Mommy," she says, "I want to go to the school dance tonight."

"You can't," her mother says.

"Why not?"

"Because you're a violinist."

"What difference does that make?"

"They don't understand you."

"They're my friends!"

"Well, they shouldn't be."

The woman in the restaurant straightens her index finger, lines up the bread crumbs near her plate and sighs wistfully. Her children are all grown.

"Just think of all the things I might have done during those years," she says. But she had a mission. "Raising children is like cultivating a garden —only, children are more complex than flowers. They need more than a bath and pruning. They must be taught values and ethics, and their talents must be nurtured. The parent must make sacrifices to raise the child. If she gets some pleasure along the way, well, that's nice, but that's not the point."

"You want your child to succeed," she says and motions for the waiter to bring the check. "A little success and the world smiles on you."

Pre-College is in session on Saturdays. The rest of the week Pre-College students go to regular school. They are between eight and eighteen years old.

Most Pre-College students consider Saturday the most important day of the week. It gives them a break from the tedium of regular school. It is the culmination of a week of practice. And they get to be around children with lives like theirs.

Pre-College students call the regular division of Juilliard the Upper School. They think the Upper School is vicious. Their teachers tell them it's really competitive, and their mothers often encourage them to go somewhere else after high school. One Pre-College student says the only thing that counts in the Upper School is being Number One. "It doesn't even matter if you're nice," she says.

Some people say that Pre-College students play better than the Upper School students. Pre-College standards are sky-high. And enthusiasm and innocence compensate for what, if anything, the Pre-College students lack in insight and technique.

The Pre-College once had children with parents intent on exposing them to the finer things in life. They went to the Pre-College the way they went to New York Philharmonic Young People's concerts and Broadway shows and had tennis and ballet lessons. Pre-College standards are now so high, especially for pianists and string players, there is little room for dilettantes.

Pre-College students not only sound professional but come with the mannerisms of world-weary concert artists. A tiny nine-year-old girl clicks in her black patent-leather pumps across the Juilliard Theater stage to play a Mozart concerto in a Pre-College competition. She is wearing a blue velvet dress with a white sash and Peter Pan collar and is carrying a white hankie. The air is still. Her footsteps puncture the silence and echo in the hall. She sits down at the shiny Steinway concert grand, twists the bench knobs until the seat is all the way up, runs her hankie from the top to the bottom of the keyboard and places it in the corner of the piano. She plays an earnest and flawless first movement, lifts the hankie and runs it across her palms and brow as she has seen grown men do. Another girl sits down at the keyboard, places her hands in her lap and stares at them, concentrated and poised. Her performance is full of wrong notes and memory lapses, but her head and body move as if the piece were welded to her. A boy gets so excited when he practices, he gets up and bows at the end of his pieces. Some of the boys wear silk cravats. Their hands pop out to shake the hands of all slightly older people. Alone with friends, they show off scars and romp around like little beasts. Around someone who matters, they click into professional gear.

A wunderkind of truly extraordinary gifts comes to the Pre-College every now and then. Word of the wunderkind's advent travels like wildfire. The mother hens—the teachers, the parents and the power brokers—gather around the nest and coo. They want to be sure the chick emerges from her delicate shell with her talent intact. They say they want her to lead a normal life.

The life of one such fourteen-year-old includes, so far, a stage name, the glitziest manager in the world, and publicity photos where she looks like a porcelain doll. Her Saturday-afternoon Juilliard recital draws an overflow crowd that includes heavyweights from *The New York Times* and the New York Philharmonic. She has performed for the President and the First Lady. Her performance at Tanglewood in the summer of 1986 is preceded by a photo with Leonard Bernstein on the front page of the *New York Post* and followed by a front-page photo and article in *The New York Times*. Her father lives halfway around the world.

She is obsessed with Snoopy. Snoopy is plastered all over her bedroom, her socks and sneakers, her mug and fork and spoon, her violin case and her music bag. The infatuation does little, however, to obscure the plain truth: Midori is no ordinary fourteen-year-old.

Midori is the newest entry in the child-prodigy register. Her professional name used to be Mi Dori, her full name split in two, but now she is simply Midori, à la Sting and Cher and Liberace. She has most of the violin repertoire at her fingertips. She knows all the major concertos, including Bartok, Shostakovich and Stravinsky. She learned the Berg concerto in four days and on the fifth performed it from memory for her teacher's class. On the way out of the class, one boy said he expected her to come in the next week and play the Hindemith forward and Schoenberg backward while standing on her head.

Midori was born in Japan, where her mother, a violin teacher, gave her her first lesson when she was four. When Midori was eight, a friend of her mother's heard her practice and asked if she could make a tape. That woman, who lived in New York City, played the tape for an assistant to a woman who teaches violin at Juilliard and the Aspen Summer Music Festival. The assistant played the tape for the teacher, who found it remarkable.

The phone rang late one night at Midori's home. The man on the other end was speaking English. It was the head of the Aspen Music Festival calling to offer Midori a full scholarship to Aspen.

It happened that Midori's mother was looking for a new teacher for Midori. Midori was almost nine and had never studied with anyone but her mother. Neither of them knew much about the Juilliard teacher, but they went to Aspen.

Midori had to audition her second day there. Every student without a teacher plays for the entire violin faculty. Midori was in a strange new country and exhausted from jet lag when she walked onto the stage of the hall where the violinists auditioned. She looked slight and frail, even for a nine-year-old. Her bangs, page-boy haircut and oversized glasses covered most of her face. Her half-sized violin was tucked under her right arm.

She stopped in the center of the stage and bowed her head.

"What do you have?" one of the teachers asked.

Midori didn't understand. Another teacher on the panel was Japanese. He repeated the question in Japanese.

"Bach Chaconne," she responded, placed her miniature violin under her chin and tore through one of the most subtle and intricate works in the violin literature.

"What next?" one of the teachers asked.

"Paganini caprice," Midori said. Paganini wrote twenty-four caprices for the violin. They are technical demons, the ultimate challenges in the violin literature.

"Which do you want to play?" the Japanese teacher asked.

"Which do you want to hear?" Midori responded innocently. She had all twenty-four at her fingertips. She played number seventeen, the hardest of all, and didn't miss a note.

Not all child prodigies fare well. Yehudi Menuhin, the most famous one of the century, blames his unnatural childhood for the breakup of his first marriage and his professional crisis shortly after that. Ruth Slenczynska made her Town Hall debut at eight, appeared with every major American orchestra by ten but had virtually disappeared from the concert stage by thirteen. At thirty-two she published her memoirs, *Forbidden Childhood*, the story of how her father tortured her to realize his own frustrated ambitions. The story is a tragic classic. The demands of life in the spotlight arrest personal development and sometimes artistic development as well. The instrument is sometimes put away forever. Those who look after Midori are trying to protect her from this fate. Her mother says that Midori is not the *only* special child. She says that all of her classmates at the Professional Children's School are talented. Her teacher limits her concerts to those that neither waste her time nor overwhelm her.

Zubin Mehta invited Midori to solo with the New York Philharmonic just after her eleventh birthday. Her name was not included in the publicity. The publicity and program said only that the Paganini Violin Concerto was to be performed, the soloist to be announced. Mehta brought Midori out as a surprise for the audience. It was Christmas time. The self-possessed little girl, not even four feet five inches tall, walked to the front of the Avery Fisher Hall stage in her pink party dress, patent-leather shoes and bobby socks. She stood there, flanked by men and women three times her age in tuxedos and black evening dresses. She tackled the work nimbly and immaculately. She looked as serene as a soaring dove. She connected with the music—with her instrument—as if only she and it existed. There was no extraneous motion, no shifting from foot to foot. She looked like an adult. The audience broke into thunderous applause, then sprang to its feet. Midori lowered the half-sized violin in front of her, nodded quickly, and searched for the exit. She looked eleven years old again. There were eight curtain calls. After the last, her teacher ushered her directly back to the dressing room, right past the green room, where the crowd would have mauled her.

Midori could not be kept a secret forever. One muggy summer night she was performing the Leonard Bernstein Serenade with the Boston Symphony, Bernstein conducting. Near the end of the complex last movement of the piece, Midori broke a string. She turned to the concertmaster, who handed over his violin. She fitted on her chin rest and continued. Then she broke another string. She once again turned to the concertmaster, who was playing his stand partner's violin. He turned that violin over. At a pause in the piece, Midori snapped on her chin rest and finished the piece. She handled the crisis with the aplomb of a veteran and played a spotless performance. The audience and orchestra went wild. Bernstein and the two men whose violins had saved the day hugged and kissed her. Tears welled up in the eyes of some of the old men in the violin section.

The international press went berserk. Suddenly Midori was a household name. *The New York Times* ran a front-page article and photo on the story, and the next day ran an interview with her. Magazines and television around the world had features on her. Midori was puzzled by all the fuss. "What could I do?" she asked. "My string broke, and I didn't want to stop the music."

Midori plays viola in her chamber music class. Her chamber music teacher says that if she played violin, there would be no students at her level to play with. She plays in the viola section of the Pre-College Symphony, the second-tier orchestra. She is too young to play in the big orchestra, and there is no rule-bending on this issue.

Midori is an only child. She lives in a simple two-room apartment with her mother and a long-haired black cat named Bee. She takes homework with her on the road. Her violin teacher gives her one or two lessons a week. She practices four or five hours a day and gets two months each year without concerts. During that time she practices—she learns new pieces and prepares for concerts—and goes to school and sees her friends.

Midori takes a stuffed Snoopy everywhere she goes. He is as soft as old terrycloth and as pliable as an antique Raggedy Ann. He wears a baby-blue T-shirt with rainbow-and-heart appliqués across the top. Midori's mother bought him before Midori was born, so he is getting old. The stuffing is coming out of his floppy ears, his paws are wearing down and his knees are skinned. When Midori and her mother wash him, he never gets as clean as he used to be. The word "Aspen" has almost completely faded from his T-shirt. But Midori still takes him everywhere. She used to take him to her concerts, but her teacher says she can't now that she is fourteen. So she leaves him at the hotel. She never leaves him in New York. She can't, she says. She can't sleep without him.

She thinks she might become an archaeologist one day, but she's not sure. She doesn't think she could live without the violin at the moment. Without a violin, she feels as if something is missing.

The lounge is at the end of the second floor.

Roger, a hulking teenager in a black parka, sinks into a lounge sofa. He has come straight from his lesson, and is upset. "It pisses me off to the highest extent of all time," he says. "The notes were fine, every last one, but there she is, yelling at me about the bow pressure and all this shit. God damn, it really pisses me off."

Joey, who is sitting on the other end of the sofa, shakes his head. Joey goes to "Horace Mann, the best school in New York," as he tells people, whether or not they ask. He is buried in a book about sports cars. Without looking up, he starts to quiz Roger.

"Faster?" Roger repeats, raises a clenched fist and flicks out a finger for each car he names. "Not Porsche, not Ferrari, not Maserati, not Lamborghini." He stops. "I take that back. I'd say Porsche. Yeah, Porsche. Faster than Mercedes-Benz."

Jimmy, who is sitting next to Joey, murmurs, "Porsche, there's no substitute."

"Mustangs aren't slow, either," Roger says, but his mind is on the lesson. "I'm depressed." He sighs. "I've got to get out of this depression. Tonight," he says, "I party."

"Too friggin' fast," Joey says, shaking his head. "Outrun the cops."

"Y'ever see *National Lampoon Vacation?* With the red Ferrari? Nice car."

"In fifty years, y'know, the world's gonna be out of oil."

Joey lifts his head. "Who said that? We have the biggest oil glut ever. We've got so much oil, it isn't even funny."

"People should drive electric cars."

"They do," Joey says, "but they go slow. Thirty-five miles per hour. How many people do you know who drive thirty-five miles per hour on the highway? Unless they lower the speed limit, they're gonna get creamed on the highway."

"To get to my flight last night . . ." Roger says.

"You fly to Juilliard?"

Roger nods. He flies from Boston every Friday night and stays overnight with his grandmother. "The cabbie's batteries ran out. We sat in the middle of the highway for five minutes. I said to the driver, 'What's goin' on?' He said, 'The batteries are low.' I said, 'I gotta make this plane.' Then this Neanderthal heavy-metal type got out of a truck and came over, and he gave us a cable. We were four miles from the airport. We got to this gas station. I paid my money and hopped in a cab that was leaving the station. Jesus, did that cabbie overcharge me! We were just sitting there, and he had the meter running! But I wasn't gonna start bargaining with him. My plane was about to leave."

Joey puts his book down. "Wanna play chess?" he asks Roger.

"Nah, checkers is my game. I'm not so hot at chess."

Joey opens his magnetic chessboard anyway and scans the lounge for an opponent.

Harley, the bespectacled pianist in Roger's trio, stands at the doorway and squints, then makes a beeline for the sofa. He is armed with a library of college catalogs. Roger and Harley, high school seniors, had recently discussed their plans for the next year. Roger wants to go to the Upper School. Harley, on the other hand, doesn't want to spend four years at a conservatory. He loves the piano, but he loves petri dishes and test tubes as well.

He sits down next to Roger and taps his thigh. "If you get into Curtis, you don't have to go the year they take you. You can defer up to five years. And if you get three AP scores over three, Harvard lets you skip a year." Harley plans to dovetail stints at Harvard and Curtis, picking up two degrees in six years.

Roger digests this. "Oh, that's cool. That's really cool."

A girl Roger knows from orchestra heads for the sofa. "Nice sweatshirt," he says. "Is it yours?"

"Uh-uh. It's Marissa's. 'Member Marissa?"

"Oh yeah, that dizzy redhead from Meadowmount." Joey folds the board, puts it back in the box and shoves the box in his briefcase. "He went out with her," he says, pointing to a boy within earshot.

The boy nods slowly, as if the mere thought of Marissa bores him. "There were two things I liked about her," he says, pointing to one side of his chest, then the other.

" 'Member Chris?" Joey asks. "He was a druggie. A really serious druggie. He had a hole in his bed for drugs. He kept them in the ceiling, too. Anyway, he used to walk around the place. Once, he ran into Marissa on a walk and he went up to her and said, 'Y'know something? You have nice tits.' "

There once was a Juilliard mother who was married to a Juilliard father who begat a Juilliard daughter, a Pre-College flutist. The father took charge of the girl's musical education and the mother played a supporting role. The father took charge because he thought he knew a thing or two about training young musicians. He and his wife were busy piano teachers in the suburb where they lived.

They think fondly of their Juilliard days, but not of their daughter's days at the Pre-College. They think the Pre-College is too competitive. They say a competitive atmosphere is inappropriate where the talent is fresh and fragile. They had hesitated to send Lauren in the first place. Lauren was a delicate girl. But she insisted, so they went along.

Lauren is twenty-three. She doesn't think about her Pre-College days much. Her father does, however, often and with vividness and pain. He and his wife were not parents to sit back. They spoke up. He believes that Lauren was mercilessly persecuted for the tactical error they made in doing so.

Tactical Error Number One: Lauren studied privately with the Pre-College flute teacher for a year before she entered the school. During the year, she and her family went to a recital of one of her teacher's Pre-College students. They thought she was a wonderful flutist, with energy, a beautiful sound and artistic power. They attended some Pre-College Orchestra concerts that year and noticed that she was not in the orchestra. Another girl always played principal flute. Lauren's father thought that girl sounded like a tin whistle and played out of tune.

At the end of one of Lauren's lessons, her parents asked why the wonderful flutist wasn't in the orchestra.

"What is going on?" her father asked.

"Why is this girl not being heard?" her mother asked.

The teacher brushed the question off. He said he had no control over orchestra personnel.

Tactical Error Number Two: Lauren got into the Pre-College with no problem, and the transition to lessons there was smooth. But Lauren's parents were as concerned about her theory instruction as they were about her flute lessons. On the way home from Lauren's first day at Pre-College, her father asked what had been covered in theory class. Lauren had trouble explaining. Her father asked to see the homework. Lauren was happy to show him, hoping that he could clarify some things.

Her father couldn't make head or tail of the assignment. He told her to be patient, that things would probably become clear the next week. But Lauren was even more confused the second week. Her father concluded that she was confused because her teacher lacked a clear idea of what he wanted to teach.

Lauren's parents went to see the head of the Pre-College. "We'd like to help Lauren," her father said. "Can you clue us in on what this theory teacher is doing?"

He got the feeling that the Pre-College head was annoyed to see them over a problem with theory class.

The theory teacher was new to the faculty that year and gone the next. Lauren's father is somewhat upset to think that he might have had a hand in the firing of the teacher, but all in all, he believes he did the only responsible thing. A school with young musical talent, he says, needs a cogent approach to teaching theory.

Tactical Error Number Three: Lauren's parents noticed that she was practicing nothing but solo flute music. Although this is the normal curriculum for flute students, they were concerned. Lauren could not sight-read. She got all flustered in orchestra unless she had seen a part ahead of time. Almost no flutists have solo careers. If Lauren was to become a professional flutist, she would have to have all the big orchestra parts under her belt.

Her parents went to see the head of the Pre-College again. They said they wanted to see Lauren spending less time perfecting the solo flute literature and more time learning the music she would need for a professional career.

The Pre-College head called Lauren's teacher into the conference. The teacher hit the ceiling. Lauren's father realized it was not wise to call her teacher on the carpet in front of an administrator and was a bit sorry he had. He liked the man. He thought he even cared about his students. But Lauren's parents felt that they were in a jam. They had sent Lauren to the Pre-College to refine her musical skills but she was not improving at all.

And Lauren was stagnating in her regular school. Her professional options, her father says, were closing daily. He and his wife began to sense that the only career for her was one in music. They wanted her to be prepared.

Tactical Error Number Four: Lauren was not doing well in orchestral auditions, inside or outside Juilliard. When she made an orchestra, she was always assigned to the back of the section. She was losing confidence. Lack of confidence can kill a performing career. Lauren could play beautifully, her father said—"God, she could play so beautifully, it could hurt your soul, wrench your guts out"—but she was becoming more and more insecure. Her parents were feeling desperate.

Her father once again called the head of the Pre-College.

"My God," the Pre-College head said, "if every parent in the school were like you, what would I do?"

"I don't give a damn about every other parent," the father said. "We've got to talk about Lauren."

They had another conference. Lauren's father complained that Lauren was not getting a chance to overcome the blocks that were killing her confidence. "O.K.," he conceded, "she did screw up in one of the orchestra concerts." (The Pre-College Orchestra performs in the Juilliard Theater four times a year.) "But she panicked."

"We can't have that in the school," the Pre-College head said.

Lauren's father was incredulous. "In the preparatory division? Are you kidding?"

"We can't have that," he repeated. "We need people who are dependable."

"Even if they're not talented?"

"Dependability she's got to have now."

"Look," Lauren's father said, "I don't know that much about the flute, but I'm learning. A young flutist needs a whole range of experience. She can't have just low- or middle-range experience. She's got to have some principal experience."

The Pre-College head was put off. "You just want your daughter to be the star."

"I do *not* want my daughter to be the star," he said emphatically. "I want her to be educated. If she chooses a career in music, she needs a variety of experience."

There was silence for a few seconds. "I'm sorry," the Pre-College head said finally. "The conductor decides who sits where. It's totally in his hands."

"Well, it shouldn't be," Lauren's father said. "You're the head of the school. It should *not* be in the conductor's hands." His fist came down on the desk with an emphatic thud. "This is not the New York Philharmonic. This is a school, and you have talented kids here. And from what I've been told, our daughter is a major talent."

"Well," the Pre-College head said, "she has to learn to hold up under pressure."

"Exactly," he agreed. "That's what we're trying to teach her to do. You have to say, 'Lauren, here's your chance. If you blow it, you'll get another chance. And if you blow that, you'll get another still.' Not 'If you blow it, you'll never get a chance again.' This is not the right age for that."

Tactical Error Number Five: Annabel was an ambitious girl who had studied piano with Lauren's father. She entered the Pre-College as a flutist. Annabel had tremendous pizzazz. Yes, she was talented, Lauren's father says, but she bluffed her way through. Yes, she got a clear sound from her flute, but only because she used a Sankyo Prima, a Japanese instrument, much easier to play than Lauren's Haynes. Annabel didn't practice much. Lauren's father believed she desperately needed to be cut down to size.

Lauren's father says Annabel was a musical bully who started knocking down Pre-College flutists she couldn't hold a candle to. She got a better orchestra seat than Lauren. Lauren's father called the head of the Pre-College for another conference. He couldn't get him on the phone, so he wrote to him.

As you may have suspected, I was trying to communicate with you while there was still time for you to do something that only you can do. Namely, to speak to the Pre-College Orchestra conductor about letting Lauren play the solo part for the Beethoven Sixth Symphony. Lauren sight-read it during Annabel's absence last week, and from all accounts, did exceedingly well (no pressure). Having tried for two weeks to reach you, I find myself numb from despair. I trust your reasons for not returning my calls, but I've lost sleep over this problem, concerned as I am over Lauren's failure to get recognition from Juilliard in the form of important orchestral parts (solos), especially because it is I who am responsible for Annabel's being at Juilliard. I resent that she's gotten so much more orchestral experience than Lauren, who needs it more. The argument that Lauren is not up to it is no longer valid. I have heard her perform magnificently under extremely pressured situations too often to accept that. I know Lauren, and it is going to take an act of faith on the part of Juilliard's administration to help her overcome her fear. Until the fear that she will never get a solo until she reads well at an audition is overcome, she is going to be trapped in an ever-increasing web of fear and frustration and self-doubt. Don't let her relaxed manner mislead you.

Before the head of the Pre-College had a chance to respond, Lauren's father decided to appeal to a higher authority. He wrote to the Juilliard president. The president forwarded the letter to the dean who sent it to the head of the Pre-College.

The Pre-College head was furious that Lauren's father had gone over his head but agreed to meet with him—along with the dean—anyway. By the end of the conference, the dean was agreeing that Lauren should be getting chances to play principal flute in the orchestra. He said that things would be different the next year, Lauren's last in Pre-College.

The Final Blunder: Things were not any different. Since Lauren wasn't getting anywhere in orchestra, her parents decided to encourage her to do what they thought she did best anyway: to play concertos. (Concertos are works for solo instrument, accompanied by an orchestra.) The Pre-College holds a flute concerto competition every four or five years. There happened to be one that year.

The competition date was announced. Annabel couldn't make it, so the date was changed. Everyone, including Lauren's parents, agreed that this was fair. The Pre-College had only eight flutists. The competition would have been a sham unless all of them competed.

There were three judges: the head of the Pre-College, the Pre-College flute teacher and a flutist from the New York Philharmonic. The competition was open to the public. Lauren's parents were there, and so was Annabel's father. The fathers nodded to each other across the hall at the start of the competition. They had met at one of Annabel's piano lessons.

The contestants all played. Lauren's father sat beaming. He thought she had won, hands down. He felt that in every category the judges could possibly consider—intonation, attack, phrasing—Lauren had outdistanced her opponents. The head of the Pre-College came onstage to announce the winner. The winner, he said, was Annabel. Lauren turned white.

Lauren and her father went straight home. Her father went immediately to the phone to call and congratulate Annabel's father. Annabel's father said he was surprised, although delighted, by the result, and mentioned that he had made a tape of the competition. Lauren's father asked to borrow it.

He took the tape to a professional flutist, an old schoolmate. "You decide who should have won," he said, handing the tape over. The players on the tape were not identified. "Let's call them one, two, three, four and so forth," Lauren's father said and chuckled half-heartedly.

He called his friend again, a week later. His friend had chosen number three—Lauren's performance—as the best.

Lauren's father wrote to the Juilliard president again, citing the blind tape test. He stapled to the letter the professional flutist's written analysis of the eight performances, broken down into categories of intonation, attack, evenness of tone, stylistic accuracy and "number of obvious bloops." The president forwarded the letter to the head of the Pre-College.

The Pre-College head called Lauren's father. "We don't judge our competitions by tape," he said. "There are other things that come into performance, like personal appearance."

Lauren's parents were devastated. Lauren was devastated. And Annabel had gotten another boost. That, Lauren's father said, was the greatest shame of all.

He wrote a final letter to the head of the Pre-College:

I want to take this opportunity to thank you for helping teach Lauren two important lessons: (1) that injustice is rampant in this life, and (2) that power institutions are not to be entirely trusted. Ironically, it is Annabel who has suffered the greatest injustice, for she has been deluded. I have discovered that she does her best work only when she thinks there is someone around who is better than she is. Now Annabel has every right to think of herself as the queen flute player of Pre-College.

CBS did a television special on the Pre-College. The head of the Pre-College chose Annabel to be a principal subject. The film crew shot Annabel and Lauren, who always came to school together, entering the building. The camera cut past Lauren as it zoomed in on Annabel. Lauren watched the documentary at a friend's house and came home and wailed. "It was so mean, so unnecessary," her father said, "and it was just because she was our daughter."

Lauren never got her Pre-College diploma. She had stopped going to theory, and the administration refused to grant a diploma without a minimal effort in that area. She didn't get into the Upper School either. She went to Curtis, where she was happy. Orchestra seats were assigned on the basis of seniority.

Lauren's parents still believe she is a major talent. They say the conductor of the American Symphony stopped the orchestra four times in a Carnegie Hall rehearsal to say, "No flutist in the world plays that more beautifully." They say Leonard Bernstein stopped a rehearsal at Tanglewood to ask, "Who is that flutist?" But Lauren, they say, is still fighting her insecurity. "I'm not trying to blame the school for Lauren's personal weaknesses," her father says, "but it's wrong for a school like that not to allow a student to make a mistake in a concert."

The head of the Pre-College once asked Lauren's father, "When are you going to learn there's no justice in this world?"

"I know there's no justice," he responded. "But you don't have to *create* injustice to prove it." Especially with kids, he says. Children need protection. If we don't protect children from ugliness and injustice, we're going to create a monster society.

————

Lauren's father has been meaning to write to the head of the Pre-College to say that he has no hard feelings and realizes that the man was probably only reflecting attitudes from on high.

The Pre-College head says the problem was simple: Lauren was simply not the best flutist in the Pre-College. He couldn't say that to her father, so he had to do some fancy dancing.

Lauren's father says he likes the head of the Pre-College and figures that the man was probably just playing the game.

The Pre-College head says, "My goodness. My dancing is better than I'd thought."

*"If Juilliard is Mount Sinai,
the teacher is God."*

A Juilliard harpist

5   THE TEACHERS

The relationship between the teachers and the students is intense.

The teachers seem godlike. Some of them are world-famous performers and others are world-famous teachers. Some are pure inspiration, and others are consummate trainers. Some are very, very old and intone in exotic accents. This adds to the godlike aura.

The teachers who are often out of town and those with an abundance of students have assistants teach some of their lessons. This widens the gulf between teacher and student and adds to the aura.

The student never forgets that he is the apprentice at the feet of the master. The teacher is often the reason he has come to Juilliard and the reason he endures his roach-infested matchbox-size apartment.

The teacher is no less concerned with the student. The teacher is an artist, and artists have egos. The student is an extension of his ego. The student is the vessel he speaks through. The student is his puppet, his lump of clay to mold, the apostle to spread his word. He lavishes attention on promising students. The others sometimes feel ignored.

Some teachers behave like army generals. They treat their students as soldiers and other classes as enemy camps. They guard their artistic advice as if it were war secrets. The student who dares to defect to another camp risks vindictiveness: his departure is often seen as an ad hominem attack on his teacher.

The teacher and the student work together behind heavy red doors one hour a week. The teacher sits and listens, coaches and demonstrates. What he neither says nor shows the student expects to absorb from his presence. The student spends the rest of the week in the practice room, the voice of his teacher echoing in his memory.

The teacher and the student communicate in music. It is a language more powerful than words. It says nothing, but says everything. It comes straight from the heart and cuts straight to the bone.

The result of all of this is that relationships between the teachers and the students are filled with the tension and gratitude of the most troubled relationships between children and their parents and with the love and hate of the most tempestuous love affairs.

Simon remembers every detail of the traumatic day three and a half years ago. He remembers that his socks were pretty close but didn't match. He remembers that the temperature jumped from 50 to 70 degrees. He remembers the moldy whole wheat crusts on the sandwich he left at lunch. He remembers everyone he called that night. (This was no real feat, actually, since he called every friend he had in New York, where he had lived only three months.)

Simon is—and always has been—independent and self-confident. He had graduated from a West Coast conservatory. He knew what he was and what he liked. But something about his piano teacher intimidated him. Part of the discomfort was that he had never before known anyone who had been on a record jacket. Still, Simon was getting used to that and feeling more and more comfortable at his lessons.

Simon brought the Rachmaninoff Second Piano Concerto to his lesson that fateful day. He had been working on it, on and off, for three years. He had hesitated to bring the piece to a lesson with this teacher, because the teacher had made his name playing that and other late and great heavy Romantic pieces.

There is a theme in the Rachmaninoff Second so lush that someone set words to it in the forties, turning it into "Full Moon and Empty Arms," a song Frank Sinatra made famous. The theme comes three times in the last movement of the concerto. Simon had an idea of how he wanted to play them. He wanted each one to be played with a little more passion: the first quietly, the second a bit more appassionata and the third (with the orchestra womping the daylight out of it) with total abandon.

His teacher had a different idea. He thought that the first should be moderately passionate, the second practically inaudible, and the third (as Simon liked it) with total abandon. Simon sat at his lesson swooning in the forest of harmonies he drew from the piano. The teacher stopped him two bars into the second statement of the theme and demonstrated how it should go.

"But don't you think," Simon asked, "it might go this way?" He turned to the keyboard and demonstrated three seconds' worth of his interpretation.

His teacher was livid. His back went stiff. "Who are you to say this to me?" he asked, fire in his eyes.

Simon thought he could deflect the rage with reason. "I really have a lot of trouble when I bring you a piece that I've played a lot; where I'm trying to do what I want to do, I have a hard time in lessons. It's tough for me to change. When I bring you something I haven't studied that much . . ."

His teacher's face hardened, his eyes narrowed. His shoulders curved like the back of a threatened cat. "I'm a seasoned professional, and you're a country bumpkin," he said. There were things about Simon he hadn't liked from Day One. All at once he unleashed his feelings about all of them.

"You're twenty-eight years old and floundering around here."

Simon sat still as a nail. "I'm not twenty-eight," he said. (He was only twenty-three.)

The teacher ignored him. In a black rage he stomped around the room spewing insults. Simon was in a daze. Half of him felt paralyzed. The other half felt sharp needles puncture his skin at small distances from one another.

The attack went on for half an hour. Then the teacher threw the music on the floor, and his voice dropped. "Get out," he said. His right arm whipped through a dramatic flourish and stiffened straight out, his finger pointing to the door.

Simon didn't budge. The teacher grabbed his briefcase and headed for the door. On the way out, he flicked the lights off. It was seven-thirty at night and as dark as the inside of a cannon.

Simon found his way to the door and started wandering around the halls like a sleepwalker. He ran into two friends who told him he was white as a sheet. He smiled and walked past them. His whole future was a haze. He wondered whom he could study with, whether he would stay in New York, whether he could go home to live with his mother and how soon he could pack and get a flight out there.

His teacher had lent him a piece of music. Simon used the return of this as an excuse to confront him. Six days had passed. His head had cleared, and his strength had returned.

He was in a combative mode. He had started wearing certain clothes when went to school. Nothing elegant, just clothes he felt at home in: a pair of brown corduroy pants and a blue workshirt. He looked very work-manlike. He thought of himself as a steely urban toughie who was not going to take crap from anyone. His father was in the military. When it's time for battle, Simon believes, you do battle. If someone crosses swords with him, he forgives but never forgets.

Simon knocked on the door of his teacher's studio. It was the middle of the day, half past the hour. His teacher was in the middle of a lesson. "I believe this belongs to you," Simon said, handed his teacher the score and turned to walk out.

"Wait a minute," his teacher called after him, "I'd like to talk to you, but today's . . ."—he glanced at his watch—"uh . . . at your next lesson."

"O.K., fine."

Simon walked out the door thinking, O.K., goddammit, if I ever have another lesson with you, I'm going to challenge you. I'm going to play your game, but I'm going to beat you at it. I'm going to bring every piece memorized and perfect. He planned to learn every piece so thoroughly he could play his teacher's way at his lessons, and his own everywhere else.

Simon's heart pounded when he went to his lesson. He sat down at the piano. He and his teacher talked for the entire hour. They touched on Simon's past and present without delving deeply anywhere. Simon got the feeling that his teacher had prepared what he would say about the last lesson. He semiapologized for the personal insults, but as for the rest, he laid on the line what he expected from a student.

"I'm not here to teach you your way," he said. "I'm here to teach you *my* way. I have a way that works. It works for me."

Simon felt strange. "I'm sorry if I offended you in any way," he said, unconsciously mimicking his teacher. "Let's see how things work out. If they don't work out, we'll figure out what to do then."

Simon went directly from his lesson to ear training. To start each class, his ear-training teacher played a slow glissando up the keyboard. Everyone was to be silent by the time she reached the top. Class consisted of a series of quizzes. Every class, each student had to get up in front of the room and perform an ear-training exercise from a book. The exercises consisted of tapping out rhythms, singing intervals or reading the music in do-re-mi syllables. The student was graded, A plus to F, on his performance.

The teacher called Simon up to do a complex rhythm exercise. Using a pencil, he had to tap a rhythm against the metal stand that held his book. As he tapped the pencil resting loosely between the thumb and index finger of his right hand, he grew self-conscious about his left arm and put his left hand in his pocket. His teacher could tell he was uncomfortable. She picked on anyone who showed any sort of discomfort.

"Something in that pocket feel nice?" she asked.

Simon looked up blankly.

"Huh?" she drawled derisively.

She made Simon feel stupid.

Hey, Simon said to himself, I'm not six or seven anymore. I'm not eighteen either. You can talk to me like an equal. He got back into his combative frame of mind and returned to his seat.

Three minutes later his hand shot up to answer a question his teacher threw out to the class.

"Mr. Smith," she said in mock-surprise tones, "you're still talking to me!"

"Well," Simon said, and addressed her by name, "why shouldn't I?"

"Well, usually when I ride somebody like that in class, he never talks to me again."

"Well," Simon said, and repeated her name, "anything you can do I can take."

A chorus of ominous "Oooooohs" from the class crescendoed around him.

There is a teacher who scares all her students. She has a temper as fierce as a hurricane. Her students seem to age a hundred years at her lessons.

Some say the tirades are for the good of the student. If she believes a student has the goods, she will do anything to get the music out. She teaches that humility is critical, that the music must be supreme. One needs an ego to perform, she says, but the music must be able to get past it.

She puts her heart and soul into the students she adores. She drags them through the mud at lessons, but as a concerned mother would. She goes to dinner with them and calls them at home to be sure they are eating properly. They call her to play snippets of pieces, and she sings back to them.

But only the hale and hardy survive. She gobbles up the weak ones. She likes students who are strong, intelligent and committed. But she has a problem with women students. She doesn't like to teach them and tells them so when they audition for her. She thinks women waste her time. She believes that only men truly commit themselves to their careers. Women go off and get married, or might as well. She believes that women are too weak for the brutality of a concert career. The rare women she does teach are both talented and aggressive.

Renata was such a woman. Or so it seemed.

Renata brought two pieces to a lesson at her teacher's house, a Bach toccata and fugue and the Ravel *Valses nobles et sentimentales.* The lesson began with the Ravel. Renata played it from beginning to end. As the last note faded the teacher rose and walked over to the piano, grimacing and muttering. She grabbed a pen from the piano ledge and started scribbling huge letters and musical notation marks. The music became unreadable.

Renata had been warned about this sort of behavior. She had even seen it in mild form at the end of lessons before hers. She had sensed that someday she would fall victim to an outburst and had subconsciously prepared herself. She would hold her head up and appear as unruffled as possible. When the teacher finished ranting about the Ravel, Renata turned to her. "I'd like to play the Bach," she said, as if the lesson were just beginning.

Renata had played the Bach at the previous lesson. Her teacher thought it had not improved at all. "You're wasting my time with the Bach," she said. "As a matter of fact," she continued and raised her chin a couple of millimeters, "you're wasting my time here altogether." Renata quickly and quietly inhaled and exhaled to harness her tears. Ask a question, she thought. A show of deference might calm the teacher down.

Renata asked something about the Bach that she hadn't understood at the previous lesson.

The teacher thought the question rude and Renata insubordinate for asking it. She threw the music on the floor and began to attack Renata, rambling on about her emotional problems and the disappointment she had turned out to be. "Dear," she said, circling behind the piano bench and around the piano, "it's a good thing you're in therapy, because you need it."

Renata started to cry.

The teacher strode into the bedroom and slammed the door.

"I'm not coming out," she called, "until the next lesson."

Renata did not know whether she was serious. Four endless minutes passed. Renata gathered her music, grabbed her sweater, slung her shoulder bag across her chest and tiptoed out of the apartment, quietly closing the door behind her. In the elevator the tears began to pour. The elevator opened at the ground floor. Renata walked past Jeannine, who had the next lesson. Jeannine did a double-take.

"Did you just have a lesson?" she asked.

Renata nodded.

"Was it that bad?"

She nodded again.

Renata walked to Juilliard, where she ran into Garrett, another student of her teacher's, who was leaving the building with the two others in his trio. He motioned for them to continue and said he would catch up with them at the restaurant.

"What happened?" he asked Renata, his eyebrows flexed with concern.

Renata started to explain, but halfway through she started to cry all over again.

"I've got news for you," he said. "She's going to call you to apologize."

He was right. She called early that evening. "Dear, I'm sorry," she said the moment Renata picked up the phone.

"Do you realize what happened?" Renata asked.

"I don't know what happened," she said. "I just felt you were being insubordinate."

"I was only trying to ask you a question." Renata repeated the question over the phone, thinking her teacher might now see how humbly and sincerely she had meant it.

"I'm sorry, I did overreact," her teacher conceded and cleared her throat. "I don't apologize for what I said, you know, about the Bach, but I apologize for the other things I said. And I certainly apologize for how I said it."

"O.K.," Renata said.

"How do you feel?"

"Do you really want to know?"

"Yes."

"I feel pretty terrible," Renata said. "I feel like I don't want to get out of bed. In fact, I'm not going to." Renata stayed in bed for two days and spent the rest of the week talking on the phone and walking around her apartment in bare feet and bathrobe. Word of the episode spread. Her classmates made condolence calls, some by phone and some in person.

Her teacher called again. "Do you think you're going to want your lesson next week?" she asked.

"You bet," Renata answered. "I'll be with you on Monday."

Judd always had the lesson after Renata. He was a new student at Juilliard. He thought of his teacher as the goddess of the piano. Judd was sensitive. He would go to the movies and cry. He would watch TV and cry. He loved the piano and loved his pieces.

The teacher both babied him and flirted with him. She told him about her old love affairs. She told him she was once in love with a tennis player who, like Judd, had blond hair. "Oh, dear," she said at one lesson, "you look very athletic. You play tennis, don't you? You have to think, when you play this phrase, that you're at the net, hitting a volley."

Judd and the teacher discussed his repertoire at the end of one lesson. She decided that he should be doing some Chopin. "Dear, she said, "why don't you bring the *Polonaise-Fantaisie* next week?" Judd knew that an instruction to *bring* a piece was an instruction to bring the piece *learned*.

Judd was always scared going to his lessons. He had the feeling that his teacher was not interested in him—that she had two or three students she liked to teach and took on people like him only to fill up the week. Judd had the first lesson of the week. If it did not go well—and it often did not —she would say, "Well, now you've set the tone for the whole week."

Judd stood at the door to his teacher's apartment, the *Polonaise-Fantaisie* in the stack of music under his arm. Renata had canceled her lesson that day. Judd pushed the buzzer gingerly. It took several minutes for the teacher to answer it. She had done a hasty job with her makeup. "Dear," she said when she opened the door, "don't look at my eyes. And excuse me another minute. I can't talk without my lipstick."

The lesson began with the *Polonaise-Fantaisie*. Judd sank into it, finished it and smiled. He was proud of the job he had done. His teacher had been quiet throughout. (She rarely let a student play straight through a piece the first time he brought it.) Judd turned around.

The teacher was reading her mail. She had in fact been reading it since he began to play. She looked up. "You have no business playing this piece," she said. "This is an artist's piece. You," she stressed, "are not even a good student." Something in Judd stopped. Rather than suffer the indignity of breaking down in front of her, he got up and walked over to the big picture window overlooking Lincoln Center. He put his hands in his pockets and clenched his fists.

The teacher came over and stroked his hair. "Now Juddy, Juddy, don't sulk," she said. "Don't be that way."

So Judd loved her again and returned to the piano. But another five minutes into the piece she said, "This is horrendous," and threw the music on the floor. Judd left the studio crying and went to another teacher the next year.

Kyoko had the next lesson. When Kyoko was choosing a teacher, this woman was the obvious choice. But her teacher at home had strongly advised against it. Kyoko was strong-willed, as strong and temperamental in her way as the Juilliard teacher. A clash of wills might ruin her playing. At any rate, her teacher didn't think the two would last long together.

So Kyoko spent her first years at Juilliard with a teacher she loved as a person who taught her little. She decided to risk devastation at the hand of the teacher she had wanted all along and auditioned for her on the sly.

The teacher gave Kyoko the speech about not wanting to teach women, but then she played and the teacher was impressed. She said "Bravo" after each piece and accepted her as a student. On the way out of the audition, the teacher asked Kyoko what she would like to study. Kyoko said she wanted to start some new pieces.

"What do you lack?" the teacher asked, referring to possible holes in her repertoire.

Kyoko had merely scratched the surface of the Russian romantic literature. That repertoire happened to be the new teacher's specialty. She told Kyoko to bring the Scriabin Fourth Sonata and Prokofiev Sixth Sonata to her first lesson.

The lesson began with the Scriabin. The teacher sat on the sofa, panting and making grand gestures from the very start. Kyoko thought they might be cues to stop but charged ahead, figuring they might be part and parcel of a demonstrative coaching style.

There was a pause in the middle of the third page. The teacher lifted the Scriabin from her lap, closed it and curled it back as if she were going to swat flies. She walked over to the piano and whipped it against the side of the instrument.

"Nothing is right," she said. "Nothing is right. You're not even looking at the score. Everything is wrong."

My God, Kyoko thought, I've had this piece a week. One week! What does she want?

The teacher sat down at the second piano and demonstrated the proper tone for the opening. "Start again," she said and returned to the sofa.

Kyoko didn't get past the first line this time. "No. Wrong." The teacher threw up her hands. "You don't feel the music. If you don't feel this music, you shouldn't play it."

Kyoko had heard about the antics and was prepared. She sat unruffled —until the teacher suggested she didn't "feel" the music. It was as if she had said, "You have no feelings, you're a vacuum, you have no chance." Kyoko, for the first time in twenty years of lessons, felt tears well up. But she held them back and turned to her teacher. "Sorry," she said. "I'm not giving up."

"Of course you're not, dear," the teacher said and was suddenly transformed into a perfect angel.

John is driving fifty miles an hour. It is raining buckets, with shattering thunder and blinding lightning. The wind is whipping rain against the car at 110 miles an hour. It sounds like pins falling in a bowling alley. The road is winding. John turns at a moderate angle. The car starts to skid.

The next thing he knows, a policeman is waking him up in the car of a total stranger. He opens his eyes. His car is twenty yards off the road, wrapped around a tree. An ambulance pulls up. Two men in clear plastic raincoats jump out, slide him onto a stretcher and into the ambulance, drive onto the highway and turn the siren up.

John passes out again. When he comes to, he's lying in a pale green hospital room with a basket of artificial zinnias in green Styrofoam on the bedside table. His glasses are there too, with one lens gone. A tube is attached to his arm. He feels like throwing up. He lifts his left shoulder to turn over but can't raise it more than half an inch. He touches his face, and his fingers sink deep before they hit his jawbone. His lips are puffed out to his nose. He feels like one massive bruise. He sees the faint image of a nurse coming at him. She wraps brown canvas around his upper arm and pumps a rubber ball that looks like the beeper on his old tricycle.

"Listen," John says in his drug-induced stupor, "all I want to do is play. All I really want to do is play."

The hospital releases him the next day. He looks like the Elephant Man. His broken nose is caked with dry blood. He is dizzy as a top, so full of Demerol his parents have to prop him up to walk him to the car. They take him home and put him to bed. His father comes around every four hours to give him another fifty milligrams of Demerol. The phone starts ringing for John and doesn't stop. He asks his parents to take messages. He is too weak to get up and too depressed to talk to anyone. When he's awake, he's lying in bed muttering, "Shit, this is it. It's over. My life's over. Kiss the horn good-bye."

John is still in bed the next day, but he feels well enough to sit up a little. The phone rings, and his father answers. John hears faint snatches of the conversation.

"Nice concert," his father exclaims. "Real real special. Bernstein looked great. The section sounded spectacular, absolutely terrific."

Jesus, John thinks, they're talking about the Philharmonic concert. Christ, that's my teacher. His heart starts to pound. He bangs on the wall between his room and his parents'. He can hardly open his mouth, but he yells as loudly and distinctly as he can, "I want to talk to him! I want to talk to him!"

The phone extension cord nearly reaches John's room, but not quite. John has not been out of bed in two days. He holds his breath, maneuvers himself upright and shuffles over to the night table in his parents' bedroom.

"Hello?" John says without moving his lips.

His teacher sounds curt and gruff, as if he has a cigar clenched between his teeth. "You'll do anything to get out of a lesson."

John grits his jaw. "Don't make me laugh," he says. "It hurts."

His teacher is always terse. He once told John not to talk too much when he was with other musicians. "Let your instrument do the talking," he said. There was a period when John called him "the excerpt crusher" because he wanted to hear nothing but orchestral excerpts, and he pounded them in. He always gives one hundred percent at lessons. John has sometimes wished he didn't.

He stands over John or walks around the room, listening, shaking his head every two notes.

"It's wrong."

John tries the three-note passage again.

"No. Look at that. Look at the rhythm. Beat your eighth notes."

John claps.

"That's a quarter."

John beats twice as fast.

"You playing that right?"

"No, I didn't. I played that two times too slow."

John tries the passage again.

"No."

John tries again.

"What'm I doing wrong?"

"You're playing eighths, right?" The teacher claps the beats. "This is your beat, right?"

John claps the rhythm of the passage over it.

"Still wrong. Sing sixteenths to this." He claps the beats again.

John sings.

"No. You're singing thirty-seconds."

John sings again.

"Now your sixteenth note is sluggish. It's lazy."

His teacher sings the passage with a quick short flick of his head on each downbeat. "Just because that's slurred," he says and points to a curve mark in the music, "it doesn't mean you slight the thirty-seconds. Wait."

They finish the etude and go on to the next. John plays. His teacher walks around the room, a half-drunk Diet Pepsi in his large right hand. He walks the carpet staring at his shoes. John finishes the etude. His teacher jangles the change in his pocket.

"The intonation," he says, meaning that it is off. "And it sounds"—he pauses—"kind of rushed. You're pushing it."

"Was the beginning too fast?"

"Yeah. Take more time. Slower at the beginning. The whole thing slower."

John plays the beginning. His teacher circles the music stand and stops, facing John head-on. He beats on the stand with the index and middle finger of his right hand. "It's dying off. It's got to be big all the way through. Sustained."

John plays.

"Sustained."

John plays again.

"No. You can't make a hole there." He sings, imitating John's hole. "The beginning," he says.

John starts again.

"Deep breath," his teacher says as the third note dies out. John inhales deep for the next three notes, but not deep enough.

"Smooth. Got to be smooth as silk."

John plays the three notes once more.

"Get some depth in the sound. You're skimming the surface. Take in some air." The teacher pats his belly twice to show where the air should go. "Don't be afraid of it," he says. "Don't be timid with it."

John plays.

"Right. That's the sound. You've got to pay attention to every little detail." John has prepared this piece for an audition tape. "On the tape," his teacher says, "they're going to listen to rhythm, intonation, and they're going to try to listen for sound and style. You've got to have all the details worked out. You've got to think about how you want to play before you start."

John absorbs what his teacher has said. "What's next?" he asks and momentarily leans against the short back of the hard piano chair.

"What didn't I hear last time."

"The Berlioz and the Wag—"

"O.K., let's hear the Berlioz."

John plays the Berlioz straight through. His teacher leans on his elbow, his thumb tucked under his chin, his index finger pressing against his upper lip.

John finishes. His teacher drops his hand and stands up. The knuckle of his index finger has left a groove over his lip. "Yeah," he says. "It doesn't have the drive. The energy. It sounds clumsy." He sings, imitating John's clumsy sound. "Drive it through."

John plays the beginning again.

"No. Everything's got to be even." The teacher lifts a palm-sized metronome off the piano, turns it on and adjusts it to the proper speed. He points to a spot in the music. "Right here." John plays the spot as the metronome ticks away in the background. He falls behind. "Is this the way you're practicing?" his teacher asks. "If you don't place that eighth note perfectly, that screws everything up." He and John stare at the music. "You've got to put some weight on it." He sings and beats on the piano. "Duh-duh-duhhhhh, duh-duhhhhhh . . ."

John tries to imitate the sound with his horn.

"The low F. Still sharp."

John plays it again.

"Still sharp."

The teacher has nicknames for his students. They are little inside jokes, meant to remind the students of their weaknesses. "The Creeper" creeps into notes instead of attacking them directly. "Dirty Harry" plays super-clean—spotless even—but almost antiseptic. "Mr. Clean" tends to be sloppy. "Spanky" slaps at the attacks to every note instead of hitting them squarely but plainly. "Moldy" sculpts every note, even those that call for no adornment.

The teacher lives out in farm country with a wife, three children and a golden retriever. He once brought his class out to play a concert at his church. At nine o'clock that Sunday morning he pulled up in front of Avery Fisher Hall and the class piled into his van. He drove them around the countryside and showed them the farmhouse where he lived while his house was under construction. When he lived there, he said, he would go to the barn at night and listen to the bulls fighting over the cows. Every morning he would go to the barn and sit and listen to the cows moo. The class sat in rapt attention. The oldest student—the only one bigger than the teacher—said, "Oh, is that where you got your concept of sound?"

"Oh, uh, yeah, Mac," he responded, "that's it."

His teacher plays one of the biggest trombones in the world. Most trombonists use a nine-and-a-half-inch bell. His is ten and a half inches. He uses a huge mouthpiece. He added a heavy crook to his instrument and screwed the rim bell to the end of that. Most trombones weigh between five and ten pounds. His weighs close to fifteen. It takes an iron grip to hold it. And it can't *just* be held, it must be held precisely so the embouchure doesn't shake and there's no pressure on the slide. The weight of his instrument doesn't faze him. John says that if it were dipped in lead, he would be even happier.

On the telephone with John after the accident, the teacher was kind. Terse but kind. John had been lying in bed, abysmally depressed. The doctor had forbidden him to touch the horn for six weeks, and he had concerts and auditions coming up. He had a contract to do the Mahler Sixth with Leonard Bernstein exactly four weeks away. He always needs a week and a half to get back into shape after a week away from the trombone—and that's after a vacation. That's not accounting for an accident and the damage it might have done. John lay there worrying. He didn't tell his teacher, but his teacher seemed to know.

"Don't worry, take it easy," he said over the phone. "It'll be fine." He spoke as if he meant it.

Lying in bed got harder and harder. The first day John felt strong enough to get up, he called his friend Natasha. Something in him said, Talk to Natasha. Natasha was not nearly his best friend, but he sensed that she would understand. She was a violinist under constant pressure.

John had to look up her number in the Manhattan directory.

"It's funny you called," she said. "I can't play either. I have tendinitis." She had been forced to take the week off. She had had to cancel two big concerts, one with an orchestra that would never reengage her. She was curt with John because her roommate was standing over her, waiting for a transatlantic call. When she got off the phone, she threw on a coat and went to the corner drugstore to buy a card John pulled from his jammed mailbox two days later. It was a Hanukkah card with flames jumping off a gold menorah and a poem about miracles and lights.

Natasha wrote on the page opposite the poem:

Dear John,

I've got the perfect idea. Start drinking and don't stop. By the time New Year's comes, you'll be totally blitzed. Then by the time you sober up, you'll be able to play.

The swelling subsided after a week, but John's muscles were still sore. His depression deepened. It was scary lying there. He spent the mornings watching game shows, the afternoons watching soap operas, and the evenings—when he was awake—watching old movies. The drugs made him too dizzy to read. He began to feel inadequate.

John called his teacher again. He thought about what to say before he picked up the receiver. He was not exactly nervous, but one does not call this man to shoot the breeze.

"Hello?" It was his teacher's wife.

John introduced himself.

"Oh John," she cried, "how are you?"

John soft-pedaled his misery. He said things were coming along, that he was optimistic about his prospects, that he was busy doing minor repairs around the house. She knew he was downplaying his agony. She is Southern, very friendly and warm. The day her husband's class came, she cooked a meal of smoked ham, crab fondue, stuffed peppers and potato salad, and pear and pumpkin pies for dessert. The students sat around drinking Moosehead and listening to records while her husband told trombone stories. She came to the doorway of the study and her husband stopped mid-story.

"Oh, he tries to act so tough and mean to you guys," she said, "but he's really a pussycat." She walked over and gave him a peck on the cheek.

The students cracked up. The teacher turned a little red. When she returned to tell them lunch was ready, her husband chased her out of the room cracking an imaginary whip.

She opened up to John on the phone. "Look, I know what you're going through," she said. "I know the whole situation. Don't get down on yourself. Don't be hard on yourself."

All of a sudden John realized that his teacher had probably gone through this sort of thing. His wife seemed to understand everything before John said anything. "Take it easy, go slowly, you'll be fine," she said. "I know you'll be fine."

She put her husband on.

"Hello," he said in one quick burst of air. "How you doin'? Play *Boléro* yet?" *Boléro* is one of the killers in the orchestral trombone-part repertoire.

John started to answer.

"Oh," his teacher interrupted before John finished the first sentence. John called again when he had been back on the horn almost a week.

He played only when his parents were out of the house. They had forbidden him to play. They worried about the damage he would do by playing before his face muscles were strong. The first time John's mother heard buzzing from John's room, she bounded upstairs and kicked the door open as if she had just heard that he was on the window ledge about to jump. John was ripe for instant gratification. Patience was hard to find. While everyone seemed concerned about a smooth recovery, John worried about his sanity. He found the waiting intolerable and decided to take his trombone out the next time his parents left the house. The first time he did he blew only through the mouthpiece, trying to recapture his old clear buzz. The next time he slid the mouthpiece into the horn and blew through that for five minutes, and felt dead. The next day he felt dead after fifteen. It was all very slow.

The teacher answered the phone this time.

"Oh," he said, "so how are you doin'?"

"Pretty good, y'know," John said, "I was working on *Zarathustra* this morn—"

"What!" the teacher interrupted, and John could almost see his eyes bulge out of their sockets. "Are you crazy?" *Zarathustra* demands tons of power to belt out the notes—just to get them, not even accounting for projection in a big hall. "Don't do that, you're going to *kill* yourself!"

"Just kidding," John admitted and told his teacher that he was sticking to easy etudes and long tones.

"Listen," his teacher said, "do things slowly. Don't change anything. Don't try to work with what you have now. It's not really you. You'll be you in a little while."

There was a time when his teacher scared him to death. The lessons were so businesslike that John had no idea what his teacher thought of him. He worried that his teacher was not happy with him. The trombone was the most important thing in his life. The worries kept him awake for weeks. He told his girlfriend he was losing sleep.

"If it's on your mind," she said, "why don't you talk to him? What's to lose?"

John raised the subject fifteen minutes before the end of the next lesson. He glanced at his watch every five minutes up to the designated hour, then asked, "Well, how do I stand?"

"What do you mean?"

"I have no idea how I'm playing. Where I stand. Whether I've gotten better or worse since I've been here. I have nothing to go on."

"Well, what do you think? Do you think you've gotten better or worse?"

"Better, I guess. But I have no idea where I stand in the big picture, compared to the others here."

"Your playing has a lot that is positive," his teacher said. "You're showing a great deal of promise. But," he said, "you're still young. You're going to have to keep working."

They talked for ten minutes about John's embouchure and intonation and rhythm. Then his teacher said something strangely revealing. "You have to understand. I'm quiet. I understate things. I'm not going to come out and tell you you're great."

John was touched.

John bounded into the studio for his first lesson after the accident.

"Hey," his teacher said.

"How're you doin'," John said, put his case on the studio sofa, pulled out his trombone, ran the slide in and out, sprayed the slide with lubricator, grabbed his music, dropped the pile next to the piano chair in the center of the room and sat down.

His teacher sauntered over to the open case. He seemed bored. He picked up a black rubber air bag lying in the case. John had bought the air bag for ten dollars at a surgical supply store. Patients with breathing problems use the bag to monitor their progress. They blow in the bag to test their lung capacity. Healthy men ordinarily have a two- or three-liter capacity. John's bag held five liters.

"Can you fill it up?" the teacher asked.

"Nah," John said, shaking his head slowly. "Nah, I can't fill it."

The teacher put the bag to his lips, took in a roomful of air and exhaled. The bag expanded and expanded. (The teacher once thought he had pulled a muscle in his back and went to a doctor. The doctor asked him to breathe out, and the doctor nearly fell over because he had never before seen muscles expand like that.) The bag would have exploded had he blown one more ounce of air. He let the air out and handed the bag to John.

John inhaled and tried to fill the bag. His teacher laughed. "What do you want," John said, defeated, and the teacher ambled across the room and settled into his green-and-yellow tweed easy chair, his feet up on the ottoman, his fingers interlocking over his belly.

John, not to be humiliated, had the last word. "But y'know," he said with a devilish grin, "it's not how big it is, it's what you do with it."

Every composition lesson began the same way. Exactly on the hour, Anton tapped three short taps on his teacher's studio door, waited three seconds, opened the door a crack and then the rest of the way, in two separate swing motions. Anton was not shy. He was just being polite.

Anton and his teacher exchanged hellos. His teacher always nodded slightly when he said hello. Anton headed straight for the piano, laid his music on the right-hand piano ledge and sat down on the black-lacquered seat.

"So," his teacher said, "what have you written this week?"

Composers have dry weeks. They can sit and stare at a piece of staff paper for hours—for days—and draw a blank. When his students had dry weeks, Anton's teacher sat and talked with them for the hour or had them do counterpoint exercises. Sometimes he gave lessons in melodic writing.

Anton never had dry weeks. He brought a new piece to nearly every lesson and always announced what the piece was scored for.

"Why not play it," his teacher responded.

Anton played it.

"Hmmmm," his teacher said, walked over to the piano and lifted a red pencil from the ledge. "Why not make it a fugue?"

The teacher tried to transform every piece Anton wrote into a fugue.

No matter what the mood or texture or instrumentation, he took the first melodic idea and at its conclusion sketched it in another register in another key. Then he pointed to the end of the first melodic idea and said, "Now write some new material here to be the countersubject." This, basically, is how a fugue is written.

Anton found this peculiar. At first he thought that his teacher was trying to ensure that he understood the rudiments of Western composition. The fugue is the cornerstone of much of Western music. But it went on much too long for that. And there were other strange things about his lessons. No composition teacher Anton had ever had—no composer he had ever known—made him play through every new piece he showed him. Most of them could look at a piece of music and hear it in their heads. People who can do this are said to have good ears. Most composers have good ears. Anton began to suspect that his teacher made him play his pieces because he did not have good ears, and that he was fixated on fugues because fugues are constructed largely by formula. Anton decided that his teacher rejected his free-form pieces because he didn't know what to do with them.

And there was something else. Unlike every other composition teacher Anton had had, this teacher never talked about pieces in terms of chords and pitch and never sat down at the piano to play bits of the pieces they discussed. Anton wondered if this was because he could not do these things. He began to think his teacher was one big fraud.

One day Anton got brazen.

"Why not make this a fugue?" the teacher asked (as usual) when Anton finished playing a piece he had written.

"This has nothing do with a fugue," Anton replied.

The teacher hesitated. "Fugue," he said, "fugue is the greatest form of art. Fugue is the summit of music."

"Well, lots of great music is not fugal," Anton said. "And I'm not interested in fugues right now."

The teacher was silent. They went on to another piece.

Anton was only sixteen when he entered Juilliard, and he was obsessed with his teacher. When he decided his teacher was a phony, he was disappointed, but he was not going to play the fool. He did what any precocious sixteen-year-old would do: he played tricks on him.

Anton continued to bring his pieces to his lessons, but he stopped playing what was on the page in front of him. He played approximations of it instead. He would look at the shape the notes made (the picture they formed on the page) and improvise. He played most of the right rhythms. Wrong rhythms are easier to spot than wrong notes. But the notes he played wrong, most of them a half step above or below those he had written. But he played them with conviction and always turned the page at the right time. His teacher never stopped him. Anton thought, He either can't hear or doesn't care, or he has blanked out. It didn't matter which. Anton was furious. He didn't know what to say to his teacher, so he didn't say anything. He just started to hate him.

Anton began to think that everything his teacher said was pompous. His teacher intimidated most of his students. Some of them liked jazz and told him so. "You shouldn't play that garbage if you want to develop a sense of musicality," he replied with bravado. He told Anton how lucky he was to be studying under him. He said he was the only one in the world who understood this and that. Fugue, for one. Orchestration, for another.

Eventually Anton stopped bringing the music he was writing. He felt his teacher would contaminate it. Instead, he brought pieces he had written when he was twelve or thirteen.

One day his teacher announced that it was time for him to embark on a new venture. It was the middle of a lesson. The teacher cleared his throat and bellowed out Anton's last name, as if he were saying Beethoven or Mendelssohn. "I think," he proclaimed, "it's time for you to write a major orchestral work."

"Yeah?" Anton said.

"Big, big orchestra."

"O.K." Anton said.

"I want a real start by next week," the teacher said.

Anton walked out of the lesson. I have to do something, he thought.

On the way out of school he noticed a sign on the door of the Juilliard bookstore. It said, FREE MUSIC PAPER.

The bookstore was giving away paper that was unusable. A midtown music store had dumped it there. It was old and frayed. Worse yet, it was green. Furthermore, it was gargantuan. There seemed to be a thousand staves on it, and the staves seemed to stretch for miles. If one got close enough to the page to see the notes on the staves, one couldn't see the whole page. If one stood far enough away to see the whole page, one couldn't see the notes.

Anton took tons of it. He got home, and even before he opened his mail, he sat down to count the staves on the page. There were eighty-eight of them. One could put *Götterdämmerung* on the paper, two systems per page.

Anton ripped the top sheet off the stack and took it to his drafting board, where he did his composing. He twisted the switch on his drafting lamp and perched himself on his wooden stool. He stared at the blank page. A big orchestra work, his teacher had said. The words resonated in his head. He decided to sketch a huge phallus. He sketched it in soft but thick lead. It took up the whole page. It was an eighty-eight-staff phallus, the color of mint jelly. Anton filled in notes along the inside, all over the place. He didn't pay attention to what they were, he just made sure they were playable. He filled in rhythms, although he wasn't sure they worked together, either for the single instrument playing them or in the context of the orchestra. Then he erased the phallus outline. Along the left margin, one per staff, he wrote the name of every instrument he could think of. He had to keep erasing the list, because there were always staves left over when he had exhausted his repertory of instruments, but in the end, he was able to fill the page. He had the whole family of every instrument that had ever been included in an orchestra piece. First piccolo, second piccolo. First flute, second flute, third flute, fourth flute. He wrote parts for two pianos and two harps. When he got down to the strings, nearly every player had a different part.

Anton brought the piece to his lesson and placed it on the piano ledge. There was silence. Anton thought, Either he's going to laugh and prove he has a sense of humor or there's going to be a scene. Either would have suited Anton. He wanted, more than anything, to break the tension.

The teacher scanned it. "This looks excellent," he said. He cleared his throat as he did when he was about to make a pronouncement. "This is the first time you've brought me a really fine piece of music," he said. "I see great orchestral sweep." Then he wrinkled his brow and bit his bottom lip. He lifted his red pencil from the ledge. "But," he said, "I don't know about this note." He circled one note with his red pencil. It was written into the first trumpet part. It was playable, but it was very high. "Isn't it a bit"—he paused slightly—"high for the trumpet?"

"I want a sense of striving," Anton said. "I don't want the player just to *hit* the note. I want him to strive. Maybe even to crack on the note."

"I see," the teacher said seriously.

Anton left the lesson livid with anger. He had brought his teacher a joke —something with no meaning—and his teacher had been impressed.

Anton once again started to bring to his lesson pieces he had written as a young adolescent. But his teacher kept asking to see more of the orchestra piece. Anton evaded the entire subject. The teacher eventually got angry. He accused Anton of not being able to finish anything and went to the administration to try to get him thrown out of school.

Anton did not know this.

Composition juries are held in the spring, at the same time as instrumental juries. Juries are like final exams. In the composition department the jury grade becomes the second-semester grade. Composition juries are slightly different from instrumental juries, where the student performs for ten or fifteen minutes at a certain date and time. A week or two before the date set for composition juries, all composition students must submit all the pieces they've written that year to the registrar. The entire composition department reviews them. The students are told to show up for a two-hour period on a certain day. They sit outside the jury room and are called in one by one. The composition faculty sits around the room, drinking coffee, discussing the scores. If there is a problem, the discussion tends to be drawn out. If there is none, they chat briefly. When the student leaves the room, the faculty discusses him and his work and decides on a grade. The composition faculty tends to be either very lenient or very rough.

Just before jury time, Anton's teacher told him he didn't need a jury. He seemed very sincere.

Anton looked at him, incredulous. "I don't need a jury?"

"No, no," his teacher responded. "You've had pieces performed all semester."

This was true. Anton had been more prolific than ever. He had written incidental music for *Waiting for Godot,* commissioned and performed by a Soho theater. He had written an Off-off-Broadway musical performed in a Hell's Kitchen basement. His classmates had performed his pieces in solo and chamber-music recitals. "The composition faculty has seen some or all of the performances of your pieces. So they don't need to see your scores."

This seemed entirely logical. O.K., Anton thought, I don't need a jury. But he decided not to take chances.

"So I assume that means I'll get my A," he said. He needed an A to maintain his scholarship and teaching fellowship. Juilliard figures that anyone who gets less than an A in his major area of study should not be teaching other Juilliard students.

"Nothing to worry about," his teacher said.

This worried Anton. His teacher hadn't said yes or no. Anton went to get his report card the day they were issued. His teacher had given him a B minus.

Anton went immediately to see another composition teacher, the man he had originally wanted to study with and, by chance, the one he thought was the friendliest in the department. (The department is small, and everyone in it knows everyone else.)

"Why didn't you show up at your jury?" the teacher asked. "Why didn't you at least give a *reason* for not showing up?"

Anton was numb at first, but by the time he finished explaining he was almost blind with rage. He went home and typed a letter to the administration, barely stopping to think:

Dear Sir:

I was denied my jury this year. My teacher told me that I didn't need one. He said that since the entire composition faculty had heard performances of most of the pieces I had written this semester, I would not have to take a jury. I assumed this meant I would get the A necessary to maintain my scholarship and teaching positions.

I have just learned that the composition faculty is under the impression that I failed to show up for my jury for no particular reason whatsoever. Failure to show up at a jury, I realize, is bad behavior, so this reflects poorly on me. But even worse, my teacher gave me a low grade as a jury grade, as if this is what I deserve.

I believe that in doing this, my teacher acted out of malice. I am not sure what he has against me, but I would appreciate the opportunity to take the jury as every other student does.

I appreciate your consideration and await your response.

Anton typed three copies of the letter and mailed them to the president, the dean and the registrar.

The registrar wrote back within the week. Under normal circumstances, where a student is pitted against a teacher, the registrar sides with the teacher, but in this case, Anton's teacher had broken the rule by telling Anton he didn't need a jury.

Dear Anton,

I am writing in response to your letter of last week. A terrible error was made in excusing you from your jury. The jury grade on your transcript is being expunged from your record. You will have no jury grade for a while. We will arrange a jury at your earliest convenience.

Please call my secretary to let us know when you are available.

Anton called the registrar to say he was available immediately, but, as the registrar discovered, most of the composition faculty were leaving town for summer homes and festivals. They decided to hold the jury in the fall.

The man Anton had gone to see after receiving his grade came to the door of the jury room to usher him in. Anton was standing there sweating in his only suit, a wool herringbone tweed, far too heavy for the suffocating humidity of the afternoon. Anton had twelve black cardboard-covered spiral-bound scores clutched between his forearm and rib cage.

The teacher leaned his head out the door and around it, like a turtle. "Your teacher is having a little fit," he whispered, then raised his eyebrows and wrinkled the right corner of his mouth, as if to indicate that he wished he were somewhere else.

Anton entered the room. His teacher was pacing back and forth in the far corner, three steps in one direction, three steps in the other. He leaned forward. One hand clutched the other at the wrist, behind his back. He looked at Anton through tense squinted eyes, as if he were going to kill him. "Richard Nixon," he spit out. (This was at the height of the Watergate period.) He started muttering. The words were indistinct at first, like interference noise on a television. Then the words came through gruff and bristly, without real tone. "This student is just like Ehrlichman, just like Ehrlichman," he said. "In fact, he's worse than Ehrlichman. He's Haldeman."

The three other faculty composers were seated at the long beige Formica table. Anton respected them all, and was anxious to switch to any one of them. He got the feeling, in that room, that they all felt sympathetic toward him. One was embarrassedly staring at his knuckles. Another was staring at Anton but was obviously lost in his own world. The composer who ushered Anton in took charge.

"Would you please," he turned and said to Anton's teacher, "let us handle the jury." He pointed to the empty bridge chair at the end of the table. "Sit down," he said. "Please be quiet."

He turned to Anton. "Let's see your scores."

Anton put the scores on the table. As he did he realized that his teacher hadn't seen any of them.

"You wrote all this last year?" the composer asked.

"Yes."

"This looks pretty substantial," he said, flipping through the pile. As he finished with each, he slid it in front of the colleague to his left.

Anton's teacher stopped pacing, walked over to the table and leafed through the half of the scores that had not been opened.

"He didn't write *any* of this," he growled. "Someone wrote them for him. I've never seen any of this."

"It's true you didn't see some of it," Anton said, choosing the word "some" over the more accurate "any," "but that's because we had problems. I wrote this, but I didn't want you to see any of it."

The composer in charge addressed Anton's teacher by his first name. "It may be true that you didn't see this," he said, "but you have to admit that doesn't mean Anton didn't write it."

"He didn't write that," he insisted in grating staccato tones. "He hired someone to write that, probably someone who . . ." He paused and reached for the scores piled on the opposite edge of the table. "Let me see those."

The composer in charge closed the scores in front of him, collected the others, handed Anton the stack and walked him out of the room.

"I'm sorry you had to see this," he said. "I'm sorry you had a year like this. I'll see to it that you get your A back."

Anton laughed, mostly to relieve the tension.

Anton switched teachers but continued to run into his old teacher in the hallways. The teacher was leaving his studio once as Anton was passing by. He grabbed Anton by the forearm and pulled him into the studio.

"I know you're giving lectures in Tully Hall about me," he said.

Anton looked at him, speechless.

"I know you're giving lectures in Tully Hall, and you're telling people all these terrible untrue stories about me."

"I'm not giving any lectures in Tully Hall," Anton said.

"Answer these questions." The teacher threw one finger out. "Do you tell your friends about me?"

Anton hesitated. "Well, I talk to my friends about you because you are part of my life, and I tell my friends about things that happen in my life."

"What do you tell them?"

"It's none of your business what I tell them," Anton said. "Whether or not any of it is true."

"You're telling your friends terrible things about me," the teacher said. "It's libelous!"

"What I tell my friends—"

The teacher interrupted. "Then I know, I know, it's a lecture hall. Maybe it's Paul Hall."

Anton left the room and went to the president. He told him that he had been mentally tortured for a year, that his teacher had been totally vicious and could have ruined his career.

"You don't have to tell me this, I know all about him," the president said. "This is nothing." He seemed at once to acknowledge the seriousness of the problem and to dismiss it.

"Does this mean," Anton asked, "that you're not interested in what he has done to me? This was the most disgraceful thing that has happened to me in my life."

The president was silent for a moment. "It takes all kinds," he said.

"What," Anton asked, "to make up a faculty?"

"It's like the world," he said, "it takes all kinds." He wouldn't say anything else.

A crowd of tired-looking people stand and sit and slouch against the pale grass-papered wall outside Room 530. They droop the way people droop at five in the afternoon, when blood sugar is at a low ebb. The tired people are waiting for their teacher. Within minutes, she comes into view, walking up the heavily trafficked corridor between the elevator and her studio. The slouchers stand up straight. She smiles sweetly at those who make eye contact with her.

"Hi," a broken chorus chimes. She smiles a longer smile and returns the greeting.

"Gregor, may I talk with you?" she asks the violinist next to the door.

"Sure," he says and lights up.

He and his teacher walk out of earshot of the others and sit on the newly upholstered sofa outside her studio.

"Do you have the Brahms?" she asks. She means the Brahms Violin Concerto. One "has" the Brahms if one has studied it and can quickly prepare it for performance.

"Yes," he answers, smiling. She has a goodie for him. She tells Gregor that a conductor has asked her to recommend a violinist to perform the Brahms with his orchestra. Gregor grins from ear to ear.

The teacher is a Juilliard institution. Her phone starts ringing at 9:00 A.M. Anyone who doesn't get through at nine is bound to get a busy signal for the next two hours. Some of her students get private lessons every week, some get private lessons every other week, some play for her only in her five o'clock daily master classes. There is always a congregation of students outside her studio. They come for emergency lessons and conferences. She has been at Juilliard more than thirty-eight years and teaches seven days a week, noon to midnight. She has taught most of the prominent young violinists in the country and her reputation has lured countless others to Juilliard. She keeps track of her students through a jumbo-sized black loose-leaf notebook. She keeps a record of each one's age, address, repertoire and upcoming concert dates.

She and Gregor complete business and break from the huddle. She walks toward the studio and reaches for the door handle when Sasha, another student, stops her with a big smile and oscillating hand. "I would like you to meet someone," he says, as if they were there alone. He introduces his mother. "You've got a wonderful son," the teacher says.

Sasha and his family emigrated from the Soviet Union five years ago.

His mother has just come from the ladies room. She has combed and puffed up her hair and redone her makeup. The prospect of meeting the teacher has her slightly nervous. She stands at an angle behind her son and places her outstretched fingers on his shoulders. She smiles at the teacher's kind words and raises her chin.

"He is our hope," she says.

Hour after hour the teacher sits in her wood-framed studio chair while the disciples come to play for her. Now, like a mother hen, she is encircled by students scrunched together on the sofa, chairs and carpeted floor.

The students are dressed casually. Rugby shirts are the current vogue in the class. The European girls are wearing wool skirts and sweaters, and the teacher is wearing a dark grey knit dress with a charcoal-grey silk scarf ingeniously twisted around her neck and fastened with an elegant brooch. And bootlets, something of a trademark.

The bodies should warm the room up. It is chillier than usual in there: 65 degrees. The central air conditioning has gone haywire.

The room is bustling. People are coming in late, looking for places to sit. The door handle keeps clicking, twice in succession: once when the handle is pushed down, and once when it is released. The teacher signals Sasha to say that since he has brought a guest, he will perform first. He prepares for his promenade to the center of the room. Sasha, the skinny six-foot-two class clown, has a naughty twinkle in his eye. He puts on a flimsy black double-breasted jacket with a bright red lapel and silver buttons that look as if they came from Woolworth bins. He reties the laces on his sleek Italian shoes. He opens his violin case. The noise simmers down. He strolls to the center of the room, twirling his violin. He tightens the bow hair and tunes.

"I am going," he announces in his thick Russian accent, "to perform" —he pauses every two words—"in my Michael Jackson outfit."

"Gon-na Thril-ler!" someone in the corner hoots.

"Knead it, feed it, beat it," someone else mutters.

Sasha slips out of the jacket, folds it in thirds and places it on his violin case. The room is totally silent.

"I am going," he says this time, "to play"—he scratches his left ankle —"the first movement of the Haydn Violin Concerto." He lays the fiddle against his left collarbone, twists to the left and signals the accompanist to begin. Her hands are poised in midair when the teacher interrupts. "I want you all to pay attention to the structure and keys of the piece," she says, scanning the room. "I am going to quiz you after the performance."

The performance ends, and there is polite applause. The teacher doesn't quiz them. She does what she always does: she circles the room asking each student to comment on the performance.

There are one or two unspoken rules when it comes to commenting on a classmate's performance. The cardinal rule is: Compliment before you criticize. This week's critic is next week's performer. The teacher says no one is allowed merely to say "Good" or "Great," but some do. Others are ruthless.

The first time Sasha played in class, he wanted to kill himself. He had played a Brahms sonata. Less than three seconds after the sound died out, a student raised his eyebrows and exclaimed, "That was *Brahms?*"

"Sometimes it kills, like in the middle of your heart," Sasha says. "You work hard on a piece. You have strong feelings about it, feelings of love. The piece becomes your child."

The teacher nods at the girl in the corner.

"I think you worked it out beautifully, and it sounds great," she tells Sasha. "Maybe it's hard with people breathing down your back, but you could have more fun with it. The character should be light." She sits very still. "Sometimes, also," she adds, "the phrasing was not clear."

"I thought it was good and clean," the next says. "But the ending of notes was too sudden. There should have been more vibrato on the ends."

"It was great," the next one begins. Her French accent sweetens the flattery. The class is half Asian and half Caucasian. The Asian students all sound American-born. Most of the Caucasian students sound foreign-born. There is a Viennese accent in there, an English accent, a French accent and a Russian accent. All of the Asian students were born in the United States, except for a girl who just arrived from the People's Republic of China.

"This piece doesn't have much contrast of theme," the French girl says. "When the phrase rises, you could vary the bow speed and vibrato. If you want a brighter sound, use less pressure near the bridge. In the arpeggios, be looser in the sound."

Eventually the teacher takes the floor.

"Paul and Dillon got something I was groping toward in your lesson," she tells Sasha. "Your style has a mixture of elements. One is lovely, beautiful. The other seems very virtuosic. This kind of thing." She wrinkles her brow and strikes an imaginary fiddle with harsh movements. "They don't work together. Get clearly in your mind what you want. Don't think, Better get dramatic, better make this interesting. That will take your mind off what the character really is."

"I think you're right," Sasha concedes.

"The style should be like Mozart," she says. "What do you think the mood is?"

"Happy," Sasha says.

"Does the word 'charming' occur to anyone?"

"You could hear trumpets," someone says.

"They would have to be little trumpets," the teacher says.

They say that anything you can play in her class you can play in Carnegie Hall. The pressure in there is intense. No one gets away with anything. Everyone sees and hears everything and compares himself with the performer every step of the way. One boy sits there and says to himself, I can do it, I can do it even better. Or he says, I cannot do that, and I'm worthless because I cannot.

Each player takes center stage. Even the least polished presents himself with poise. Each appears comfortable with the fiddle and comfortable performing. Not everyone plays in tune and not everyone plays elegantly, but almost everyone plays with security.

The last performer puts her fiddle away while the next dashes out to get the music for her accompanist.

The teacher tells a story about a violinist making a Town Hall debut back in the 1920s, an era when violinists played concertos in recitals. The accompanist would play the orchestra part. Every concerto has a cadenza, an extended solo passage where the soloist gets to show off his virtuosity. Before the cadenza, the orchestra usually plays alone, giving the soloist a chance to get his bearings before plunging into the cadenza. The orchestra ends the section with a long sustained chord. The Town Hall pianist built up to the chord, then threw his hands from the keys with great drama. There was silence. One second, two seconds, three seconds. The silence seemed an eternity. The pianist looked over his shoulder to see what the violinist was up to.

The violinist had left the stage. He was so discouraged with his performance, he saw no point in continuing.

This teacher's students know to finish a performance come hell or high water. They learn to finesse mistakes, hold their heads up, analyze problems and look toward the next performance.

The girl returns with the music for her accompanist. She performs, takes criticism and sits down.

Everyone in the room scheduled to play has played. But there are more names on the list. The teacher recalls that Gregor, the fifth on the list, has left the room. "Could someone get Gregor?" she asks. The student next to the door darts out and produces him within seconds. He had been sitting outside, his violin cradled in his lap. He had slipped out to practice.

Gregor is flying high from the Brahms offer. He scans the room. "Oh my God, a crowd," he says and announces that he is going to play an Ysaye sonata, a work for unaccompanied violin. He charges through it.

The teacher asks if he would like comments from the class. He nods.

"I have nothing to say," the first says.

"Oh, c'mon," Gregor says, "I was *forcing*. I was *nervous*. I was *shitting in my pants*." Gregor takes the liberty with his language because he is buzzing over the Brahms. The teacher doesn't blink an eye.

The girl sits mute.

"I don't know the piece," the next girl says but goes on to challenge Gregor's phrasing and sound.

Gregor nods and refers to another flaw in his performance. "I didn't really do this right. There's a cantus firmus going through the whole movement. You're supposed to bring it out." He shakes his head. "It's hard. There are four voices."

The teacher is reassuring. "That'll come in time."

"I liked it very much," the next says. "Watch the intonation in the second movement. I thought the ending could use short, separated bow strokes." He reconsiders. "Not so much separated. It could be more expansive, and more, um . . ."—he makes a broad arc with his right arm—"more connected."

The girl from China is next. "I thought . . ." she says, and falters, still struggling with English.

"We'll give you a little time before we ask you to speak," the teacher says.

Sasha is next. "I thought you had a good idea of structure," he says, using words reminiscent of those Gregor used to describe his Haydn. You scratch my back, I'll scratch yours. "In the last movement the repeating passage might need a little more bow speed."

Gregor shakes his head. "I'm rushing and don't have time to take more bow. Good point. I was practicing in this shitty little practice room and promised when I came in here I wouldn't overplay. And what did I do?"

The teacher has the final word. "Gregor, the one way in which you and I think alike has to do with the order in which we perceive things." She points to a painting on the wall. "What do you see?"

Gregor describes the scene in a few words.

"Some see the sum total first. Others see detail first. We hope the groups end up in the same place. When I think of you people," she says and turns to them, "I think of details and try to generalize from there. Those who see the big design pick up the details later. Same conclusion, different order. Gregor, you've looked at the details here, but not at the big picture. Not what it leads to."

Gregor nods. "That's what you've been talking about for years." It is not clear whether he says that for the benefit of the teacher, the class, the visitors or himself.

"You've got to start looking at the big chunks," the teacher says, "how they relate."

Gregor scans the room. "That's it? No more?" His limbs buckle in relief. "Thank you," he says. He does a three-quarter pivot, aiming for his violin case. He takes a voluminous scarf out of his case, wraps his fiddle and tucks it away.

"How long have you been working at the Ysaÿe?" the teacher asks.

"Two weeks." He snaps the case with two brittle clicks. "I have it scheduled for my Paul Hall recital November nineteenth. Dillon bet me a Peking duck dinner and drinks I wouldn't have it ready by then. So I bet him he wouldn't find a bow by then. But he's just about found a bow, and I've just about finished the Ysaye." He smirks. "I guess we're going to have to go Dutch."

"When you're preparing a piece, start at the end," the teacher says. "Back up through it so the end gets strong. Concentration is most intense when we begin a task. We should begin with the most difficult things."

She asks the students if they would like a break.

"Let's keep it going," says Gregor. "It's already a quarter to seven." There are two students left to play and an orchestra concert at eight.

The teacher offers more advice while the next performer unpacks her fiddle. "Each of us has an order of priorities in performance. The things we think important we generally do best. We've got to even things out, get the weak things strong. With some, it's a rhythm problem. With others, it's intonation. With others, it's making a passionate statement. If you listen to any world-class artist, you'll find all of these in order. The only person in this room who came to me playing in tune was Elena. Everyone else came playing out of tune. How did the rest of you fix up your intonation?" She looks around the room. "Dillon?"

Dillon, sitting cross-legged against the studio closet, drops and shakes his head. "I'd get so embarrassed . . ." He lifts his head. "But *really,* anyone can do anything at a slow enough speed. I'd bring the speed down and get everything perfect. Then I'd slowly bring it up. If you bring it up little by little, you don't realize you're bringing it up to the real tempo. Anyway, that's how I approach all my weaknesses."

"Very good," the teacher says. "Slow it down so you can cope with it. Then bring it up gradually. The important thing is not to get impatient and give up and decide just to play *musically.* "

The two last performers play. It's seven-thirty. One girl who hasn't played this time bolts out of the room. She says class meetings always bring her down to earth. "I feel like Salieri in there," she says.

No matter what time they end, she heads straight for the practice room.

"How many Juilliard students does it take to screw in a light bulb?"

"One hundred. One to screw it in and ninety-nine to say they could have done it better."

A Juilliard joke

6 THE COMPETITIONS

The Juilliard Christian Fellowship Association had the right idea. The small but ardent band of believers were stuck for a tactic to lure students to their poorly attended meetings. Then someone thought up an ingenious poster. In bold letters at the center it said:

HOW TO WIN EVERY COMPETITION

The time and place of the meeting was printed in smaller letters on the lower right-hand corner. In even smaller letters, tiny letters visible only with 20/20 eyesight, the poster revealed the subject of the meeting in full:

HOW TO WIN EVERY COMPETITION
...OR LOSE GRACEFULLY

Competition. The word grabs and transforms the students. It raises their blood pressure, focuses their energy and gives their existence purpose. They know (they know well) the competition high: the high from single-minded dedication to preparation, the anxiety tempered by the excitement, the chance to express themselves on stage and the chance to win. They pin their hopes on competitions. This is how the unknown burst onto the scene. They by and large believe the cream will rise. The runner racing others runs faster than when he runs alone. The musician in competition rises to higher peaks, too.

Juilliard students know the thrill of victory. When they hear of a competition they're eligible for, they momentarily suppress the memory of the agony of defeat.

Juilliard holds competitions all through the year. The winners appear in Alice Tully Hall as soloists with the Juilliard orchestras. The excitement of winning a concerto competition stems partly from the chance to perform a great work of music with a first-rate orchestra in a first-rate hall. But beyond that, the winners become instant celebrities at school. The students regard concerto-competition victories as giant steps in the ascent to worldwide fame and fortune. They complain about the process—the pressure, the pain and the unfairness—but they thrive on it. The concerto competitions are such charged events that competitors recall the details of them with vivid accuracy years later. When they do, they often relive the pain and euphoria that lay dormant in them for years.

Each competition revolves around a different concerto. There are about fourteen concerto competitions each year: four for piano, three for violin, two for viola, two for cello, two for winds and one for brass instruments. Details of the year's competitions—the scheduled concertos, the competition dates, the concert dates, and the conductor and orchestra scheduled to perform each concerto—are printed on posters hung around the school.

Each teacher may enter up to two students in a competition. The entrants draw lots to determine the order of appearance. Each contestant gets only fifteen or twenty minutes to play. The Concert Office publishes the cuts they are to take in the concertos. If there are more than ten or so entrants, there are two rounds: preliminaries and finals, held on consecutive days. Three contestants advance from the preliminaries to the finals. One of them becomes the winner, and another the alternate. The alternate plays the winner's concert if the winner is unable to.

Most departments impose rules on top of these. The piano department does not allow first-year students to compete and closes preliminaries to the public. The cello and violin departments do not allow faculty members to vote. Most departments prohibit students who have won one concerto competition from entering another.

Each rule is fodder for conflict. And, as always at Juilliard, the rules get bent and broken. When they do, cries of foul play always fly. The process is ripe for charges of unfairness. Judges often know the competitors. In some cases, they teach them. Those they do not know personally they often know by reputation. The competitors, prone to heightened sensitivity, look everywhere for evidence of injustice. There are big egos at play. Competitors don't want to lose in front of their friends. Emotions run at fever pitch: after months of round-the-clock work, winning seems a matter of life and death. The world does not exist beyond the Juilliard walls. Rising to the top there—winning a concerto competition—renders them winners in life. Defeat, by the same logic, renders them losers.

The competitors look for an edge every step of the way. Each step seems decisive. The two-student-per-studio rule often favors those from smaller and "weaker" studios, where competition is less intense. The manner of choosing the entrants sometimes influences the outcome. Some teachers select entrants through studio competition. One teacher initially had her noncompeting students judge the play-offs, but this posed problems of bias and bribery. Others enlist their assistants, former students and random students. Some teachers endorse the first two students who ask to enter. Others assign students to competitions when the pieces are announced. Some students opt out of the process altogether. Discouraged by teachers who tell them they are "not yet ready," some wait years to enter. Others wait for the "right" competition. Some enter the competitions of obscure concertos, where they expect competition to be less intense. Others, knowing they can win only once, wait for the concertos they love best.

Some people think competition order is decisive. Playing first is considered disadvantageous: judges tend not to be struck by an exceedingly strong first because the first sets the standard. Playing last is also undesirable: judges are tired by the end of the competition, and each may already have chosen his winner. How good any contestant sounds also depends partly on who has preceded him.

Passages from each concerto seem to seep from every nook and cranny of the building for months before each competition. More students prepare for than ultimately enter a competition. Just *who* is preparing to enter, however, is never clear. Before competitors' names are announced, those suspecting others who may enter pass in the hall and avert glances. Or their eyes meet and they half smile, betraying a pernicious anxiety. Competitors see one another in classes and in the cafeteria, and the competition inevitably comes to mind. They walk down the fourth floor, hear someone practice, think, "Those octaves are faster than mine," and then spend days between sleepless nights working them up to the other's breakneck speed.

Some students keep mum about the competitions they plan to enter. They lull their competitors into complacency while they slave away in secret. But there's more to it than that. Competitors are superstitious. They don't want to incite others to enter. And they want to minimize the humiliation accompanying a potential defeat.

It's a hard secret to keep, however. Teachers talk, and gossip travels. And before the competition, the contestants perform the pieces in class meetings and studio play-offs.

The class-meeting performances are often uncomfortable. It's hard to play for those who know a work inside out, to listen to someone play a piece one has one's own convictions about and to expose the nuances that distinguish a performance. It's disconcerting to listen to someone breeze through a passage that had always seemed an obstacle course. But despite the discomfort—*because* of the discomfort—teachers encourage their students to perform the pieces. Performing under pressure, they say, is good practice for the competition.

Outsiders are not always welcome to sit in. Walter once invited his roommate Sam to a class meeting where he was to perform a concerto he would play in a competition later that week. Sam's teacher had no students in the competition.

Sam walked into the studio scrunched in a pack of students who took lessons there. He snuggled in the corner of the plush studio sofa, and minutes passed before the teacher noticed him. When he did, he smiled and asked Sam if he would please step outside for a talk.

The teacher and Sam knew each other well enough to say hello in the hallways. They had never had a conversation, but Walter had introduced them, and the teacher had sat on Sam's juries. There was definitely a good feeling between them.

"Sam," the teacher said and shifted his considerable weight from his right to his left foot, "uh . . . this is a family affair. You know . . . uh . . . just among ourselves." He gave Sam an "I'd love to have you, but . . ." look. Sam realized how awkward the teacher felt and left.

The play-offs can be even more grueling than the finals. They pit students against their brothers and drinking buddies: the friends they hang out with in practice rooms and confide in over the telephone. Whether the results are announced in public or posted on the studio door, there is always condolence from the winners to the losers. Sometimes, even at this stage, there are tears. This is the stage the students expect to breeze through: the competition has not even formally begun.

Peter was the first contestant.

Peter felt he had to win. He was a student whose reputation had preceded him at Juilliard. He had amassed a staggering array of victories

in international competitions where, in most cases, he had been the youngest entrant. He already had a big career. He had soloed with major American and European orchestras and had done several European concert
tours. He had recently performed with members of the Juilliard faculty in
a chamber music concert in Carnegie Hall. He was under the management
of one of New York's top impresarios. Peter had a reputation to uphold.

Emma was the third contestant.

Emma wanted to win. She didn't exactly feel she had to, the way Peter
did, but she wanted it with all her soul. She knew Peter was expected to
win. Even her teacher had said so. "I know Peter is slated to win," her
teacher had told her, "but I think you can go out there and do a creditable
job." By the time the competition rolled around, Emma thought so, too.
She figured there was a slim chance Peter would pull out at the last minute.
A sprained finger, maybe, or a sudden out-of-town engagement. At any
rate, Emma was twenty-four and this was her last year at Juilliard, her last
chance to solo with the Juilliard Orchestra. She decided to give it a shot.

Randall was the fifth contestant.

Randall didn't expect to win. He hoped to, but he was mostly concerned
with getting through the competition piece, the knotty and strenuous
Shostakovich First Cello Concerto. The Shostakovich is a technical
demon, with almost every virtuosic trick in the book. It is also an endur-
ance test: three of the four movements are played without pause, twenty
minutes of uninterrupted intensity. Randall felt confident about his preparation—he had practiced the Shostakovich between seven and ten hours
a day for half a year—but one never knows what will happen onstage.

Randall had not had good luck in competitions. He had won a few in
his hometown, but he hadn't gone past the semifinals in any national
competitions. Randall was seventeen, a first-year student. Like everyone
else, he knew Peter was the odds-on favorite.

Peter was scheduled to play at four. He stood before the chipped mirror
over his bedroom dresser. He stretched out his right hand, palm up, poured

some clarifying oil on the four extended fingers, then slapped the oil, gently but thoughtlessly, on his right, then left, cheek. He slapped it on quickly so the oil wouldn't trickle down his wrist. He couldn't risk dirtying his dress clothes. It was three-thirty. In his navy suit, white shirt creased from the dry cleaning press and olive-and-mustard paisley hand-me-down tie from his father, he left home with an entourage of his girlfriend, his roommate and a close friend. They got off the Juilliard elevators at Paul Hall, one floor above the ground. Peter went backstage to warm up.

A cleaning woman had been there. The furniture stood at perfect parallels and perpendiculars to the walls. The dust that had been a thin white sheet on the carpet was now in the dark cavity of the Hoover bag in the equipment closet two flights up. Peter dropped his coat, took his cello out, and warmed up with some scales and thorny passages from the Shostakovich.

The Shostakovich was Peter's baby. He had performed it with orchestras in Munich and Geneva and had won top prize playing it in a competition in Carnegie Hall. A month before, he had spent an entire week getting it back into his fingers. It had felt like an old friend. He practiced it sporadically after that: he had to prepare new pieces for some out-of-town recitals and perform a Boccherini concerto with an orchestra just three days before the competition. This left only two days—the two before the competition—to devote exclusively to the Shostakovich. He spent them working only moderately hard. He wanted to preserve his energy for the competition.

Peter was annoyed to be doing the competition. He somehow felt it was his right to perform the concerto without doing the competition. He was nonetheless confident that he would win. Not just because the Shostakovich felt so comfortable. He thought he was in good standing with the administration: the administration treated him differently from other cellists. Every year he (unlike every other cellist) was excused from orchestra, but there was always an A next to orchestra on his report card. Everyone at Juilliard considered him a cut above the other cellists there. He, in fact, was surprised that eight cellists were signed up to do the

Shostakovich competition. He hadn't thought that that many could handle the piece.

Had Peter felt less confident, he would not have entered. He cleared his calendar for the winner's concert.

Peter ran through the Shostakovich in Paul Hall that morning. Contestants get time to try out the hall. Most of them bring someone to evaluate the projection in the hall. Peter came with only his accompanist. He had played recitals there and knew the acoustics. He tried the hall only to test the onstage balance with his accompanist.

There were three judges: the associate dean, a musicology professor and the conductor engaged to conduct the winner's concert. They sat in a row in the center of Paul Hall, two seats apart. No one sat in the two rows behind and in front of them. The hall was dark.

At 4:07, one of the judges signaled the backstage monitor to begin the proceedings. The monitor in turn motioned to Peter. Peter darted over to the full-length backstage mirror to make sure his tie was straight, brushed his thick mane of hair back with his hands and darted back to his instrument. Quickly and quietly, he played the opening passage of the Shostakovich. The last thing he always plays backstage is the first he has to play onstage. The hardest thing to play onstage is the first note. One can't anticipate the feeling onstage. The combination of audience and lighting and space is sometimes relaxing, sometimes unnerving. Reviewing the first note or first troublesome passage backstage gives Peter something to hang on to, some feeling of confidence: anything he can do backstage he can do a minute later onstage. Peter mounted the five stairs to the stage. The monitor pulled the creaky wooden stage door back, slowly but deliberately. The noise broke the tense silence. Peter strode onstage, his accompanist a step behind him. He was frowning and carried the cello as if it were a weapon—end pin first, the body of the instrument before him, gripped tight with a tilted wrist.

He got to the middle of the stage. "Where's the podium?" he asked angrily. "It was here this morning."

"Well, there's no podium here now, but there's a great big audience," one of the judges bellowed from the middle of the hall. His voice bounced off the walls.

Peter moved the heavy backless stool away from the piano. He rammed his end pin into the floor with a violent stab and started playing. He was angry to be subjected to this public trial. He had won competitions on three continents, and none had felt this uncomfortable. Paul Hall was like a funeral parlor—dark and shallow, cool and quiet. A coffin and white gladioluses would fit perfectly, Peter thought. He felt a hundred pairs of eyes on him as he played. They were not warm, encouraging eyes. They were eyes that scrutinized. They were eyes that knew the agony of being up there, but felt no empathy.

There is no mistaking a competition for a concert. The contestants in the concerto competitions are not interrupted, but the cuts in the pieces break up their natural shape. The event is solemn. There is no applause. The contestant does not know whether he's getting anything across. He finishes a piece with a rousing climax and gets stony silence. He cannot let his guard down. The audience cannot absorb the music. They can hear it, but not get lost in it. The time and space are not the performer's to control, as they are in a concert. Music, in this setting, is merely a means to an end. The prize is always in the back of the contestant's mind.

There had already been controversy in this competition, controversy over Peter's participation. Peter had already won a concerto competition. At the request of his teacher, the administration granted him special permission to enter this one.

Randall's teacher was furious. He went to the administration to try to get Peter eliminated. He had even tried to elicit the support of Emma's teacher. There was more to his wrath than concern for the rule forbidding former winners to enter a second competition, and more than the protection of Randall's interests. He and Peter were not on good terms. Peter had once studied under him. Peter had played a debut a year before the competition and had accidentally left the teacher's name out of his biography. The teacher happened to be at the concert. Someone came backstage before the concert and pointed out the missing name to Peter. Peter knew the teacher was sensitive, so he asked the concert sponsor to make an announcement about the omission. The announcement was made, but the teacher was not satisfied. He believed the original omission was intentional.

Peter had hurt his feelings more than once. He had started in his class, left it, come back to it, and then left it again. Peter, in fact, had hurt many feelings along the way. As a friend once said of him, Peter doesn't burn bridges behind him—he blows them up.

Peter was angry while he was playing, but strangely detached from his anger. He was thinking about the irony of his anger over the Montagnana he was playing, an instrument valued at $500,000. A foundation had lent him the precious eighteenth-century Italian cello with a big rich dark sound. The head of the foundation had told Peter it was high time he retire his Lupot, a nineteenth-century French instrument with a sweet small sound, an instrument valued at $80,000. Peter loved the Lupot, and wished, as he sat onstage, that the Lupot, rather than the Montagnana, were under his fingers. He felt bullied all the way around.

Peter played well despite his anger. Maybe because of it. Maybe the anger made his playing extra expressive. He made little adjustments as he played, reacting to his accompanist. He pushed when she fell behind and bore down when she was drowning him out. There were two small mishaps: he scratched a high note in the second movement and blurred a fast passage in the third-movement cadenza. Other than that, his performance was both clean and charged.

The echo from the last chord died, and Peter got up to leave. He hadn't enjoyed playing, but he felt he had done well.

Roughly half the audience filed out of the hall.

Some of the spectators, including old friends of Peter's, came backstage to say hello. Peter hadn't seen some of them for years. There were bear hugs and fraternal slaps on the back. Everyone told Peter how impressively he had played and that, of course, he had the prize wrapped up.

Peter's girlfriend was the last to meet him backstage. After the friends and well-wishers left, she hugged him. They stood backstage talking, then he checked his pocket for the key to his teacher's studio, and they went upstairs to hang out there.

Emma worked on nothing but the Shostakovich for three months. She didn't practice scales or even etudes. She didn't think she needed to. She figured that getting through the tortuous passagework would keep her fingers in shape.

By the time the competition rolled around, Emma had grown to love the Shostakovich. When she was in high school, she had played in an orchestra that performed the piece, but she remembered almost nothing of it from that. So when she decided to enter the competition, she went out and bought the Rostropovich recording. (Shostakovich wrote the concerto for Rostropovich.) She listened to the recording three or four times before she sat down with the cello. At first she got depressed. She didn't think she would ever get a handle on the piece. When she went back and listened the week before the competition, it didn't sound half so difficult.

Emma tried to isolate herself from her competitors. She avoided the fourth floor. Her orchestra-stand partner—another contestant—played through hard bits of the Shostakovich during warm-ups and breaks. That annoyed Emma. She didn't know whether he was looking for encouragement or trying to psych her out, but either way, she was annoyed. She kept hearing that people were holding Shostakovich play-throughs, mini-recitals to try the piece out in public. One teacher encouraged all his students in the competition to hold play-throughs. Emma had been invited to some but had declined. Her teacher had advised her to keep her distance.

Emma's boyfriend was a Juilliard pianist. The night before the competition, he lay belly-down on their bed, the music in front of him, coaching her through the piece. This was the first time he had sat with her through a practice session. He made her play the piece slowly, way under tempo. They went through the entire cut version. He stopped her where she was out of tune and where she needed polishing. She was nervous. She expected the level of playing to be high. His coaching comforted her. He had been through the concerto competition mill, and he assured Emma there was nothing to worry about.

Three hours of practice was enough. "If I don't know it by now, I'll never know it," she said, getting up to put her cello to bed for the night.

As Emma snapped her cello case shut, her boyfriend walked over to the cavernous bedroom closet and grabbed a flat rectangular box covered with high-gloss green paper and tied with a red-and-green striped bow.

"Merry Christmas," he said, two weeks early, and handed her the box.

Inside was a pale pink blouse with a ruffled Victorian collar, ruffled cuffs and cleverly concealed buttons. A perfect blouse for the competition.

Emma had spent weeks complaining that she had nothing to wear for the competition. She had been playing all her concerts and competitions in a French lace dress, but she had soured on it. It had lost her too many competitions. It was definitely a bad-luck dress. (She had even started thinking of wearing it to recitals of people she wanted to jinx.) Every time she opened her closet for the two weeks before the competition, she had hinted, more and less subtly, that she wanted a new blouse for the competition. Her boyfriend had just gone to buy it. Emma knew where he was going when he left the apartment but pretended to be surprised when she opened the package.

Emma woke up nauseated the morning of the competition. Neither she nor her boyfriend was surprised. She always felt sick to her stomach on performance days. Instead of sitting at breakfast with food she couldn't get down, she went straight to the cello and practiced for two hours. First she played the Shostakovich straight through, up to tempo. Then she played only the rough passages, under tempo. That afternoon she tried to relax. She sat on the living-room sofa, staring at the wall. She walked around the apartment and moved things, as if she were cleaning, but she didn't make much of a dent in the mess. She forced herself to eat a can of tuna and two slices of melba toast. She ate the tuna straight from the six-ounce can, stabbing each little section and depositing it in her mouth in precise mechanical movements, as if she were on an assembly line. She drank half a bottle of Perrier with the tuna. She had heard that Perrier calms the stomach. She hates Perrier.

At 4:08, just as Peter was onstage cutting into the first four notes of the Shostakovich, Emma put on her new blouse, her pink-tinted pearls, grey pleated skirt and low-heeled black pumps. She admired the outfit in the mirror on the back of the bathroom door, standing close and far away and then close again. She thought it looked just right. Neither splashy nor cutesy. Serious, but not solemn. She left for school.

She went straight to the fifth floor and stormed into her teacher's studio. Her teacher, who was sitting on the sofa filling out forms, had postponed her four o'clock lesson until Saturday.

"I want to pull out!" Emma cried. "I can't do this. I'm going to embarrass you up there, I *know* it." A creepy feeling had overcome her on the way to school. She had imagined blacking out onstage.

Emma's teacher, fresh from the hairdresser and wearing a butterfly-shaped diamond brooch on her flashy fuchsia dress, told her to lie on the couch. Emma slipped out of her shoes and lay down. She knew what was coming. Another student of her teacher's had just played a debut recital and had told her.

Her teacher walked to the door, flicked off the lights and returned to the sofa. She stood a comfortable six inches away from Emma. "Relax your brains," she said. She always had a soothing quality about her, but especially now. "You have three brains. The cerebrum, cerebellum and medulla oblongata." Very slowly and quietly, in even, lulling tones, she explained the function of each. As she spoke she gave Emma a very light shoulder-and-arm massage. She lifted a piece of onionskin paper from the piano and fluttered it across Emma's arms. Emma felt as calm as a baby.

"Relax your brains," she said again. Her speech slowed down, sensitive to the deceleration in Emma's internal rhythm. "Your brains are always working. I want you to relax them now. You can even sleep if you want to. I'm going to go out to the hall to check the time."

She left the room for five minutes. Emma was half asleep when she returned.

"O.K., you can sit up and start to warm up now." She had Emma take out the cello and do slow stretches, then scales. "I can tell you're ready," she said after a while. "I can tell just by the way you're reaching for those notes."

The teacher carried Emma's cello downstairs. They took the stairs so that Emma could get her blood flowing again. Peter was still onstage when they got to the hall. They each put an ear against the door at the side of the hall.

"Oh, he doesn't sound very good," the teacher whispered. "I don't think you have anything to worry about." Emma had never heard her utter a critical word before.

The contestant scheduled to play between Peter and Emma was practicing in the backstage area. He caught their attention. He was playing fast. Sloppy but fast.

"Oh my God," Emma said, "I'm doing the wrong tempo."

"Don't be silly," her teacher assured her. "Listen to how unfocused he is." She wished Emma good luck, and they parted.

Peter came offstage, a thick bead of sweat slowly descending the right edge of his face. The rest of his face, especially his forehead, shone with a thin film of perspiration. Emma thought he looked pleased with himself. Peter and his girlfriend hung around backstage even after his well-wishers had left. That made Emma self-conscious. She wondered whether he was there to distract her, but tried to suppress the thought. She sat down to practice. Before long—before she had really sunk into her instrument— the second contestant came offstage. The monitor motioned to catch Emma's attention.

"O.K., your turn," he called to her three times, each a little louder than the one before.

Emma tried to locate her boyfriend in a quick scan of the audience. She spotted him, and she spotted the shiny blond crew cut of his best friend, sitting on the other side of the hall. She remembered someone once telling her that people who get nervous focus on negative things. People who get nervous, she had been told, see the audience as unfriendly. Relaxed people see the audience as responsive: prepared, even anxious, to be entertained. Emma tried to focus on the people she thought would enjoy her performance.

She left the stage pleased, as pleased as she had ever been. The Shostakovich had felt comfortable. The slides she had worried about had come off. The hall had been quiet. She felt as if the audience had been with her.

As time passed, Emma thought there was a better and better chance that she would win. She packed her instrument and went to sit in the dimly lit foyer outside the hall. She wished that her boyfriend would come out to keep her company, at least talk to her for a minute, but she knew there wasn't much chance he would. He wanted to hear the whole competition, and there were four contestants left to go. A new student of her teacher, a sixteen year old girl, left the hall. She noticed Emma, galloped over to her and motioned for her to slide along the bench.

"Oh, you were the best," she said, nodding furiously.

The door to the hall slammed. Emma looked up and saw the contestant who had played just before she did. He passed the bench where the two girls were sitting and smiled at them. They smiled back.

When he reached the elevator, the young girl leaned over to Emma. "March of Dimes," she whispered maliciously. They giggled, Emma nervously.

The competition was not so emotional for Randall. He was not nervous because he had no expectation of winning. He and his teacher had decided he should enter just to get his feet wet.

Randall had been very methodical in his preparation. He had never heard the piece live, but he had listened to the Rostropovich recording over and over. Two weeks before the competition he sprained his wrist helping a roommate move a cardboard box full of books and had to go cold turkey for two days. After that, he practiced enough to keep the piece in his fingers but not so much that he would aggravate the sprain.

The weekend before the competition, Randall tried to picture himself on stage, competing. Now and then he thought about how nice winning would be, but mostly he concentrated on all the things he would have to do to play well. Everything that seemed a little shaky he went over an extra hundred times.

Randall practiced in the jacket he planned to compete in. It was big and loose. Randall always performs in slightly over-size jackets, with enough arm and back room to enable him to get around the cello with ease. From the audience, his shirts seem to have only a right sleeve. He rolls up and irons down the left sleeves just above the elbow. They stay there rigid, as if starched. That way, they don't dangle and don't impede his ability to reach notes high on the fingerboard.

Randall was in a daze backstage before the competition. It wasn't fatigue. He was careful to get a solid night's sleep and to eat a hearty breakfast. After breakfast, he ran through the whole concerto, under tempo. He had a light lunch and a nap. He wasn't tired, he had just tuned out the world.

He went through his performance routine. Like Peter, the last thing he plays before he goes onstage is the first thing he has to play out there.

The Paul Hall door creaked open. The sweaty fourth contestant came offstage, relieved. He wished Randall good luck and left.

When the door creaked open again, Randall walked out half dazed, followed by his accompanist. He sat down on the bench in the center of the stage. It had crept quite far from the piano, but Randall was too nervous to notice just how far. The pianist gave Randall an A to tune. Randall placed his bow on the A string. The moment he did, the C string suddenly unwound, like a swollen balloon that had just been deflated. Randall had been afraid that would happen. The peg had been slipping at home. To prevent it from happening onstage, he had coated the peg with chalk, figuring the friction from the chalk would hold it in place. It didn't. Randall decided the competition was over for him. Now he just wanted to get through the piece and out of there.

He tried not to look out at the crowd. Whenever he looks out at an audience, he sees people he thinks look bored to death. The two times during the Shostakovich he couldn't help looking out, he saw friends and parents of his competitors. He thought they looked amused, not bored. He saw them smile at one another as if to say, Not to worry about *this* guy. The back door to the hall slammed after one treacherous arpeggio. Was it so bad someone had to leave? Randall wondered, then realized that someone might have just walked in, not out. Oh no, he thought, he is about to hear me mess up.

He left the stage relieved and spent the next hour pacing the floor outside Paul Hall. He stopped to listen through the door, but he didn't listen closely. His relief was overwhelming and gave him a sort of euphoric buzz.

At one point he caught Emma's eye. He sat down with her and told her he was upset with his performance. "My playing lacks bravura," he said. "My Shostakovich sounded like Mozart."

Emma consoled him. "Maybe they'll like that approach. I'm sure it was clean." Randall smiled. He waited until it was comfortable to leave, then left.

The eighth and last contestant left the stage. A competition clerk, an efficient-looking woman from the admissions office, asked that everyone leave the hall for jury deliberation.

People in big and small clusters loitered in the foyer. There were contestants, friends of the contestants, teachers of the contestants, students of the teachers, friends of friends of the contestants and people with no ties to the contestants at all. Some stood silent, some made small talk. Some greeted teachers and friends they had not seen for a while. The air was heavy with anticipation. The contestants were all told they played beautifully. Those standing out of earshot of others were told they would win. Where contestants stood together, the subject of winning was avoided. Emma huddled in a corner with her boyfriend. He told her that she was the best, but that the judges might choose Peter. He ranked the competitors, one to eight. Emma, who had sworn off cigarettes, bummed a cigarette off a total stranger.

Some contestants avoid the charged moment when competition results are announced. It can be creepy. For the so-called losers, there's public humiliation on top of the sting of rejection.

Everyone is interested in the results, but for different reasons. The contestants all want to win, but with varying degrees of urgency. The teachers want their students to win. The friends of the competitors want their buddies to win. For some of the others, who wins and who loses is irrelevant. Some come just for the high they get from the announcement of the results. They love the horse race, the sporting-match aspect of the competition. They feel vicariously for both winners and losers. This is life-affirming stuff. They revel in both the thrill of victory and the pain of defeat. For some, the defeat—especially of a worthy contestant—is good dirt, fodder for talk. Watching good contestants lose satisfies them the same way that watching violent movies does. Civilized man must control his base instincts. He can't inflict certain types of pain, but he can watch others do it. And relish it.

The concerto competitions are extra charged for the student spectators. They identify with the contestants while avoiding the torment of actual participation. Those who have lost a concerto competition take solace in watching worthy people lose. For others, the competition results clarify the student hierarchy. The winner affirms his place or becomes the new target, the new one to watch. The losers, to some extent, are eliminated from consideration.

Ten or eleven minutes passed, and the Paul Hall doors opened. The judges filed out, chatting, laughing and ignoring the crowd. They were glad to be out. They had heard eight Shostakoviches, back to back. They went straight for the elevator. Heads turned, and heartbeats quickened. The competition clerk followed the judges, carrying a clipboard with notes the judges had scribbled.

"We have results," she announced. The crowd fell silent. "The alternate is Emma." There is a split second between the time the alternate and the winner is announced. To the contestants this seems an eternity. Now they are either top prize winner or outright loser. Randall was anxious to learn who had won, as if he were a step removed from the process.

"The winner"—she paused a second—"is Randall."

There was a dead silence.

Those who knew Randall gathered around to congratulate him. The other contestants politely shook his hand. Almost everyone remarked on how he had beaten the odds. He was stunned. Not ecstatic, just stunned. It took him time to realize he had actually won and would be performing the Shostakovich in Tully Hall in a month.

He would have to cancel some appointments to clear the date.

The victory did not sink in until he got home that night. The concert both added to and detracted from the euphoria. He wanted to do the concert but was terrified at the prospect.

Peter and his girlfriend left his teacher's studio twenty minutes after the results were announced. His shirt was disheveled, and her makeup was smeared. Not far from the elevators, they ran into a cellist Peter knew, one who was not in the competition. He was walking with a pianist Peter had never seen before.

"Hey," Peter called out.

The cellist's face lit up. "How did the competition go?"

Peter wasn't sure whether he was asking "How did you play?" or "Did you win?" or "What was it like?"

"O.K., I guess," he said, wanting to avoid the subject.

Unbeknownst to Peter, the competition results had already been posted all over the school. The pianist had seen them.

"What's your name?" the pianist asked.

Peter told him.

"Too bad," he said and scooted off to find a practice room.

"Let's get out of here," Peter said and headed for the stairwell despite his proximity to the elevator.

Peter went home. Before he even considered changing his clothes, he called a friend and asked if they could meet at the local Cuban-Chinese diner. He took off his suit and dashed to the diner. Over a heaping plate of yellow rice, black beans and guacamole salad, Peter and his friend talked about the competition and other things, but Peter couldn't think of anything else. He went home and immediately headed out again, for a drink with his brother.

Peter felt more than disappointed. He felt rejected in a very direct and immediate way. A performer defines himself on the basis of how well he plays. Even worse, on the basis of how well others think he plays. There's a funny interplay between them. The contestant who loses but thinks he played well feels both better and worse than if he had not liked his performance. "They happened not to like my style," he could say, "and there's nothing I could have done about that. I played cleanly and thoughtfully." Maybe he can chalk the rejection up to politics.

On the other hand, he wonders whether he's deluding himself.

Peter went to bed exhausted. He felt like a wet rag that had been wrung dry. The phone rang as he reached for the switch to put out the light. It was his girlfriend.

"How're you feeling?" she asked.

"I feel like crying," he answered.

Peter was a student of the musicology professor who had been one of the judges. The professor had asked him—weeks before the competition —whether he would be entering. The professor was organizing the contemporary music festival the Shostakovich concert was to open, and he asked Peter if he would play chamber music in the festival if he decided not to do the competition. "Sure," Peter had said, but added that he was pretty sure he would be entering. "From what I know of your playing," the professor had said, "I don't see how you can lose." Peter assumed that the professor wanted the festival to benefit from his playing.

Peter happened to have musicology the morning after the competition. When he walked through the door, the professor asked him to stay after class for a conference.

Peter was grateful for the chance to talk to him. He respected him as an intelligent man and musician. The pain of rejection had subsided with the night's sleep, and Peter was able to think about the previous day's events with greater clarity.

His first reaction to the competition result had been surprise. Then he thought that the person who had won (whom he didn't know) must be truly extraordinary. All that changed when he spoke to the professor. The professor said that he had found Peter's playing spectacular but detached. Remarkably masterful but unconnected to the music. Peter had heard such criticism before. In another competition—where he had won second prize —he had heard that the judges were offended by the "efficiency" of his playing. Peter interpreted these feelings as reactions to his onstage manner. He gives off arrogant vibes when he plays. He holds his head high, almost haughtily, and hardly moves. "Fuck-you vibes," someone once called them. Peter felt that something about his demeanor had alienated his professor just as something about Randall's must have appealed to him. Peter believed that the professor's dissatisfaction had nothing to do with either his cello playing or his performance of the Shostakovich.

This made him feel better. He thought the criticism was completely subjective. If the professor had criticized his technical mastery, then he would have been upset. Peter sometimes felt insecure about his technical proficiency. But as for depth—as for connection with the music—Peter felt this was his strong suit.

He left the classroom feeling exonerated.

Emma had prepared herself to understand if Peter won. When she heard that Randall won—"some snotty freshman" she called him—she was outraged. Her boyfriend said that of all the unfair Juilliard competitions he had seen, this was the most obscene by far. That didn't help. Emma's outrage turned into depression. She felt as if a heavy viscous mass covered her body, and it lingered for weeks. The Shostakovich was all she had thought about for months. She woke up thinking about it. She practiced thinking about it. She even sat in front of the TV thinking about it. Suddenly there was nothing to think about.

The morning after the competition, Emma brought a Christmas card to the dean who had been a judge.

"This thing's been stuck in my throat," he said.

Two contestants had already been in to complain. One had heard that Randall was a personal friend of the conductor on the jury. The other complained about the elderly woman in the front row who coughed up phlegm through his whole performance. (His father had called from Chicago that morning to chastise the administration for failing to remove her from the hall.) The dean told Emma that he had voted for her. Later that afternoon Emma told a girlfriend what he said. "Of course he said that," she responded. "He's in the business of getting people to like him."

Emma was happy he had said it, even if it was a lie.

All of a sudden everyone knew Randall. People who had heard the competition and people who hadn't, cellists and noncellists. They congratulated him in the elevators and the hallways and on the street. Randall liked the attention, but it made him realize that he now had expectations to meet. The concert would be much harder than the competition, where he had been anonymous.

Randall put everything but the Shostakovich out of his mind. During the Christmas break, between the competition and the concert, he and his mother drove for four hours to get his slippery peg repaired. When Randall got back to New York, he spent all his time tending to the upcoming performance. He rented tails, prepared a bio for the program and called out-of-town friends to invite them to the concert. He let his dirty laundry pile up, ate all his meals out and stopped returning phone calls. He became a recluse. He tried to stay calm and focused. He avoided anything that could upset or frustrate him.

The day of the concert, Randall woke up at eight as usual but lay in bed for a while. He got up, took a quick shower, put on his most comfortable polo shirt, and went through the entire Shostakovich, slowly. He tried to preserve his energy. He tried not to think too much about the concert. Doing so made him nervous.

There was a dress rehearsal in Tully Hall that afternoon. There had already been several rehearsals in Room 309. By the last, Randall had overcome his fear of playing in front of the cello section, where six of his competitors sat. (Each of them knew the Shostakovich cold.) Randall's teacher sat in the back of Tully during the rehearsal. Randall sat on the wooden podium onstage. This is a nice hall, he thought, with wood paneling that looks like matchsticks blown up a thousand times. It's a big hall, too, he thought. Well, medium-sized, maybe, but the orchestra is loud. Randall worried that his sound wouldn't cut through the orchestra. He had considered borrowing an Amati from Juilliard but decided that without at least six weeks to adjust to it, he might have trouble getting around it under pressure. Randall met his teacher after the rehearsal. His teacher said he would have to dig in deep, much deeper, to be heard.

Randall went to the American Restaurant at Broadway and Sixty-ninth Street and ordered goulash to go. He took it home, gobbled it down and undressed for a nap. He was due at a six o'clock cocktail reception at the president's office. He didn't want to go. He didn't want to have to perform before he got onstage. Under the circumstances, though, he felt obliged to.

He made the rounds. Everyone (including the conductor) wished him good luck. Nearly everyone asked how he thought the performance would go. "Hopefully, well," he answered every time. Randall is straightforward. In less formal circumstances, he would have said, "Either it will go well or it won't."

Randall noticed that everyone was drinking. He poured himself some ginger ale and put ice cubes in his glass so that no one would think he was drinking wine.

He was the last to leave the party. He had wanted to leave after he had been there five minutes but worried that might be rude and ended up staying until a cleaning woman started wiping the hors d'oeuvre table. He went home and took another nap, careful to set his alarm clock before putting his head on the pillow. He drifted off for about five minutes but woke up gripped by the fear that hours had passed. He took a scalding shower that made his heart speed and his skin turn scarlet, dried himself and put on his tails. He took his cello out and warmed up. He felt withdrawn. When he got to Lincoln Center, he went through the Juilliard entrance to Tully Hall and headed for the soloist's room. The orchestra was coming offstage for intermission.

Emma was one of the first offstage. Emma played principal cello in the orchestra. Watching Randall play the Shostakovich had depressed her early in the week. By the end of the week she had stopped thinking of the Shostakovich as hers, but possessive feelings returned that evening as she sat onstage. She and her stand partner—partners also in defeat—consoled each other that neither of them would be sitting on the soloist's podium that night.

Peter was at the concert. It was difficult for him to be there, but he decided to go for the sake of his image and self-esteem. He wanted to prove to himself that he was strong enough not to run the other way, and he wanted to show his teachers and peers that he was a gentleman. He knew he would not have to make an effort to make his presence there known. If just a couple of cellists saw him, in two days every Juilliard cellist would know he had been there.

Peter and his girlfriend had left his apartment at eight-thirty. They arrived at Tully just before intermission, crossed the lobby and sat down on a cushioned bench. An acquaintance of Peter, a German girl who studied cello, had seen him cross the lobby and approached him.

"Hey, Peter," she called out, catching him off guard.

"Hi, Gretchen," he said, smiling.

Her program was folded back to the page with the concert program.

"Some competition," she said, pointing to the program to the Shostakovich. "Crazy thing." Her laugh had a sarcastic edge.

Peter looked at the spot she was pointing to. "I was in it," he said with forced enthusiasm. He knew she knew he was in it, but he was geared up to be the forthright soldier, just another in the crew of contestants.

"I know," she said, and there was a dull silence. "I hear he's not so bad, this Randall," she said. Silence again. "Of course, not *that* good," she added, trying to lighten the atmosphere. She gave Peter a jab on the shoulder and walked away.

The crowd started to empty the hall for intermission. Peter decided to go for a walk outside. He crossed the lobby at a brisk pace, his girlfriend a step and a half behind him. Outside, he tried to divert his attention from the concert and launched into a monologue on the Calvin Klein underwear ad that shone in an illuminated display case near the Broadway curb. The ad displayed the torso of a woman in a pair of men's briefs. She was arched backwards. The briefs were pulled up on the sides to expose her hip, and the top of the photo, cropped just below the nipple, showed the lower portion of her breast. Peter talked about his annoyance at the ad's manipulation and about how it made him miss his girlfriend during the period they were apart. They walked past Avery Fisher Hall and around the frozen fountain in the center of the Lincoln Center Plaza. The air was strangely still, considering that there were performances on at Avery Fisher Hall, the Metropolitan Opera House and the New York State Theater, thirty yards to the north, west and south. Peter suddenly sensed that the Tully crowds were heading back to their seats, and he turned.

He and his girlfriend headed for the balcony. He tried to avoid eye contact with the crowd when a beaming violist who had won a concerto competition that morning tapped him on the shoulder. "Hey, you missed this one," he said with animated sympathy, cocking his head to the side, reeling with the glory of his own triumph. "Next time," he assured Peter, nodding.

Peter sat in the last row of the balcony, by chance three seats from Randall's teacher, who failed to acknowledge his presence.

A stagehand knocked on the door of Randall's warm-up room. "It's time," he said.

Randall stood backstage and felt the momentum start up. He was strangely at peace with himself. In a sense, the performance had begun. He played the first passage, quietly, then walked on stage.

Randall was relieved when the concert was over. He thought he had played well. Friends, administrators and total strangers came backstage to congratulate him.

He couldn't believe the whole thing was over. The thirty minutes onstage with the Shostakovich represented six entire months of his life. When the euphoria wore off, he couldn't figure out what to do with himself.

Concerto competitions and tennis matches both have winners and losers. But there are differences. The winner of a tennis match is the one who serves the most aces or returns the most balls. It is a numbers game. The music competition is not. A musician can play a note-perfect performance and lose the competition.

Competitors try to make sense of the results. Those who are rejected want to know why. Either something is wrong with them, or something is wrong with the process.

Ramon is a Juilliard pianist who considers the process the problem and decides to do something about the way the piano concerto competitions are run. He drafts a petition, gets more than one hundred pianists to sign it and sends it to the president.

The piano concerto competitions are not run like those of the other departments. The preliminaries are closed to the public. The piano faculty judges both rounds, although teachers with students in the finals don't vote in them. Judges vote yes or no on a contestant. At the preliminaries, the three contestants with the most yeses advance to the finals. At the finals, the contestant with the most yeses wins the competition. Voting is by secret ballot. The department chairman, witnessed by another faculty member, counts them.

Ramon's petition proposed that

1. faculty judging be eliminated
2. the "yes-no" voting system be changed
3. preliminaries be open to the public
4. secret voting be eliminated

The president decides to meet with the students. His secretary hangs posters announcing the time all over the school.

The meeting is called for 4:00. By 4:02, nearly every bridge chair in the room is full. Even some flutists and violinists are there. At 4:04, as the flow of students entering the room reduces to a trickle, the impeccably groomed president strides in, the chairman of the piano faculty a step behind him.

Ramon drops his head into his hand. The meeting has been called, at least in part, to discuss corruption in the piano department. Ramon is afraid that the chairman's presence will chill the exchange.

It is quiet. The president puts his hands together and lowers his head, as if he were searching for an opener, then raises it and says he understands the emotions competitions arouse. "Vince Lombardi once said, 'Show me a good loser and I'll show you a loser.' " There's no response. "You don't even know who Vince Lombardi is, do you?" Here and there a few people chuckle. "He was the coach of the Green Bay Packers in the fifties and sixties."

The president defends the honor of the piano faculty. "The distinguished record of the piano faculty is one of public record," he says. "Juilliard has earned its reputation through its faculty as *well* as its students."

The president admits he's not a hundred percent behind the competitions. He says he believes their value is questionable, especially in the context of an educational institution, where individuals should be nurtured. He says he does not think the competition process is always fair and objective and that he thinks competitions may even harm more contestants than they help.

But that said, he endorses them for two reasons: to choose soloists for the orchestra concerts, and to give students an idea of what they'll face when they leave Juilliard.

The department chairman scratches his ear, steps forward and says that for at least a quarter of a century the piano faculty has been grappling with the question of how to make the competitions fair and efficient. He then addresses the petition proposals, one by one.

On outside judges: He says the faculty recently voted to have outsiders judge the competitions, but only the finals. It would be difficult to have outsiders judge the preliminaries as well, he says. It would be difficult to find enough judges willing to sit through twelve performances of a piece one day, and three more the next. It would be hard to find enough judges "beyond suspicion," enough judges unconnected with one or another faculty member. Under the new system, he says, faculty members will not vote on their own students, but the comment, meant to reassure the students, prompts one girl to whisper to her neighbor that a faculty member could still skew the result by giving a good contestant a low grade, decreasing the competition for his own student.

On the rating system: The chairman says the faculty recently voted to switch from a "yes-no" to a numerical rating system where the top and bottom grades are dropped, to discount the "extreme" or "questionable" vote.

On open preliminaries: Open preliminaries are out of the question, he says. Allowing the public to enter and leave the hall between contestants would disrupt the proceedings and throw the timing off. Preliminaries should also be closed, he says, to protect the weak competitors.

On open voting: Open voting is out of the question, he says. The faculty wants to be able to vote without fear of retaliation. He confesses that on occasion he might even want to vote against a student of his own, one who is not ready for a Juilliard Orchestra concert in Tully Hall.

The president takes the floor again. The talk about secret voting reminds him of an incident from his student days. He was a clarinet student and lost a concerto competition. A teacher who he knew didn't like his playing had been a judge. For years after the competition, whenever he saw the teacher, he thought of the prize he believed he had kept from him. He eventually became the man's colleague. One day when they were chatting, the subject turned to the competition. "Why did you shoot me down in that competition?" the president asked. The teacher had only a vague recollection of the event, so he went to check the records. He had given the president the highest grade.

There is a gasp from the crowd.

"There must be some element of trust," the president says, "or we might as well close the door and turn off the lights." But he has not convinced everyone. The girl who whispered to her neighbor before whispers to her again, then raises her hand to ask if the preliminaries could be played behind a screen.

"We put up a screen, and then we have to forbid women to wear high-heeled shoes, so the judges don't know who is male and who is female. Next, we have to demand that the contestants walk in and out of the hall a certain way. We would get to the point where a contestant who has to cough will have to leave the stage to do so." The return on the investment, he says, would not justify the gymnastics.

"Juilliard is a community where there must be mutual trust and respect. Anyway," he adds, with a wry smile, "where will we find a big enough screen?"

The chairman takes the floor to say that he personally opposes preliminaries behind a screen. A screen, he says, denies the judges the pleasure of seeing the contestants. Without that, the competition is like listening to twelve recordings of the same piece, only not as good. And after all, he adds, the way one looks is part of the show.

The drama does not really begin until Ramon rises to speak. Ramon, a self-styled Che Guevara, senses that his moment has arrived. He has been gathering his strength during the half hour of questions from the floor. He raises his hand. The president nods to him. He stands, takes two steps away from his chair, faces his constituents and clears his throat.

"First of all," he says, pulling his cardigan down to eliminate creases, his thick Spanish accent enhancing the drama, "I want to thank you very much, all of you, because you have been incredible." He speaks as if this were an election-night victory speech at campaign headquarters. "I mean, it's incredible to have all of you here. There's something I want to say, something very important. You have been talking about what you feel about the competitions. I have been talking with all of you." He prepares a fist for the next sentence. "I have felt such strong energy, a great feeling you have." On "great" and "feeling," the first comes down for emphasis.

There is a dramatic pause. His voice drops. "We are the ones who go out there and play. It is suffering. It is very important for us to say what we feel."

He brushes back a lock of hair. "My personal feeling is that a number of teachers' students never win." He calls the feeling personal, but he has attempted to prove that it is the undeniable truth. He has compiled a chart showing how many competition winners each piano teacher has had since 1955. (Some of the teachers are dead, and some are new to the faculty.) Ramon believes that the chart—evidence of the uneven distribution of winners—proves that something unseemly is going on.

"How to judge all the things is their responsibility," Ramon says, "but we have ideas and feelings. The most important thing for our feelings is to express them."

The president interrupts. "I think we're appreciative we have this opportunity for you to express your feelings. Feelings are feelings, though, and as I said before, not everyone can be a winner in a competition. I wouldn't make an argument that certain teachers don't have winners, therefore there's some activity on the part of the judges—"

Ramon's arm shoots up. He takes another step toward the president. "I beg your pardon. One of two things. Either they are bad teachers or they have bad students. That's logical."

"That's *not* logical," the president says. "That's just like saying all dogs have tails, cats have tails, therefore cats are dogs. Let me put this in perspective. A suggestion has been made that the studios provide the soloists. A cycle. Each teacher would pick the soloist from his studio. But I think the consensus is that that system would be far removed from the reality of the music profession and that we should create a process at Juilliard to help the student understand what the rigors of the profession are." He advises the students not to measure their abilities through competition results. It would be a mistake, he says, to make competitions the focus of life at Juilliard.

Ramon grants him that. "Most of us think competitions are not the best things. They are not perfect, but they can be improved. But we need to agree that something is wrong."

"We agree," the president says, although it is not clear whether he is agreeing to the need to agree or agreeing that something is wrong.

The faculty chairman, who has been leaning against the bridge table, shifts his weight to his feet and speaks. "We are your teachers and totally sympathetic to your agonies. We have the duty as faculty members to select a winner. And regarding teachers who may or may not have winners, the competitors are the students. I don't think we're concerned with who studies with whom. Nobody says, 'The first contestant studies with x, the second with y.' I don't know who teaches most of the competitors. I'm judging what a student is doing."

He throws out theories to explain why some teachers have more winners than others. "Some teachers don't enter many students. Years went by when I didn't have a winner. Sometimes the Yankees win all the time . . ." He stammers, then asks for the name of another team. "And sometimes the Mets lose all the time. Unless you go to a system where you assign a particular concerto to a particular teacher, there's no guarantee anybody's student will turn out a winner."

There is a rumor that Ramon's teacher has proposed such a system.

Ramon, who has been politely dancing around the issue, gets to the point. "Before competitions, some teachers decide to vote in a particular way. If two people always vote the same way, you have to draw certain conclusions." He introduces the term "bloc voting."

The chairman looks confused. "What do you mean by bloc voting? How can you prove I'm dishonest by how I vote in a competition?"

Ramon is stuck. If he spells out his theory in any more detail, he will be calling the faculty a bunch of petty connivers. He sits down.

The president takes two more questions from the floor. They are, mercifully, on remote subjects. He answers them thoughtfully but quickly and adjourns the meeting. He has another to attend. "I'm not going to wish you good luck in your concerto competitions," he says, "but I wish you luck in your education." Everyone applauds. He leaves the room. The rest follow.

An angry girl is waiting outside for Ramon. He promised, when she signed the petition, that the names of the signers would not be revealed to the administration. But as she discovered at the meeting, Ramon turned in the entire list of signatures with the petition.

"You lied to me," she says, "and I am very upset. *Very.* I would never, *never* have signed it if I knew they were going to see it." Ramon doesn't say anything. He walks straight to the elevator, where he suffers the misfortune of running into the chairman.

The chairman once again asks what he means by bloc voting. "How can there be bloc voting—how can you say a teacher always votes the same way when he is always voting on different students and different pieces? I don't understand."

Ramon hesitates. What he wants to say is that teachers vote for and against *teachers,* not students. Students come and go, but teachers don't. Ramon believes that teachers gang up or swap favors, the students mere pawns in the game.

"Well, just look at the chart," Ricardo says uncomfortably.

An elevator arrives. The chairman makes no move toward it. Ramon decides to take it.

"Everyone here is somewhat human. There are, of course, exceptions."

A Juilliard cellist

7 THE CAFETERIA

If Juilliard were a human body, the fourth floor would be the heart, the place to test for vital signs. The fifth floor would be the brain. The second floor, where the cafeteria is, would be the guts. There, away from their teachers and without their instruments, the students are themselves. On the second floor, the dams break and emotions spew forth.

Some people go to the cafeteria to eat. Some go to play bridge. Some go to ogle the young lovelies. Most go to gossip. The cafeteria is the lounge and game room and therapist's office rolled into one.

Some spend nearly all day in the cafeteria. (Peter Schickele, who discovered the nonexistent composer P.D.Q. Bach, says he majored in cafeteria. He says in fact that P.D.Q. Bach was born there.) Some spend endless hours drifting from table to table. They live on coffee and cigarettes: a drag on the one, a sip of the other, a flick of the ashes, a blow on the steam. The confused and paranoid find kindred spirits there.

People in the cafeteria say "I really should be practicing" more often than they know. The person who says it sometimes gets up to leave. Sometimes someone else at the table does. The utterance usually just raises the level of anxiety.

The cafeteria is a sea of white Formica tables and black chairs. Windows run the length of two walls and overlook the streets below. The cafeteria is one of the only places in the building to see the sun and a friend at the same time.

The cafeteria is also the one part of the building where dancers, actors and musicians coexist. The societies within each group coexist, too. But none of them mingle. Each one stakes out a territory and exudes its essence. The cafeteria is like a circus, a different show at each table.

The cafeteria is the ultimate Café des Artistes.

When the cafeteria opens at eight in the morning, the sun cuts a bright, sharp angle through the big Broadway window. The cafeteria manager ambles in, the *Daily News* morning edition tucked under his arm. He unlocks the canteen grate and gives a shove from underneath. The grate squeaks all the way up, then falls back an inch and comes to rest on a hook. He retreats to his office behind the serving area, leaving a Hispanic woman buttering bagels to man the fort.

A Jamaican busboy with a tray of plastic salt and pepper shakers walks the aisles, placing a set at the center of each table. They used to be glass and sat on the tables overnight. Then they started to disappear.

People come through to load up for the morning. Half of them leave with their food, half sit down with it. A French organist with slicked-back hair and a soft leather jacket sits beside the Broadway window and pulls from a wrinkled paper bag a tub of cottage cheese and a plastic spoon. Two girls sitting against the Sixty-sixth Street window rip open small dry-cereal boxes, pour the contents into identical yellow Styrofoam bowls and saturate them with milk from identical red cartons. A balding blond man with a reddish beard, sad blue eyes and a big soft belly sits down and pulls out a leather-bound copy of *Madame Bovary*. Three composers and a conductor at another table are wolfing down three-course breakfasts of eggs, sausages, bagels and farina. One of them bangs on the table and exclaims, "But there's no B in the E flat diminished chord!" "But there *is* in the G sharp!" another responds. A girl with tortoiseshell-framed glasses conducts an irregular meter with a pencil, mouthing syllables between the beats, bouncing her head on the downbeats.

It doesn't smell like breakfast. The cafeteria smells the same all day and all night. The air cooler sucks the odors in.

Jennifer comes in. Her left arm is in a cast. She broke it running for a subway. She stuck her left hand out to break her fall and to protect the cello in her right hand. The cello survived, but her left wrist broke. She can't play, so she sits in the cafeteria. She plans to catch up on overdue homework. Maybe a friend will come by.

A ballet dancer struts past her, toes turned out like a duck. Her bony derrière swivels to the right and left and right and left. She goes up to the unofficial School of American Ballet table next to Jennifer's and plops down. Two boys are curled up there, one with his ballet-slippered feet on the table.

"Oh God, I'm so *tired* I could *die*," she moans. "I need an intravenous feeding of caffeine."

Jennifer wonders how she manages to look so pert.

The drama students on the other side, waiting for diction class, are talking about suicide. Jennifer heard on the radio this morning that a Westchester teenager killed himself last night. One of the drama students —the girl with the lead in the upcoming production of *The Rose Tattoo* —doesn't know her lines. She tries to concentrate, but even she gets seduced into the debate.

"We're all going to go anyway. What's the difference if it's now or later?"

"Big diff."

"If it hurts that much to be alive . . ."

"Today it hurts, but tomorrow could be heaven."

"Hey, man. You spend ten years feeling like you got a razor cutting through you, cutting in slow motion against the grain. You don't wake up the next day like you're in a heart-shaped bubble bath in the Poconos."

"It's against the law."

"Oh. So they going to hang a dead man?"

"It's also incredibly selfish."

"I slit my wrists and that's selfish? How 'bout if I wipe the kitchen knife clean before I bow out."

"Very funny. You never *really* considered it."

"I have."

"And?"

"I couldn't decide whether to go with the kitchen knife or the sandwich baggies."

"No, seriously."

"Look at it this way. It's the ultimate painkiller. And it doesn't even hurt. There's no difference between the feeling at four in the morning when you're asleep and at four in the morning when you're in a coffin six feet underground. You're sleeping peacefully—only, the sleep goes on and on forever. It's just turning the light out on pain. You turn the 'on' switch 'off.' " He bends the flip top from his can of grapefruit juice. "You don't like the game? You drop out. You don't like the play? You leave the theater."

"Nice poetry, but when you leave the play, you leave the theater and go get a sushi dinner. There's no sushi in heaven."

"There's no sushi down here for some people. Look. Someone's been handed a bad script. There's no way out."

"He's still got his imagination."

"If he's doubled over in pain, I mean if someone's scrapin' his heart with a razor, what good's an imagination?"

"Pain passes."

"That's easy for you to say."

Jennifer wonders whether he really has considered suicide, or whether he's needling them to get a reaction. Actors do that, she thinks. He looks wholesome—not like someone who would put a razor to his wrist—but whenever a teenager kills himself, his teachers and friends say, "He was such a sweet quiet boy." Jennifer decides you can never tell.

It is the middle of the morning. Jennifer wishes she were practicing. These are the most precious hours of the day. When she misses her midmorning practice, she feels as if she has lost the day.

An enormous pianist, his hair damp along the edges and his cheeks still red from a vigorous scrub in the shower, is scanning *The New York Times*. He takes extra time at the sports section. His breakfast consists of a bag of potato chips, a can of apple juice, an orange and a pickle.

A boy sneaks up from behind. "Hey, big guy. What's in the news?"

He smiles. "Hey, have a sit."

"I've been sitting all my life."

The other smiles again. "Did you have your morning coffee?"

"No."

"Well, you can always wake up by paper," he says, and shoves the sections he's finished with in the other's direction.

A busboy in a fresh white uniform with a white half-apron does the rounds, kicking a jumbo-sized bag-lined plastic garbage can around the cafeteria. He kicks the can with his right foot, grabs trays and dumps residue with his left hand, and wipes the table with a damp cloth in his right hand. He reaches for Jennifer's tray. She puts a flat hand over it. He moves on.

A violinist and his accompanist stroll into the cafeteria totally frustrated. They have spent the last thirty minutes in search of a practice room. The violinist is nine days away from the finals of a competition that could win him professional management and a New York debut. He is edgy. He hasn't rehearsed with the pianist since the semis, a week ago. They spot another violinist, sitting at a center table, scratching out a harmony assignment due in theory class at noon.

It is Saint Patrick's Day. The fiddle player with his homework in front of him is wearing a green corduroy shirt.

"Happy Saint Paddy's Day," the accompanist says. "You Irish?"

"Uh-uh. My father is from Finland."

The accompanist, who is black, doesn't believe him. "Yeah, and I'm half-Jewish."

"Top half or bottom half?"

"Wouldn't you like to know."

"You and Zubin."

"He's not Jewish."

"Sure he is."

"No. How could he be? No, he's not Jewish. He's Indian."

"He *was* Indian, but now he's Jewish."

"Really? Now he's Jewish?"

The third boy scrunches up the side of his face. "No," he wails. "You guys got it wrong. He once *said* he wanted to become Jewish, but he wouldn't do it because the operation would hurt too much."

He smiles. The others wonder what on earth he's talking about.

"Everyone's Jewish. Every musician is Jewish."

"Not everyone. Not Rostropovich."

"Sure he's Jewish. He's Russian. All Russian musicians are Jewish."

"Not von Karajan."

"Sure he is. He's German. All German musicians are Jewish."

Jennifer remembers that someone told her von Karajan was once a Nazi.

"Not Yo-Yo Ma."

"Yo-Yo Ma the First," says the boy who believes himself an expert on the subject of who is Jewish. He writes "Yo-Yo Ma I" on a piece of staff paper and flips it around for the others to see. "Read that backwards."

"I Am Oy-Oy." He chuckles.

"Are you going to tell me a guy whose name spells oy-oy backwards is not Jewish?" They all chuckle.

"Oy-yoy-yoy-yoy-yoy," says the first boy.

"I got one. Pavarotti. Pavarotti's not Jewish."

"I said all *musicians* are Jewish. Pavarotti is a singer."

A flutist whom the violinist and his accompanist ran into five minutes before passes by. "Did you find a room?"

"No, so we came down here."

"You might find one now. I saw people leaving."

They stay where they are.

The noise level rises. A horn player sets his case on a table of brass players, unsnaps it, removes the instrument and hands it to another horn player who runs his fingers down the valves, resisting the temptation to blow. A boy easy to picture in Israeli army fatigues studies the ads in a Hebrew newspaper. The canteen line grows long. A clarinetist in the middle of the line orders a bagel with schmeer and eats half of it before he gets to the cashier. Behind him, a male dancer in beige leotard and tights pulls a carton of milk from the cooler, shakes it and drops it. The girl behind him pretends she hasn't noticed. The composer behind her pulls out his wallet, finds it nearly empty and asks her whether he can pay with his American Express card. An opera coach who ordinarily eats in the faculty dining area spots two singers and wanders over to tell them he'll be with them in two minutes. He has hot gossip.

Another singer walks into the cafeteria waving two tickets for tonight's *Tosca* at the Metropolitan Opera. Montserrat Caballé is scheduled to sing the leading role.

"Lookie, lookie," she says, flapping the tickets in the faces of the others like a fan.

"I hope you have back-up tickets to *A Chorus Line* or *Sunday in the Park*," someone says. Caballé is famous for last-minute cancellations. She cancels so often there is a joke going around that her manager has announced that Miss Caballé will be available for only a certain number of cancellations this season.

"Or Ringling Brothers. Maybe you'll catch her there. Maybe she's moonlighting as the fat lady in the circus."

"She's had to cancel for sinus trouble recently."

"*She* cancels for stubbed toes."

"I don't care. If there's a two percent chance she'll sing, it's worth my evening."

"That toad? She does death scenes like she's a slice of American cheese and love scenes like she's a hard-boiled egg."

"Her high pianissimo notes are to die from."

"Well, she shouldn't waste our time on dramatic roles. If they're going to wheel her out to perform, she should do a recital of her hot little high notes."

"Her high notes are like spun silver."

"She doesn't pronounce her consonants."

"Her equipment is magnificent."

"She doesn't know her languages."

"Her voice is pure as Alpine air."

"She doesn't know her words."

"She's always on pitch."

"She's nothing but a voice box."

"Her high notes are hors concours."

"I'm very sorry. A high pianissimo does not a singer make."

Jennifer can't believe how bitchy they are.

Noon comes, and the cafeteria turns into Grand Central Station. One boy goes up to a tableful of his friends, waving a small white envelope of pills. "I just got these from the nurse," he says. "A dollar for all these, isn't that amazing? Look at this!" He holds the packet on a downward tilt a hair away from the table, and green and gold translucent pills pour out along with the white aspirin. "A dollar for all these multis and irons. And she didn't even charge me for the aspirin!"

He lifts two aspirin and looks for the water fountain. "My headache is *killing* me," he says.

"You should go work out," someone says. "That'll take care of it."

"I know," he says, without moving. "I went to a reception. "You should've seen it! It was fantastic! They had all this food—caviar and smoked salmon and truffles—but everyone was crowded around the bar. Everybody started drinking and it's like . . . my head this morning is like, *killing.*" He puts down the aspirin. "I must have looked awful. I was lying on the couch going 'Ahhhhhh . . .' She gave me five packs of aspirin and said 'Get out of here.' I was cracking up because there was this Korean girl leaving the office, and the nurse was telling her, 'Never take a Q-tip and shove it in your ear!' " He raises his voice to make strident feminine sounds.

"You think she lost it in there?"

"The nurse said, 'You've got a perforated eardrum. You've got to go see a doctor today.' She's talking to this girl slow and loud because the girl doesn't understand English. The girl's going 'Ya? Ya?' like she doesn't understand a word. The nurse waves her index finger and goes, 'Never use a Q-tip to clean your ear. Always use a washcloth.' "

"I love to use'm on the inside. It's so erotic."

"Especially if the tip is wet and it goes in really deep."

"Is caffeine good for headaches?" the boy with the aspirin asks. "Does it shake the headache out?"

"No," someone says, "but I think it helps the hangover."

Jennifer takes her theory homework out. She runs her finger down the semester assignment sheet and realizes she is two months behind.

The boy sits down. "Where is that bewitching dancer?" he asks, scanning the cafeteria for a girl who is usually there at this hour.

"Yeah, the Spanish dancer, the one with the big gazebos."

"Yeah, they're so huge! They'll probably force her to get an operation sooner or later."

"They must hurt her."

"They must weight five pounds each."

"Maybe the doctor can drain them."

"Maybe they can slice'm up and auction off the leftovers."

The boy with the headache rests his head on his crossed arms.

"I missed Joan Rivers last night," someone says.

The boy with the headache lifts his head. "I saw Mary Tyler Moore the other day." No one responds, so he says, "The woman, not the TV show."

"Is she ugly?"

"No, she's beautiful! She came into the pizza joint on Seventy-first Street and walked right by me. She ordered fries."

"Why would she go into a place like that?"

"Because the fries are good."

"Don't you think she's worried people'll see her?"

"If you looked like Mary Tyler Moore, would you?"

He shrugs. "Has she had ten face-lifts?"

"No way." He reconsiders. "Maybe one or two."

"God, I love Mary Tyler Moore," says a boy speaking for the first time.

The cafeteria din holds at a high pitch. The traffic shuffles, the trays clash and the vending machines gurgle. People raise their voices in order to be heard.

Jennifer wonders whether the arm in the cast is white and wrinkly. It has not seen the light of day for a week. She realizes that her mind is wandering from her assignment. At this rate, she won't get through a single week of homework. She switches to the other side of the table, where her back is to most of the cafeteria.

There is an exodus from the cafeteria at one o'clock. The overall volume drops by half, but the volume at each table seems to rise. The violinists at the table in front of Jennifer distract her. They are engaged in a burping contest. The object is to take a mouthful of air into the lungs and utter a sentence but burp before its last syllable. Whoever misses drops out. All three contestants are going strong when a girl at the table gets up to leave.

"Hey, it was nice talking to"—burp—"you," one of them says as she walks away. She continues walking. He dumps his chocolate pudding onto the half of the chocolate cake he hasn't touched and takes a sip of Perrier.

The burping contest evolves into a free-for-all for pundits and budding poets.

"My parents are nice, except for my mother and father."

"I'm a bastard and my brother is my son."

"Hey, want to hear a poem I wrote for class? It's called 'Inside Mom's Womb.' " He raises his head. " 'Inside Mom's Womb.' " He pauses, to set the title off from the poem itself. " 'Quiet, serene / Nothing to worry about. / What I wonder is / Where will all the rodents come from?' "

Jennifer puts her theory homework away. It requires more concentration than she can give. She takes out two copies of the Dvorak Cello Concerto. One has fingering and bowing markings, the other is clean. She sets them side by side and starts to copy the markings from one to the other.

Two Korean girls at the next table distract her. They are giggling over the names people choose for their chamber music ensembles. There is a subtext to their chatter. They encountered each other last night at Studio 54. Sung Ju saw Hae Sook smoking. Hae Sook has smoked for years but conceals it from her Korean girlfriends. If one of them finds out, word could filter back to her parents. But there is something more than the smoking. Sung Ju caught Hae Sook holding hands with her Japanese boyfriend. Hae Sook is not allowed to date anyone but Koreans. If her parents find out she has a Japanese boyfriend, they will pull her out of school.

When the girls bumped into each other at the cafeteria doorway, neither said anything about Studio 54.

Hae Sook pulls the annual edition of *Musical America* from her music bag and turns to the "ensembles and groups" listing in the index. *Musical America* lists the names of virtually every musician under management. Hae Sook has been studying the list for days. Kyung Wha, another Korean girl, sits down next to her.

"The N-O-T Trio!" Hae Sook says. "Why would anyone name a group N-O-T? It looks like 'Do-NOT-come-hear-this-trio.'"

"What are you doing with that?" Kyung Wha asks, pointing to *Musical America*.

"Well, we have this trio, and we had to think of a name for it. We need this name because we enter competition. And we came up with 'Nabi Trio.' Nabi mean 'butterfly' in Korean. It is word that is different in every language. She liked it," Hae Sook says, meaning the woman running the competition. "She said, 'How do you spell it?' I said, 'How about n-a-b-i?' And she said, 'That's so simple! Easy to remember! And for Americans it has a ring to it. It kind of sounds feminine. That's good because it's three girls.' So I thought, O.K., Nabi Trio. But the thing is, I tell Nabi Trio to

Koreans, and they crack up. They go, 'Ha, ha, you kiddin' me?' But I tell Americans, and they take it pretty seriously. They think it sounds pretty good!"

She pauses, then smiles defensively. "If we make a stage in America, I don't care what Koreans think."

Kyung Wha elbows Sung Ju. "Sounds like she's on a talk show, explaining the whole thing." They all laugh.

Jennifer turns to check the time. The violinists sitting against the window behind her are gossiping. One of them looks out the window and down to the street, where a battalion of teenagers is clumped against the brick wall of Tower Records. It's a typical heavy-metal crowd. The hes and shes meld together in a sea of skintight black leather pants, pointy black boots with chains at the heels and long scraggly hair in Day-glo pink and green and peroxide white. Some are cutting school. One is leaning against the wall, eyes closed and chin up. One is lost in the cover story of the *East Village Eye*. Some are gyrating to the music on their walkmen. At the front of the line is a velvet magenta rope suspended between two waist-high silver poles. There is a cop waving a billy club in front of the rope.

The violinist starts waving at the crowd. Two girls in line notice him and nod in his direction. He runs down to the street to see what the commotion is about and walks the line back and forth and halfway back again before he finds one of the two girls. It takes that long because he's kept an eye out for two peroxide mohawks, and one of the girls has disappeared.

He taps the other on the elbow. "What's going on here?"

She glances his way just long enough to see who he is. She inhales quickly and powerfully. "We're waiting for Joan Jett." Joan Jett is the queen of rock 'n' roll, in town for a series of concerts at the Beacon Theater, but he doesn't know her.

"Who's Joe Jett?" he asks.

"It's a *she*. She's gonna sign records." She pulls from an unmarked brown bag Joan Jett's latest album, *Glorious Results of a Misspent Youth*. "See what I mean?"

"Yeah." He flips to the back, looking for a bio, but all he finds is a grainy black-and-brown-and-white photo of three grisly hoodlums and a woman who looks like a bank robber. "Pretty exciting," he says and hands it back. There is an awkward silence. He wants to slip away but feels unsettled. He points to Juilliard, to the window they made contact through minutes ago. "You know what that is?"

"Uh-uh." She wishes he would leave.

"That's Juilliard."

"Julie *who?*"

He finds this very funny. In no time, he's back upstairs, repeating the exchange verbatim.

The busboy makes the rounds again. He is working fast, but not fast enough.

A singer with bronchitis is studying the life line of a singer who is trying to avoid her coughs. If she catches the cough, she'll lose her role in the American Opera Center production set to open next week. She decides to stop breathing for an instant when the girl with bronchitis coughs. "You will live to be one hundred and—" the girl says, and sneezes into her palm.

Jennifer gets up to buy an apple. She passes a table in the middle of the room. People are double-parked around it. Everyone is speaking Spanish, extra fast. Jennifer taps the shoulder of a girl at the table.

"Hi," the girl squeals as if she had been looking for Jennifer all day. She introduces Jennifer to the boy at her left. He raises his eyebrows and smiles as if he had been waiting months to be introduced.

"Are you a dancer?" he asks. Jennifer looks as much like a dancer as Harry Truman did. She tilts her head.

"No, why?" she asks.

He smiles, revealing a wide set of slightly yellowed teeth.

"Is that an insult or a compliment?" she asks.

He straightens up. "Why, a compliment of course! One should always make compliments. I never forget anyone who makes me a compliment."

She moves toward the canteen. He grabs her hand and kisses it. "*Adiós,*" he says and winks.

Jennifer winds past the cashier and bumps into Lana, a girl who ambles in rocking from side to side like a sharpshooter in the Wild West. Lana scares Jennifer. Lana walks tough, talks tough and wreaks havoc wherever she goes. She once brought a cage of pigeons into the lobby and released them before a black-tie gala in the Juilliard Theater. She once stole some Juilliard stationery and typed a teacher a note saying that Vladimir Horowitz would like her to call. (She got his telephone number through connections.) There is a cellist who has irritated her for some time, and she is at breaking point. He thinks he's the hottest thing on two feet. Lana has studied his lunchtime moves for weeks. She sits down at a table of violinists. They all say hi but she turns her chair away from them, faces the canteen and crosses her arms.

The cellist comes in on schedule, drops his stuff at an empty table and goes to the end of the canteen line. She cuts in line and makes off with a cottage cheese and fruit plate—his daily choice—then circles to the condiment station for two packets of ketchup, grabs her purse from the back of her chair and goes to the back of the room. Jennifer watches her put the plate on the dirty table, pull a tampon from her purse, rip the wrapper off, rip open the ketchup packets and saturate the tampon with ketchup. She dangles the tampon with her left hand as she unfurls a corner of the delicate wrap from the plate, slides the doused tampon between the two orange slices, reseals the wrap and hurries the plate back to the canteen shelf. It is the only cottage cheese and fruit plate left.

Jennifer is stunned. She considers buying the plate herself. She considers telling the cashier. But she doesn't do anything. She turns her back to avoid seeing who pulls the plate from the tray.

A master class given by Renata Scotto is ending. Two of the sopranos who sang there come to the cafeteria to unwind. It was a tense affair for them, onstage under the scrutiny of the Metropolitan Opera diva with the Mediterranean temper. People come by to congratulate them. A Russian violinist pays his respects en route to the vending machine.

"You sang beautifully," he tells one.

"And you sang beautifully," he tells the other.

"But *she*," he says, referring to Renata Scotto, "she has a Strad here." He points to his Adam's apple and continues on.

The room darkens. The clouds outside seem ready to burst. The Joan Jett groupies are agitated. Some leave the line. Others move closer to the wall, as if that will shelter them. The wind picks up momentum. Stray pages of a *New York Post* swirl into the street. People start walking briskly. The people in the cafeteria start to move slowly. They don't feel the wind, only the weight of the darkness.

Six ballet dancers get up and collect their bags. One leans over to another. *"Ciao,"* she says in two syllables and gives the other a peck. The dancers bounce out, leaving behind a week's worth of soda cans and candy wrappers. They are skinny. They are beautiful, and they know it. They walk around as if life were one long movie, starring them. They smoke, but look like naughty children when they do. Their hair ribbons are different colors, but no one deviates far from the model. They wear a tight bun high on top of the head and earrings that flirt and soften the austere coiffure. They dress in layers. They make themselves up like models and walk around the cafeteria half naked, but they act annoyed when people stare.

Mia and Mary are left behind. Both are sixteen. Mia presses her legs against her chest and throws her head back, as if she dared someone to approach. Mary is drawing on the white Formica tabletop with a soft lead pencil.

The Italian horn player behind Mia smacks a pack of Marlboros against his table. She turns around. "Can I have a cigarette?"

Mary mimics her. "Can I have a—*cigarette?*"

He gives her the first cigarette from his pack. When she's got it between her lips, he flicks the lighter up against the end of it. Mia inhales deeply and turns back to Mary. "I'm really nervous about *Swan Lake.*"

"Yeah, they're supposed to post parts on Monday."

Their eyes drift off.

Another dancer comes by, drops her stuff and turns toward the canteen. "I'm so hungry," Mia moans.

"Want something?"

"You eat too much. You're too fat," Mary says. Mia looks as if she weighs less than ninety pounds.

"A plain yogurt."

The third girl comes back with the yogurt. Mia neither thanks her nor pays her for it.

"I have cramps," Mia says.

"Y'do?" Mary says. She is writing Mia's name in a heart with a boy's. Mia pushes her hand. "What is *wrong* with you?" she says angrily. "You drive me up a wall."

Mary smirks.

"I'm not joking. You can really be annoying. What you were doing drives me up a wall."

The orchestra is on break. People rush into the cafeteria to grab snacks. Everyone talks of the flutist who has just been reduced to rubble.

Two pianists sit down near the dancers. Tom has been working on a program for the Chopin Competition in Warsaw. He tells Michael he is worried about playing the mazurkas in Warsaw. The mazurka is a Polish national dance. Some people think only Poles can do them justice.

"Oh come on, the Poles aren't going to play them any better than we do."

"No? The Germans think—"

"Yeah, like the Germans think they can play Beethoven. They play it worse than we do!"

"But the Poles and the mazurkas—"

"Just because they're Polish doesn't mean they can play them!"

"Of course it does."

"It does *not*. They only *think* they can. And speaking of Germans and Beethoven, I'm sick and tired of them telling me I play Beethoven like an ugly American."

Tom throws his head back and laughs.

"I play Beethoven as well as they do," Michael says. "Better."

Tom pushes the salt shaker to the edge of the table.

"And me playing Beethoven is one thing. When *Hae-Kyung—*"

Tom interrupts. "I don't think you can compare playing Beethoven in Germany to playing Chopin mazurkas in Poland. Beethoven is a more universal composer. Me playing mazurkas in Poland is like a Norwegian playing ragtime in New Orleans."

Michael laughs. "Well who knows? Maybe a Norwegian would do it better than a honky-tonker from down South! I'll tell you something, Misha's Gershwin is damn good. He bangs the hell out of it."

Tom cracks up.

"It's gross, but it's not bad! You should hear his sforzandos!" A sforzando is an accent. "When he gives you a sforzando, it's like hammering a chisel in your ear. When he plays fortissimo, that spot, buh-buh-buh-buh-bum . . . with the sforzando? It sounds like Prokofiev!"

They both crack up.

"The only problem is he has only one approach."

"Yeah! He does the same thing with everything, whatever it is. Whether it's Bartok or Gershwin or Beethoven."

"Or *Bach.*"

Arthur comes by and clunks a pile of music on Michael's head. Arthur is a fastidious boy with a wiry build and sweat stains in the armpits of his white shirt.

Tom grabs a record from Arthur's book bag. "Oh my God, the famous Friedman recording of the mazurkas. Nobody does it better."

Arthur grabs the record back, opens his music and shows Michael a mark his teacher has made.

"I wouldn't hiccup there," Michael says. "You've got to hiccup at the sforzando!"

"What do you mean by hiccup?"

Michael demonstrates. "Bum, bum, bum, buh-buh bum—bum!"

"That's an agogic accent!" Arthur says.

"Well, I don't care what you call it. You've got to do it."

"But there's a difference between a hiccup and an agogic accent! Listen." He demonstrates. "Bum, bum, bum, bum, buh-buh-bum. That's an agogic accent. Now this is a hiccup. Buh-dup, buh-dup, buh-dup."

"Well, you have to do the hiccups too."

"What did she do to the Brahms?" Michael asks.

"Oh, she thought it was too harsh. She wants a gorgeous tone on the opening."

"At the beginning?"

"Yeah, at the beginning. In the bass she wants a mezzo forte, except on the sforzando. On the sforzando she wants a gorgeous tone."

Michael laughs. "You know what *that* means. It means don't play too loud."

"Yeah, that's all it means. Well, maybe I was overdoing it a little."

"Yeah," Michael says. "That's what I told you."

"You know the second theme?" Arthur asks.

Michael whistles it.

"I mean the third."

Michael whistles that.

"Well, she had me bring up the inner line."

Michael whistles the inner line.

"Yeah, that's it."

Michael pushes his paper plate to the side.

"You going to go to practice?" Arthur asks.

"Yeah, I got to go practice," Michael says.

The dean stands at the doorway. He goes to a table of Christian Fellows and tells them that some people are offended by the poster announcing the next Fellowship meeting. It headlines 'The Jewishness of Jesus' and advertises a speaker from Jews for Jesus. The dean says the sign was ill conceived.

"We certainly didn't mean to offend anyone," one of the Fellows says. "I'll take them down immediately."

The dean thanks him and leaves.

"How could anyone find the poster offensive?" asks a Fellow who overheard the exchange. "It's a historical fact that Jesus was Jewish."

A Japanese girl in a pink silk blouse, grass-green vest and string of knotted pearls sidles up to a composer and asks if he would do her theory homework for tomorrow. He has been eyeing her for half an hour, and she knows it.

"What time you want it?" he asks.

"What time can you have it?"

"First thing A.M.," he assures her.

He is sitting with six other men, all of them victims of Yellow Fever. Yellow Fever is a disease that infects Juilliard men with a passion for Asian women. The Asian women like the attention but keep their distance.

The girl leaves the table, the composer blanches and the rest of the table breaks into a chorus of "Yellow Fever." One does the backup, a basic koto tune with rock syncopation, slapped out on the table edge.

Sittin' in the café
Sippin' coffee, tokin' cigarettes,
Imitatin' clichés
Learned in the West.
Such darlin' little creatures
With manners so mild
They got Oriental features
Driving me wild . . . !
I got Yellow Fever!
Asian Flu!
I got sushi gonad
Wanna feed'm to you!

Four pianists at the next table are sitting mute. One of them refuses to talk to anyone before two in the afternoon. (He communes with dead composers until then.) One of the girls looks as if she has walked out of a Gothic novel. (She wears white pancake makeup and insists she is descended from the illegitimate offspring of Cosima Liszt and Richard Wagner.) The other girl breaks into a cold sweat when anyone mentions the name Franz Schubert. (She says that she, like him, is destined to die before the age of thirty-five.)

Three violinists at the table beside them are studying a pamphlet containing the roster of artists under ICM, the concert management. One of them is poring over it as if contained the key to the meaning of life.

"God, look at all the conductors under ICM." He reviews the list of conductors. "Where's Slava?"

"Slava who?"

"Rostropovich, peabrain."

"Under Columbia, probably."

"God, Captain Kangaroo is under ICM."

"Did he go to Juilliard?"

"Yeah. He's a famous pianist. He went here."

"He did?"

"Yeah, Robert Keeshan, man. He flunked ear training, so he went into kiddie porn."

"Cristina Ortiz," he reads. "Now, *she* is gorgeous. The only female pianist or musician who is really attractive. She is *gorgeous*. She won the very first Van Cliburn. She's like in her early forties. She's married to—"

"She's the only pianist or musician who is gorgeous. His majesty has spoken. What about James Galway?"

"Maybe you go for guys. I don't. Look, Pinky Zukerman *and* Eugenia Zukerman. I wonder if they met and got married at ICM."

"Yeah. ICM is like a dating service. They even got a guy to marry'm if they hit it off. James *DePriest.*"

"Look, Baryshnikov is the only one listed under ballet. How can they have just one person under ballet?"

"If they want a ballet, he does all the roles, and they superimpose him on a movie screen."

The guy with the pamphlet can't decide whether the other is teasing him. He slips the pamphlet into his bookbag.

Two tuba players in the corridor are pushing a third around on a percussion cart, creating a rumpus that suddenly stills the cafeteria. The boy on the cart is playing the Vaughn Williams tuba concerto while a trumpeter behind them is unfurling a roll of toilet paper in their path.

The tuba sounds fade away. Another table of violinists distract Jennifer.

"Hey, did you hear about the violin competition yesterday? Now *that* is a fuck-up."

"What? What violin—"

"The Mozart competition. You know what I'm talking about. It's the most unfair thing I've ever seen. One of the contestants was eliminated in the preliminaries but was put in the finals at two the next day and won the competition."

"Yeah, you just know everyone's going to act like it didn't happen."

"It's really fucked up. Now, my bow arm isn't that good, but—"

"That's not the point. The point is not who won. The point is that she was eliminated in the prelims. Then her teacher went and talked to the dean, who happened to be one of the judges. Then she gets put in the finals, plays worse than anyone and wins."

"You said it. I heard Marta, I heard Sherman and I heard Ta-Kuang. Marta was the only one in the whole competition who couldn't play the piece."

"Ta-Kuang should have won."

"Oh, I like Sherman's playing better than Ta-Kuang's any day."

"Sherman has intonation problems."

"Yeah, in the second and third movements."

"He had problems all the way through."

"Not with intonation."

"Yes he did! His thirds, the leading tone is always low. I mean he played well, but . . ."

Jennifer tunes out. She hears this debate after every concerto competition.

The two guys beside the violinists are disheveled. One is resting his chin in his palm. The other is resting his cheek in his palm. A third shuffles over, his shirttails hanging beneath his linty sweater.

"I got stoned out of my mind last night." He points to one boy and addresses the other. "I called him and bitched him out for an hour."

"Yeah! All you did was bitch, bitch at me for nothing."

"Were you talking about your problems with Alice?"

"No, she's so mad at me. She thinks I'm the world's biggest dick."

"Who told you that?"

"Richard. She told him I was a prick with ears."

"To tell you the truth, I did hear about that."

"See, the thing is just that I made her feel like I thought she was my girlfriend."

"Well, why did you?"

"Because I was stoned out of my mind! I smoked a whole mother fuck-in'. . ."

"Sometimes when people are stoned and drunk they say exactly what they mean. And then they cover up by saying they were stoned."

Jennifer has never been stoned. She has been drunk, but never drunk enough to do something she would regret. She imagines that smoking pot bends people out of shape more than drinking does, but doesn't believe it turns anyone into a whole new person.

Clarissa, a statuesque girl with messy hair, stands at the cafeteria entrance looking for Lana. She goes into the cafeteria for a napkin to blow her nose on. Lana spots and signals her.

"Boy, am I glad you're here," Clarissa says. "I got this lesson at four and the last movement of my concerto is a *mess*. He wants to hear the whole concerto this week."

"Don't worry about it," Lana says and takes a bite of her sandwich.

"Don't worry about what?"

"The concerto."

"That's easy for you to say."

"Don't worry. I'll take care of it."

She asks Clarissa how the other two movements are. Clarissa says they're O.K.

Lana wipes her mouth and her gears start moving. "What time will you be starting the last movement?"

Clarissa glances at the clock. " 'Bout four-forty-five, I guess."

"O.K." Lana looks up with a business-as-usual glance. "At four-forty I go up to the roof, to the box that controls the lights in the building and I throw the fifth-floor lights. That way the lesson'll end twenty minutes early."

Clarissa giggles half with delight, half with fear. She looks back at the clock. "Damn, it's four."

"Don't worry," Lana says.

Clarissa leaves.

It stops raining at dusk. The sun is setting over the Hudson River and the Mormon Church across Broadway catches the reflection of the sun. The streets are damp.

Clarissa returns to the cafeteria at five. Her lesson was miserable. She fumbled her way through the last movement of the concerto. Her teacher told her not to come next week if she is unprepared again. Maybe she should have been up-front with him, she thinks. Maybe she should have told him her alcoholic roommate had fallen into a coma, that she hadn't looked at the last movement.

Lana ambles in.

"What happened?" Clarissa says.

"What do you mean, what happened?"

"The lights."

"They didn't go off?"

"Uh-uh."

Another girl joins them. "Y'hear what happened?"

"What."

"On the fourth floor."

"What."

"All the lights went off. It was pitch-black. It was so dark it hurt your eyes. Everybody's coming out of their practice rooms screaming, 'Help!' " She laughs.

"Holy shit," Lana says.

Nearly everyone looks burned out when two freshly scrubbed and coiffed girls come in and buy canisters of juice. They stand at a table and motion to the busboy to wipe it before they sit down. These are old-fashioned girls. They wear cardigan sweaters and hair pinned out of their faces. They bring bag lunches and bag snacks to school. They always have their figured-bass assignments done. They complain about the rock music blaring through the speakers at Tower Records. One of them wrote a polite letter to Tower Records management asking, please, if they would be so kind as to turn the volume down.

They pull plastic containers of cucumber and tomato salad from brown paper bags.

"Were you in History of Western Culture today?"

The other girl nods.

"The teacher seems to like pictures of naked girls." (The class got a lecture on Botticelli. The teacher showed slides of his paintings of naked women.)

"When he shows us pictures of naked girls, he says, 'Oh, look at this. It's so beautiful.' Remember the painting of the girl with a man? The girl looked so tense and he goes, 'Oh, she looks so beautiful.' "

"He always runs his pointer along the curves of the woman's naked body."

"I saw him at the elevator after the lecture. He said, 'Did you watch the dirty movies?' "

"He never runs his pointer along the curves of a man's body."

"Man doesn't have any curves, silly."

Jennifer forgot to go to the class and is annoyed. She's doubly annoyed because she likes the art lectures.

Three Japanese girls with take-out Chinese food are grabbing the last chunks of dinner between their chopsticks, discussing a friend with a three o'clock lesson at her teacher's house. The administration had called to say her teacher broke his foot and was teaching at home. She called her teacher to ask to change the lesson time because she had a four o'clock theory class and worried she wouldn't get there on time. "Don't worry," he said, "I'll give you cab fare to get you there quickly."

"How much do you think he gave her?"

No one says anything.

"I'll give you a hint. He lives at 103rd and Riverside."

"Ten dollars."

She shakes her head.

"Twenty dollars."

"No. You won't believe it. Two dollars."

The girls' eyes open wide.

"Oh, my God."

"That's too little."

"Is he Jewish?"

"Shhhhhh," one whispers, and points to a girl behind them. "She's Jewish."

The one who asked if he was Jewish covers her cheeks.

The other shakes her head. "Two dollars is still too little. Not enough for a taxicab."

"Well, the bus would have been a dollar anyway. So the two dollars is really worth three dollars."

The busboy circles the cafeteria, collecting the salt and pepper shakers he distributed ten hours earlier. One table has three pepper shakers and no salt shaker. The one next to it has two salt but no pepper shakers.

The woman behind the canteen counter puts thin plastic wrap over the metal bins of food. The food that spoils goes in the refrigerator and the food that keeps goes in the cupboard. A girl asks her if she can buy a piece of fruit. The woman tells her all the fruit is locked away.

Two boys with violins and bows in hand wander in. The calluses on their necks are extra red. One of them sits down. The other circles the room asking if anyone has an aspirin.

The cafeteria manager comes out of his office. He stands on tiptoes and pulls the canteen grate down. It slams. He snaps the padlock.

The fluorescent lights buried behind slats in the ceiling seem to burn brighter than they did during the day. It's pitch-black outside.

The cafeteria grows quiet. The midday din seems a distant past. Here and there, people sit and talk. Every word is audible from every corner.

The whole place looks war-ravaged. Chairs are clumped together at some tables, turned upside down at some, and wholly missing from others. Toothpicks with colored cellophane flowers on the ends are stuck in the cork ceiling like darts. There are mounds of garbage everwhere: plastic bags, cigarette cartons, Styrofoam cups and dented soda cans. The black vinyl floor is full of white skid marks, cigarette ashes and bits of paper.

The vending machines go *click-click.* Those practicing late come in for a quick sugar fix.

A girl at the Broadway window takes a long drag on a cigarette to seal off the day. It warms her lungs and relaxes her. She sits mesmerized by the white lights of the traffic coming up Broadway, the red lights of the traffic going down. The cafeteria behind her is a ghost town. She takes a last drag on the short stub of her cigarette, exhales, extinguishes the cigarette in the pool of coffee lying next to an overturned cup and heads out.

Jennifer follows her.

8 ORCHESTRA

The Juilliard Orchestra is hard to please.

The string players don't want to be there. They intend to be soloists or chamber musicians and don't like playing as part of a pack. They consider their time better spent practicing. Orchestra consumes six hours a week: three-hour rehearsals every Monday and Thursday afternoon. Too much, too precious time.

The wind and brass players want to be there (orchestra is their bread and butter) but complain that the principal parts are not evenly distributed. (The dean who distributes them admits that this is true. There are more good players, he says, than good parts. And some parts he automatically gives to those he considers the best players.) There is perpetual complaint over who gets what parts and damning explanations as to why. The players try to make deals with the dean. (True.) They ask him out to lunch. (True.) If girls, they wear low-cut sweaters. (Questionable, although the dean says that girls who wear sweatshirts and jeans the rest of the week often show up in his office in dresses.)

The orchestra finds the repertoire repetitive, often inferior, and the conductors (who are rotating guest conductors) boring or condescending or nasty or sluggish or too theoretical or downright incompetent. The boring conductors drive the orchestra to watch the big round clocks at either end of Room 309. The condescending conductors tell them what to do without explaining why. The nasty conductors make personal attacks where musical suggestions would do. The sluggish conductors, like the one who spent three hours on the slow movement of Brahms' Second Symphony, make them squirm. The intellectual conductors, like the one who talked about the 'theory of sound,' also make them squirm. The orchestra has no patience with philosophy from the podium. The orchestra is there for business, and business means playing. The incompetent conductors lose their place in the score. If they are nasty as well as incompetent, they blame the orchestra.

The obnoxious students make a stage of Room 309 and an audience of the rest of the orchestra. They whip through concerto excerpts and Paganini caprices during rehearsal breaks and pauses between pieces. They continue to play when the conductor cuts them off. Orchestra is ideal for one-upmanship. The players outblow, outbang and outpluck each other.

The Juilliard Orchestra, nonetheless, nearly always plays well. One gets into the orchestra through merit, not seniority. The Juilliard Orchestra is the rare student orchestra with string players agile enough to handle knotty Strauss and Mahler string parts. (The media noted with awe that Pinchas Zukerman was sitting in the violin section of the Juilliard Orchestra the day after he won the coveted Naumburg Competition.) Player for player, in the string sections at least, the Juilliard Orchestra could compete with any orchestra in the world. Even when rehearsals are unpromising, the orchestra comes through in concert. Perhaps it is adrenaline, perhaps youth. Perhaps the players practice the parts between the afternoon dress rehearsals and the evening concerts. Perhaps they fake well. Perhaps they concentrate under pressure.

When inspired rather than burdened, the Juilliard Orchestra makes magic. A magical encounter at Juilliard drives out the memory of the hours of loneliness, the pain of rejection and the battles with ego. Competitors become brothers and sisters who jointly remember the point of making music in the first place: the joy of it all.

The Juilliard Orchestra made magic one week. The ingredients for the encounter were so perfectly combined that the absence or alteration of any one of them would have upset the delicate chemistry. It was nearly spring, the first sweet-smelling days in New York City that can induce a glimmer of hope out of a well of despair. The repertoire was meaty. There was no concerto, no soloist to back up, no ego to eclipse the others and no egos to eclipse the music.

The conductor was said to be a gem. Those who had played under him when he was last at Juilliard knew he was a gem. The administration had made concessions to get him back, but it was considered worth it: Stanislaw Skrowaczewski (Skro-va-chev-skee) had done wonders. The orchestra adored him, and the concert had been well received. *The New York Times* critic said:

. . . nor was there anything but quality to be heard from the Juilliard Orchestra under its guest conductor. . . . Skrowaczewski drew from them splendidly committed performances . . .

The main concession concerned the rehearsal schedule. Skrowaczewski, who has an orchestra in England and engagements around the world, could not commit to the standard three-week rehearsal period to prepare the orchestra for concert. This was a problem with all "name" conductors. Juilliard had tried to get others to do a concert—Georg Solti and Leonard Bernstein had conducted single rehearsals—but none could commit to the regular rehearsal schedule. None had the time.

The administration decided to try an experiment: to compress rehearsals into one week. This meant six three-hour rehearsals and a concert between Monday and Friday: two rehearsals on Monday, rehearsals on Tuesday,

Wednesday and Thursday, and a dress rehearsal and concert on Friday. All this on top of regular classes, lessons and practicing. There would be no time for emergency rehearsals. To prepare the program in a week and keep it sounding fresh would be a challenge. The administration figured that if anyone could meet the challenge, Skrowaczewski could.

The dean called Skrowaczewski to raise the possibility of doing a concert with rehearsals compressed into a week. Skrowaczewski, who had found previous Juilliard encounters gratifying and was free the proposed week, agreed to the plan without hesitation. He marked the dates on his calendar. They decided to discuss the program another time.

Skrowaczewski called the dean at home months later. They tossed around ideas for a program.

"Stan," the dean said, "why don't you do *Zarathustra* and 'Eroica'?" There was dead silence.

"That would be a conductor's dream," Skrowaczewski responded. Not just a conductor's dream, an orchestra's dream as well. And so it was settled.

It was apparent that something was up for weeks before Skrowaczewski even got there. Brass excerpts from *Zarathustra* echoed through the stairwells. The horn section got together to rehearse the *Zarathustra* parts. String players checked parts out of the orchestra library. (The library had flown Skrowaczewski's annotated parts over from England.) In the cafeteria, the players debated the merits of the Ormandy–Philadelphia Orchestra and Von Karajan–Vienna Philharmonic recordings of *Zarathustra*, wagering guesses as to which would be closer to the Skrowaczewski interpretation. The concertmaster, with *Zarathustra* solos that soar up the fingerboard and above the orchestra, put his money on Ormandy–Philadelphia. He listened to the recording enough to learn the piece, but not so much that Ormandy's ideas would harden in his mind.

The student assigned the principal trumpet part was acting strange. He had waited all his life to play *Zarathustra*. There are trumpet parts with more notes, but few as exposed. The exposure makes the *Zarathustra* part devilish, a mental as much as a physical challenge. Lick after lick, in tortuous leaps and scales, the trumpeter sticks his neck on the line. There is one extraformidable hurdle—the famous octave C jump—a jump so revealing that trumpeters are asked to play it at orchestra auditions. The flutes set the stage with a flutter figure. The trumpeter, hanging on for dear life, tunes out the world and goes for it. Just three notes and a jump, like a run and spring leap on a diving board. The diver never misses the water, even if he lands on his belly. The trumpeter often misses the high C. When he does, he might as well pack up his instrument and go home.

The trumpeter had been practicing like a madman ever since he found out the part would be his. He bought the score to follow as he listened to his Solti–Chicago Symphony recording, to see how his part fit into the whole. He had never before done such thorough preparation. He had been a UCLA frat boy with a terminal case of tunnel vision, blissfully unaware of what went on around him. Just hacking away. Just playing the trumpet.

People were spreading the word that this guy Skrowaczewski was really good.

The first rehearsal was scheduled for one-fifteen, regular rehearsal time. Skrowaczewski entered Room 309 shortly after one to arrange special seating for *Zarathustra*. He put the trumpets next to the timpani and the harps between the violin sections. Almost no one filing into the room noticed that Skrowaczewski was already there. He had retreated to the back, where he was chatting with the dean.

Nearly everyone was in place at one-ten, roughly five minutes earlier than usual. There was none of the customary last-minute scrambling for seats before the concertmaster gets up to ask the oboe for an A to tune. Room 309 was a sea of instrument cases and music bags at the feet of the players and the edges of the room. In their aged T-shirts, spanking new sweatshirts, misshapen sweaters, ripped flannel shirts, colored sneakers and fashionable boots, the players sat ready for work, all manner of pocket-books, denim jackets and parkas slung across the backs of their chairs.

At precisely one-fifteen, just as the red second hand on the clock hit the twelve, the concertmaster got up to ask the oboe for an A. The winds tuned. The brass tuned. The strings tuned. Normal operating procedure.

The dean came forward. The room was silent. He introduced Skrowaczewski in a few words, as he does each distinguished guest conductor.

"We're pleased to have with us Maestro Skrowaczewski, who used to conduct the Minnesota Orchestra and now conducts the Halle Orchestra in England," he said. "I'm sure we're all looking forward to what's going to be a wonderful week." There was the standard polite bow-tapping on stands and shuffling of feet to welcome him.

Skrowaczewski stepped onto the podium and gave the concertmaster a hearty handshake. He is a big man, about six foot two, and sturdy, muscular, barrel-chested but thin, in strikingly good form for a man over sixty, even for a man over fifty. His face is strong and rectangular. There are no wrinkles, but there are deep lines that suggest strength and wisdom. His thick bush of carefully groomed grey-black hair was combed straight back, in dramatic conductorlike fashion. His hair recedes on the sides, making the crop in front look like a breaking wave. He was wearing thick, wire-framed glasses, a dark blue turtleneck and grey pants. The first-stand string players picked up the scent of his musky cologne.

"As always," he said, his Polish accent laced with traces of American and British, "I'm looking forward very much to this orchestra. So let's begin with, how do they call it, '2-0-0-1.' " This was a reference to the film *2001, a Space Odyssey,* the Hollywood extravaganza that imprinted the *Zarathustra* opening on the American public's consciousness. The orchestra cracked up. They had been ready to play, taut like a stretched elastic. The *2001* reference released some of the tension but none of the drive.

Skrowaczewski gave the downbeat. The orchestra played for about three minutes, to a little past the *2001* material, before he stopped them. They liked that. It made them feel that he trusted them, that he wasn't going to tell them what to do every step of the way. The orchestra was used to two types of conductors at first rehearsals: those who stopped at the first missed note, and those who plowed through to the end, come hell or high water. This middle ground seemed natural and unworried.

Skrowaczewski went back. He went over the first full orchestra entrance, the upbeat every conductor does differently. The trumpets play an open rising call, and the rest of the orchestra enters with a dramatic upbeat, downbeat. Skrowaczewski likes the upbeat slow and aggressive. "I want it very much in tempo," he said. "Very incisive, with short bow. I subdivide that beat." He conducted the spot again. This time the orchestra came closer to what he wanted.

The eyes of the trumpeter were glued to the conductor. The long build-up to the first *Zarathustra* rehearsal made him feel as if it were a concert. He had been assigned good parts that year, but not enough to suit him. He felt raw. He had walked into Room 309 feeling edgy. He had said "Hi" to the people sitting on his right and left, but by reflex. If, midway through the rehearsal, he had been asked who they were, he would not have known. He thought of nothing but the part.

He nailed the C jump. Skrowaczewski smiled. The trumpeter calmed down.

Skrowaczewski always went right to the point. A few words, and everything fell into place. He knew exactly what did and what did not need to be rehearsed.

It was clear that the players had listened to recordings of the piece. Most of them had never played *Zarathustra,* but they knew of things (like changes of tempo) not marked in the music. At two-thirty, Skrowaczewski called a fifteen-minute break. Half of the orchestra left the room. Some of the players sped down to the cafeteria for vending-machine fuel, and some went to rest rooms to empty bladders and freshen up. Four tuba players just outside the rehearsal room stepped into four different bass lockers—eight- by three- by two-foot closets—and closed the doors. Someone outside yelled "Go!" and each of them played the *Ride of the Valkyries* theme in a different key while the crowd outside rolled on the floor with laughter. The rest of the orchestra hung around the rehearsal room, practicing and chatting with friends.

Some of them approached Skrowaczewski with questions.

"Do you want this up-down, up-down?" one violinist asked, pointing to a smudged bowing in his part.

"Did you find my solo O.K.?" a flutist asked.

"I hear you're from Poland," a violinist said. "Do you speak Russian?"

The second part of the rehearsal began at two-forty-five, precisely where they had left off. It was as charged as the first. The big shots were sitting up in their chairs. The violists who had been playing magnetic chess on their music stand all year had put the game away. There were ten minutes left to the rehearsal period when they finished the piece. They hadn't been playing as well as they had at the start, and they expected Skrowaczewski to go back and work on the last section.

He didn't.

"Thank you," he said, "you've been playing wonderfully. You're a wonderful orchestra. If you don't get it the first time, you get it the second time. Thank you, let's call it a day. I'll see you tonight with the Beethoven."

There is usually polite applause for the conductor after the first rehearsal. This is orchestra protocol. Skrowaczewski got a big ovation, foot stamping and whistles.

Skrowaczewski talked with some of the players, then headed for the dean's office.

The dean's office is like Grand Central Station. His door is always open, and he keeps no appointment book, so students file in and out when they like. Traffic gets heavy just before and after rehearsals. People come in to get excused from the next rehearsal, to complain about their seats or parts, to thank him for their seats or parts, or to ask that they be assigned the same stand partner for the next concert. When Skrowaczewski appeared in the dean's doorway, the two students there nodded to him and left.

The two big bearlike men smiled at each other. "You know, technically it's all there," Skrowaczewski said. "Now it's just a matter of shadings and style." That would be the rest of the week's work.

They talked for a few minutes. "You know," Skrowaczewski said, leaving the office, "I had forgotten a little bit how good they are."

The second rehearsal began like the first. At exactly seven, the concertmaster tuned the orchestra. Skrowaczewski hopped onto the podium with a big smile. He gave the concertmaster a warm handshake.

The rehearsal was on the "Eroica." Skrowaczewski worked carefully on the first movement, focusing on five different passages. He did a difficult section, then said, "O.K., let's go to the next major section." He conducted thorny string passages, went back and polished, then jumped to another thorny passage and polished. Some conductors spread rehearsal time evenly over an entire piece. Skrowaczewski worked only on the difficult parts and moved on, as if he were painting details on a huge canvas without stepping back to see how they fit into the whole. He trusted the details would fall into place. When he reached a passage similar to one they had rehearsed, he skipped ahead. Every comment seemed to make a world of difference.

In the Beethoven, Skrowaczewski seemed mostly concerned with the dynamics, especially with getting the softs soft. He got the orchestra to play so softly that heads turned when someone in the back of the room unwrapped a Snickers bar. Skrowaczewski explained not only what he wanted but why. "We need to let the oboe play softly, we need to be so soft that you can hear the oboe play softly." A double bassist leaned over to her stand partner and whispered something about how wonderful it felt to play that softly. "It's so much work," she said, "but it's worth it."

Skrowaczewski worked on the first movement meticulously. By the second, the players were caught up in his rhythm. He had them in the palm of his hand.

They went through the Beethoven movement by movement. They reached the finale with fifteen minutes to go, just enough time to read it.

They began it. A conducting student on the side of the room leaned over to another and whispered, "People are actually listening to themselves." When the orchestra reached the movement's slow section with about five minutes to go, Skrowaczewski clicked the baton for them to stop. They plowed ahead. He clicked it again.

"Thank you," he said. "I'd rather stop before someone makes me stop. It has been a wonderful evening. You are playing wonderfully. We're all very tired. Let's call it a night. I'll see you tomorrow."

There was no need to play to the end of the movement. They were playing well. He thought so, they thought so. In a funny way, though, they were disappointed to be stopping. They were enjoying themselves.

As at the end of the first rehearsal, there was stamping and whistling and hooting.

A half-dozen string players met at the elevators and left the building together. Those who lived uptown headed up Broadway. The street was buzzing with people leaving theaters, cinemas and concert halls. The musicians sang and whistled bits of the "Eroica." On any other day they would have hopped over to Columbus Avenue for a beer, but they were exhausted, and a long week lay ahead.

And so it went. The energy never flagged, the momentum never broke. Every rehearsal was as charged as the first two. The daily rehearsals allowed for a continuity absent from the regular rehearsals. Word about the miracle in Room 309 spread. Even students who were not in the orchestra started coming to rehearsals, standing or sitting on bridge chairs set up across the back and sides of the room. The pieces were getting to the point where they seemed to be playing themselves. Rehearsals became more and more rewarding. A horn player commented on how much Skrowaczewski seemed to enjoy himself on the podium. A violinist said that orchestra might even be fun if someone liked Skrowaczewski conducted all the time.

Skrowaczewski told a joke in the middle of Wednesday's rehearsal. It was the only time in the week he broke the concentration on the music (and the first joke since the *2001* quip).

He was in the middle of "Eroica." He wanted the orchestra to begin at letter G. "O.K.," he said, "let's go to letter G. Minuet in G." The orchestra stared at him, confused and curious. He was forced to explain.

"Victor Borge tells this story, and I'm not Victor Borge," he said, trying to worm his way out of telling it. They moaned, disappointed. His body relaxed slightly: his right hand dropped to his waist, but his elbow stayed bent, as if to indicate that this interruption would be short.

"Beethoven was sitting there composing. His cleaning woman comes in. 'Gee, that was a nice tune,' she says. And so Beethoven transposed the tune into G and it became the Minuet in G." Some of the players smiled, and some turned to their neighbors for an explanation. Most stared at Skrowaczewski, totally confused. The rehearsal continued.

On the way out, people tried to identify the quality that made them adore Skrowaczewski.

He was a gentleman. Never in the six rehearsals was there a nasty or sarcastic word, never an angry mood. He was respectful of the players. When they made mistakes, he smiled and said, "O.K., let's start again." He explained what he wanted clearly. The orchestra responded by playing well. The orchestra always wants to play well for someone who shows respect.

He was efficient in his rehearsal technique. Rehearsals never felt three hours long. He lulled the players into having a good time. He didn't lecture and didn't rehearse the life out of the pieces. He started rehearsals by saying what he planned to cover. At the beginning of one "Eroica" rehearsal he asked the orchestra what they thought needed work. "Fugato," came a chorus. He zeroed in on problems and criticized them in positive terms. He never dwelled on a point. Some conductors overrehearse a troublesome portion. Skrowaczewski let trouble spots rest after he worked on them. Or he went back to them in another rehearsal. Everyone knew what needed to be cleaned up.

He let the musicians play. His gestures were clear but left the players breathing room. They were aimed at the big picture, the grand architecture of Strauss and Beethoven, but were always clear and precise. The players were awed.

He seemed to be there, first and foremost, to make music. He seemed to place the music ahead of himself and ahead of the orchestra. He conducted without mannerism. At Juilliard Orchestra rehearsals, when an instrument has a solo lick in the middle of a piece, the orchestra registers approval by stamping and shuffling feet. Skrowaczewski didn't seem annoyed by the ruckus, but he ignored it, as if it wasted time. As if the point were making music, not massaging egos.

The dress rehearsal was in Tully Hall. There were firsts to contend with. The organ was playing in *Zarathustra* for the first time. (Room 309 has no organ.) Skrowaczewski wanted the organ's opening low note an octave lower, on a thirty-two-foot stop. He had to settle for a sixteen-foot stop: that was the longest the Tully organ had. At another point, he wanted the organ tone color to be more subtle. The organ changed from oboe to flute stops.

The brass players were in a new formation. Where Room 309 is shallow and wide, Tully is narrow and deep. The brass were arranged in rows, on risers. The trombones and tubas, who had been to the left of the trumpets in 309, were now behind them and had to adjust to sound coming from a new direction. The trumpeters couldn't hear themselves well. Some brass players overblow in the acoustic strangeness of Tully. These brass players knew where to lie low. They knew what was projecting and what was getting lost.

There was a short break after the *Zarathustra*. Some of those who didn't play in the Beethoven left the stage and went to sit in the hall. Others spent the break working on difficult passages and chatting with friends. Fewer than usual left the stage area. This was Tully, the chance to adjust to the stage and the lights and the extra space between the seats. The concert was five hours away.

After the break, the orchestra played straight through the "Eroica" for the first time all week. At three-fifty-five, with five minutes left to the rehearsal, Skrowaczewski put his baton on his stand and motioned to indicate that he had some final words before the concert.

"Thank you," he said. "It's wonderful for me in my professional career to get to work with people who are so passionate about their music making. Thank you." There was silence for a split second. Then the orchestra broke loose. They started clapping, whistling, stamping and hooting as they did at the end of every rehearsal, but this time they wouldn't stop. Appreciative clapping goes on for just so long. This went far beyond that. The orchestra's feeling for Skrowaczewski had gone beyond appreciation to love.

As the orchestra sat and demonstrated unbridled affection, one violinist's memory carried him back to another experience with a conductor at Juilliard, an experienced as charged as this, but charged with resentment instead of appreciation, hostility instead of warmth, contempt instead of admiration.

The orchestra was the Juilliard Philharmonia. The concert was all contemporary music written since 1920. The music was not the "accessible" type, like the music piped in on classical music channels on airplanes, but to students who had grown up with contemporary music, it was manageable at the very least.

The conductor may have found it less so. Perhaps his preparation had been superficial. But in the first few rehearsals, he missed meter changes, misread entrances and misread notes. The orchestra got the feeling he was learning the pieces at the rehearsals.

There is one sin graver in an orchestra's eyes than nastiness: unpreparedness. Either alone enrages an orchestra. The two together, and the orchestra goes on strike.

The orchestra had played under this conductor earlier in the year, and things had not been smooth. Some of the players had written to the Juilliard president to complain. They thought the conductor wasted their time. Most conductors schedule to the minute the time they plan to rehearse each piece. This conductor refused to do so. He often said he was going to rehearse two pieces, then decided to do only one, but still required those in the other to sit there.

The orchestra was surprised to find that he had been reengaged.

The rehearsals for the contemporary music concert were spread over two weeks. By the second rehearsal, the conductor had become abusive. "Why can't you play?" he asked a flutist. "You're terrible," he told an oboist. "You don't belong here," he told a bassoonist, "here" presumably meaning "at Juilliard." The bassoonist, a first-year student, started crying. As far as she knew, she was playing all the right notes.

Two more rehearsals of this, and the orchestra sought revenge. The brass players, instead of blowing through their instruments, removed their mouthpieces, turned them around, and went "nyuh, nyuh, nyuh, nyuh" through them, like a horse neighing, or like Curly of *The Three Stooges*. They continued to play after the conductor cut them off. Sometimes when he cut them off, they played the theme songs from *The Flintstones* or *My Three Sons*.

The conductor threatened to cancel the concert. "If this continues," he snapped, "I'll have to cancel the concert. I can't play with such an orchestra." He blamed the concertmaster, the traditional orchestra spokesman, for the pranks. The concertmaster kept his cool and tried to reason with the conductor as diplomatically as possible. The conductor ignored him. He continued to threaten to cancel the concert. "Excuse me," the concertmaster said and addressed the conductor by name, "if you just wait, everything will calm down. Everything will be O.K."

"No, no," the conductor spat back. "I'm canceling the concert." And he stormed out.

The orchestra was silent for a second, in shock. Then all at once, everyone exploded in laughter. Two minutes later the door to Room 309 swung open. The conductor stormed in, as furious as when he had stormed out, marched over to the podium, grabbed the music from the stand and turned to walk out. All at once the brass section stood up and clapped. The rest of the orchestra followed.

The door closed. They sat down.

After another minute, a trombonist, struck by the pointlessness of sitting there, got up to put his instrument away. The others followed, one by one. But the concertmaster stayed put. Five players huddled around him.

"O.K., we're in trouble," he said. "We've got a concert in three days." They decided to form a committee to deal with the problem. The committee was composed of the concertmaster, the four other principal string players and a tubist, to represent the wind players.

The committee went straight to the president's office. They figured the conductor had already been there. Yes, they were told, he had. No, the president was no longer there. The concertmaster decided to write the president a note. The committee went to the cafeteria to discuss what the note should say.

The concertmaster, in two paragraphs, explained why the orchestra was not at fault. He referred to the conductor as Maestro. (The committee thought this was a clever touch.) He suggested that the president talk to them rather than respond in writing. They wanted a chance to elaborate on the note and clarify questions he might have. Each committee member signed the note and wrote his phone number next to his name.

The president's secretary called the concertmaster at eight-thirty the next morning.

"The president requests your presence in his office at ten this morning."

"I'll be there," he said. He hung up and immediately called the tubist.

The tubist had already been called, as had every student who had signed the note. The concertmaster and tubist decided to corral as many orchestra members as possible for the meeting, figuring there would be strength in numbers. They also wanted to collect grievances and discuss a presentation strategy. They expected the conductor to be there.

They rounded up seventeen players. Everyone was told to be in the cafeteria at nine-thirty. The first two players showed up at nine-twenty. By nine-thirty the entire crew was there. They decided exactly what they would say. They expected the conductor to yell and scream and carry on. They would present their case calmly.

The conductor was not at the meeting. Only the president and the dean were there, the president seated behind his handsome desk and the dean in front of it. The concertmaster entered the office and shook the president's hand. If the two men were surprised at the number of players who trailed in after the concertmaster, they didn't show it.

The president spoke first. "I understand that you are dissatisfied with the music you're playing this concert."

"No, it's not that," the concertmaster replied. "We don't object to the music. We don't particularly love it, but we've played worse. The music isn't the issue," he said. "The issue is the conductor. We're professional enough to do our job. He," the concertmaster emphasized, "was not professional enough to do his."

The president seemed to understand but was concerned with the context in which this was happening. "The concert has to go on," he said.

"All right," the concertmaster said, "but you should understand that he's been unprepared and abusive. And things are going to fall apart."

The president said that the conductor had been brought in on two weeks' notice—the conductor originally engaged had fallen ill—and assured them that he would never again be engaged to conduct at Juilliard.

There was a rehearsal that afternoon. The president came in shortly after it began and stood against the wall, ten feet from the door. The conductor was on good behavior.

The next (and last) rehearsal was the dress rehearsal in the Juilliard Theater. The conductor behaved like a new man. He complimented the orchestra where compliments seemed strangely inappropriate. During the break, he made small talk with the committee members. He talked with them about the program, their instruments and their teachers. He had seen the note they wrote to the president. He knew who had signed it.

They did the concert. The hall was half full, a decent-sized audience for a program of contemporary music, and full of composers, including the entire Juilliard composition faculty. The orchestra played well. The conductor made some of the errors he had made in rehearsals, but the orchestra ignored them and played what was on the printed page.

The conductor was all smiles.

The New York Times usually reviews the contemporary music concerts

at Juilliard. It didn't review this one, but the *Daily News* did. The opening
line said the conductor "has no command over the standard literature,
much less the modern literature. . . . The orchestra suffered from a definite
lack of leadership from the podium." A percussion player in the orchestra
clipped the review and made forty copies on the way to school. He pinned
one to the bulletin board outside the orchestra library and distributed the
rest at the next rehearsal. He wanted to send one to the president but
abandoned the idea. He figured the president had seen it anyway.

The Skrowaczewski concert was sold out. Juilliard Orchestra concerts
usually sell out. The popular program almost guaranteed that this one
would.

There was no stand at the conductor's podium. Skrowaczewski was
conducting without music. This meant there would be no stand for a spare
baton. At seven-fifty-five a stagehand in a white shirt, black dungarees and
shiny black shoes came out onstage and placed a baton and note on the
principal cellist's stand. "Skrowaczewski's extra baton," the note said. The
stagehand said, "he wants this wand on your stand." The cellist secretly
hoped that Skrowaczewski would drop his baton so she could hand him
the spare.

The trumpeter was nervous. He was as nervous as he had been at the
first rehearsal. He had played the hard licks four or five times that week
(as much as he could have hoped for), but concerts are unpredictable.
Adrenaline can make or break a performance. His parents, who had arranged New York business around the concert, had just flown in from Los
Angeles. He spotted them in the dead center of the fifth row and tuned
them out.

By eight, the stage was full of players. The women were decked out in
formal black chiffon and silk and velvet, and the men were in tuxedos. The
house lights dimmed. There was a quiet intensity, almost a buzz in the hall.
Within a minute, Skrowaczewski appeared onstage. He looked taller than

he had in rehearsal. There was sweat on his brow even before the downbeat but still a cool aura about him.

The beginning of *Zarathustra* was razor-sharp. It was evident how excited the orchestra was. Every player sounded connected to every other, conscious of how his part fit in the whole. The players' eyes weren't glued to the page, as they often are. The page became a mere road map for the journey to speak to the audience, in chorus with the other players, guided by the conductor. The players felt a special bond with one another, expressing themselves in the eloquent words of Strauss and Beethoven. Making music aroused in them the emotions associated with making love. With the adrenaline on top of the enthusiasm, the results were magnificent.

The players applauded vigorously when Skrowaczewski came out to bow after each piece. He motioned for them to stand. No, they indicated, this is your performance. After *Zarathustra,* he signaled the soloists to stand. No, they indicated, this is your performance. He reached over to shake the concertmaster's hand. No, he indicated, this is your performance. He didn't act humble or embarrassed, just uninterested in his solo bows. Skrowaczewski turned to the audience and put his hand on his heart. He clasped his hands together and gave a wiggle of thanks. He smiled. He stretched his left arm out, touched the podium rail and bowed almost into himself, with a slight tilt toward the orchestra. He turned to his right and stretched his hand out to the concertmaster again. This time the concertmaster stood up. Skrowaczewski and the concertmaster did the dance of mutual appreciation again after the Beethoven. The orchestra had never behaved this way before. There was pandemonium, onstage and off.

A young man who had missed the concert arrived in the lobby just after the Beethoven ended to pick up a friend. He stood outside a back door to the hall. Hearing the wild, endless applause, he turned to an usher standing a few feet away, her arms crossed.

"What's going on in there?" he asked. "A strip show?"

The applause finally ended. The players packed their instruments, and some of them went to the green room to thank Skrowaczewski. He was effusive. He kissed the girls on both cheeks. He shook hands with the boys. The players left the hall exhausted but immensely gratified. There was spring in their step. They were laughing.

As Skrowaczewski packed to leave the hall, the dean collared him. "What've you got on for next year?" he asked.

Skrowaczewski didn't even stop to think. "I have one week in my schedule. November four to eight."

"O.K., put a hold on it," the dean said. And they parted.

"Well, you know, you got to look out for Number One."

A Juilliard flutist

9 LOVE LIFE

The girls say the boys are immature. The boys say the girls are uptight.

Juilliard is no love nest. The students say they have neither time nor energy for romance, that they couldn't tolerate running into a sweetheart all day in the halls and that breaking up would upset their daily routine. They say that no one meets their standards, that two artistic temperaments in a relationship is one too many and that they need to guard the demons that drive their art. They protect themselves to protect their work.

The boys who prefer boys and the girls who prefer girls complain of the same things.

It is hard to tell who prefers what sometimes. Some people aren't even sure about themselves.

The layout of the building doesn't help social interaction any. Juilliard is built in cubes. Each division and each department is in a separate cube. Musicians sit and talk in the cafeteria, but the cafeteria is off the beaten path. People sit alone or with their regular buddies there anyway. Sitting down and striking up a conversation with a stranger seems as much an intrusion as if a perfect stranger did so on the street. Those already acquainted lack the privacy to become better acquainted. Two students managed to find privacy on the roof of the building, but the rooftop visits ended abruptly when an administrator summoned them to say that someone from the ten-story Chinese embassy across the street had spotted them up there, in flagrante delicto.

The students, despite what they say, go to great lengths to ensnare the objects of their hungry hearts. One girl moved three times, trailing a conducting student who barely knew her, only to discover that his last move was into the apartment of his new bride. Another girl, with a massive crush on a trumpeter, agonized for months over how to meet him. She memorized his address, phone number and schedule and noted the friends with whom he entered and left the building. She thought she had no connection to any of them, until she discovered that she had a friend in his theory class. She began standing outside the classroom at dismissal time, pretending to be waiting for her friend but actually aflutter at the prospect of brushing up against her heartthrob.

She told her friend about the crush. Her friend set out to discover what she could about the trumpeter and found out that he spoke French.

The smitten girl approached the trumpeter in the cafeteria one morning. He was sitting alone, staring out the window, sipping lukewarm coffee.

"Um, excuse me," she said, "but I understand you speak French."

"Yes, I do," he replied and smiled.

"Well," she said, "I'm trying to learn French, and I'm wondering if you could help me with a couple of things."

"Of course," he said. "Have a seat." He tipped back the chair catty-corner from him.

She sat down. She told him she was going to study in France, at the Paris Conservatoire. She improvised a tale of sunset concerts at the Sacré-Coeur, recording contracts with Erato and recitals with Jean-Pierre Rampal. Stuck on a question about the arrondissement she planned to live in, she broke down. "Um . . ."—she geared up for her confession and blushed—"actually . . . um, I have to admit I lied when I said I was interested in French lessons." She scanned the room, registering nothing. "Actually, I'm interested in more than French lessons, and I'm interested in more than being your friend."

He got the idea. "Well," he said, trying to suppress a smirk, "I think you are the most beautiful girl in all of Juilliard. I have been admiring you for months. The problem is, I have this girlfriend I live with, and she—"

"Oh, I didn't realize," the girl interrupted, embarrassed.

"Of course, if there were anyone in the whole school I would love to get to know better it would be you, but I couldn't betray the trust she's placed in me." He had betrayed the trust with countless women, but he had the smitten girl convinced. His protests of fidelity only made her think more highly of him.

Another girl—the passion of countless men—once got on an elevator with her boyfriend three floors below street level. The elevator stopped five times en route to the fifth floor. At nearly every stop a former boyfriend of hers stepped on. By the time the elevator reached the fifth floor, the bulk of her romantic past was there with her. Some of the boys knew the others. Some pretended they didn't know any.

She started to receive poems in the mail. They were beautifully inscribed on elegant cards with scenes of Gothic women dressed in elaborate robes, outdoors, bent over flowers, gazing at the moon, taking in the atmosphere. Her boyfriend chuckled over the cards and dismissed them as the cries of some pathetic heart. She, however, spent months trying to determine who was sending them. He must be from Juilliard, she thought. The postmark said New York City. Everyone she knew in New York was connected with Juilliard, except for the checkout man at her Korean fruit stand.

She was standing on a subway platform just before Christmas, heading for a flight home, when she caught the eye of someone who looked familiar. She had no idea who he was or what he did, but she thought she recognized him from Juilliard. "Hi," she said in hearty Christmas spirit.

"Hi," he replied and smiled.

She returned to Juilliard two weeks later. That day the mailman brought a card that had a question instead of a poem inside: "Why am I good enough to say hello to in the subway station, but not at Juilliard?"

The mystery was solved, but now there would be awkward confrontations. The first one came at the second-floor elevator bank, where she was waiting for an elevator. He came off the first to arrive. Their eyes met.

"Oh, hi, how are you?" she asked with all the enthusiasm she could muster.

"Fine," he said and turned beet-red. He was a teaching assistant who always wore a three-piece suit. He walked off the elevators with two full-fledged teachers. This was no place to chat.

"Uh," she said, as he took one indecisive step away from her, "where will you be later?"

He almost lost his balance. "I'm usually in the lounge at five, grading papers."

"Maybe I'll see you there."

He smiled. "O.K., then," he said as her elevator doors closed.

They happened to cross paths in the middle of the afternoon and went out for cappuccino. He said he had fallen in love with her, watching her talk with friends in the Juilliard lobby. He had wanted to meet her for years. Expecting to meet her, he had once volunteered to assist at the master's degree table at registration. His heart sank when she walked up to the undergraduate table to turn in her cards.

They became friends of a sort. He helped her with theory and prepared her for a comprehensive examination at the end of her fourth year. The test enabled her to graduate despite nearly a full year of absence from class.

After that, they lost touch.

The relationships between the students are never divorced from the relationship between the students and music.

Young Sun avoids Lincoln Center. If someone offers her tickets to a concert she wants to go to, she shows up just as the lights are dimming. She does her best to avoid people she knew at Juilliard.

Her father calls her to say he has bought two tickets to a Serkin recital in Avery Fisher Hall. All Beethoven. A birthday present to himself.

"Will you come?" he asks.

"O.K.," she says.

"Will you meet me for dinner?"

"O.K."

"Can we eat at the restaurant I mentioned yesterday?" It is the only Japanese Restaurant on the Upper West Side he has not tried.

They meet at six. He has come straight from work. His tie is loosened at the collar and his hair is tousled. Young Sun is disheveled, too. She has taken the train from Philadelphia, after a day of mostly unproductive practice. She gives her father a peck on the cheek.

"How're you doing?" she asks.

They walk up Broadway. It starts to drizzle, and Young Sun pulls a collapsible umbrella out of her tote bag. "Here, Dad," she says as she runs the metal band up the umbrella pole and lifts it to shade each of them.

The restaurant is mostly empty. It looks different from the way it used to. There are ficus plants on the windowsills and Chinese paper lanterns over the tables and French harp music coming through the speakers. Young Sun wonders whether the harp music is supposed to pass for Japanese koto music. The thought makes her laugh.

They are shown to a table. Young Sun turns to drape her coat over the back of her chair, and her heart stops. She sees someone she has not seen in three years to the day. The date coincidence occurs to her instantly. She had thought of him that afternoon, reading through her datebook.

She considers pretending she hasn't seen him, but she is pretty sure he's seen her. He is with his brother. "Excuse me a minute," she says to her father.

"My God," Matthew says, "I hardly recognize you."

"Well, it's been a while," Young Sun says.

"How you been?"

"Well, y'know, O.K."

" 'Member Scott?" Matthew juts his chin toward his brother. He knows she remembers Scott. He wants her to say hello.

"Yeah. Hi." She forces a smile.

"I was thinking of you the other day," Matthew says.

"Yeah?"

"Yeah." He pulls his chopsticks out of the white paper wrapper and separates them at the seam. "I was cleaning out my desk drawer and I came across this picture of us."

"Really?"

"Yeah."

Scott says he has to go to the men's room and leaves.

Young Sun stares at the ficus trees. "There's something I wanted to say."

"Yeah?" Matthew says. He lifts his handleless teacup to his lips.

Young Sun turns back to the window. "I was a real jerk," she says. "I'm sorry."

"What for?" Matthew asks.

"You know," she says, "the whole thing."

"Oh."

There is silence.

"Doesn't matter," Matthew says finally. "It was good for me. Toughened me up."

A waiter comes by with a small white pitcher of sake and two cups not much larger than thimbles. Scott returns.

"Listen, you guys, I can go around the corner and get a paper or something," he says.

"No, it's all right, I'm eating over there with my father. I should go."

Young Sun gives Matthew a kiss on the cheek and nods in Scott's direction. She returns to her father, who pretends he hasn't seen anything.

Young Sun was five when her mother decided she was going to be a concert pianist. Not a pretty little girl who played the piano, a real artist. The piano would free her from an unhappy adulthood. Young Sun's mother had an unhappy marriage. Her marriage, like that of all Korean girls of her age and social class, had been arranged through a matchmaker. She was a star piano student, and her prospective husband was a young executive in his father's business. On paper, the marriage looked ideal, and for a time it was happy. But Young Sun's mother came to realize that she and her husband would never enjoy the bliss she had dreamed of as a child. A Korean woman, at the time, could neither avoid marriage nor separate from her husband, so she turned her attention toward her children. Young Sun was the youngest of them. Her mother claimed that she loved them equally, but, as she always said, some children need more attention than others.

Young Sun was raised like a princess. She had to practice, but that was all. And Young Sun did not think practicing was a chore. She thought it was something everyone did. A chauffeur picked her up at school every day and brought her directly to a piano lesson. After that, he brought her to another, with a woman who taught her nothing but scales and etudes. She practiced two hours after supper and another before school the next day. She worked hard and did as her teachers told her. She was talented, too.

Her father's business went bankrupt when she was thirteen. Her parents decided that Korea was too unstable for raising children and moved to the United States. They settled in a Korean neighborhood outside Philadelphia. The older children went to public school, and Young Sun to an all-girls Catholic school. Her parents sent her there to keep her mind off boys and on the piano. Young Sun thought about nothing but the piano during that period. She adored clothes and loved to shop, but she even chose clothes with the piano in mind. She bought dresses that were comfortable enough for practice, formal enough for recitals and festive enough for receptions.

Young Sun auditioned for the Juilliard Pre-College. She was immediately recognized as a star. She had developed such facility that even Upper School students stood outside her practice room and marveled at how she tossed off the hardest works in the piano literature. She became famous for two Chopin etudes—the "Revolutionary" and "Winter Wind," two of the demons in the set. Whenever possible, she practiced in Room 426. The rooms on either side had no pianos, and the action on the piano in there was hard. The action was so hard that when she released a key, she could feel the weight of the hammer jerk back to rest position. The hard action made her fingers work.

She didn't like Catholic school. The workload was heavy, so doing even the bare minimum took time. Too much, her mother thought, to leave time for adequate piano practice. Her parents considered sending her to the Professional Children's School, but they lived more than two hours away. The commute would exhaust her and cut into the extra practice time.

Her mother called her piano teacher about the practice problem. Her teacher mentioned that a number of Pre-College girls went to an out-of-state girls' boarding school, where they had plenty of time to practice. Her family visited the school, and she played for the head of the music department, who called the headmistress. "I suggest we do everything possible to get this girl enrolled," he said. Young Sun was offered a full scholarship and a deal: if she played one recital a month, she could take three hours of class each morning and spend the rest of the day practicing on the school's nine-foot Bösendorfer.

Young Sun had time to practice, but the rest of the experience was traumatic. The school was full of girls from broken homes, girls Young Sun thought of as "All-American." They were rich and sophisticated, dressed like models, had second and third mothers and smoked pot. When they weren't talking about clothes and ski vacations in St. Moritz, they were talking about sex. The girls liked Young Sun and tried to draw her into their little societies, but Young Sun thought they liked her only because she was a novelty, the token weirdo.

Despite that, Young Sun was starting to feel some independence from her mother. One weekend her mother asked her to come home, and she refused. It was the first time ever she had said no to her. Her mother was not only hurt that Young Sun refused to come home but frightened that she was losing control over her. So when spring came and Young Sun said she wasn't sure she wanted to go back to the school, her mother agreed that she should come back home.

They decided to try the Professional Children's School. Her father now had a job in New York City and drove there and back every day.

The PCS venture turned out well. Young Sun left school at two every afternoon and went to Juilliard to practice. Her teacher gave her two lessons a week. She was entering competitions and always winning first prize. She loved to perform and was never nervous. She was anxious before concerts, but anxious with excitement, like a child whose roller-coaster car door has just been shut. Her social life was happy too. She was spending days around children with lives like hers. Some Upper School Korean girls became like big sisters to her. She didn't know many other students, but the silent bond made her feel good.

One morning in French class, Young Sun got a message from the PCS principal: Call your piano teacher immediately. She borrowed a quarter from the girl sitting next to her.

Her teacher picked up on the first ring.

"Hi, this is Young Sun."

"Get to Juilliard immediately. I'll meet you at my studio."

Young Sun took a cab.

Her teacher showed up five minutes after she did, breathing fast.

"O.K. I want to see you at four this afternoon. Bring the Liszt Sonata, "La Campanella" and the "Appassionata." You're going to play an audition tomorrow."

"Really?" Young Sun asked. "Where?"

"In Philadelphia. At the Academy of Music. Pre-College recommended you." The soloist scheduled for a Young People's Concert with the Philadelphia Orchestra had canceled. Young Sun was to be auditioned as a replacement. The concert was three weeks away.

"Great," Young Sun said and scurried off to Room 426. She usually noticed when people peered through her practice-room window, but she concentrated so hard now, she barely knew where she was. At four she was back in her teacher's studio. Her teacher found the pieces presentable and told Young Sun to meet her at the Academy of Music stage door at two the next afternoon.

"Remember to wear a nice dress," she said. "And bring a hankie."

The door closed. It opened again when Young Sun was five steps away. "And don't forget to smile."

The audition went well. An assistant conductor and a number of orchestra board members were there. They all seemed pleased. The conductor asked Young Sun whether she could prepare the Prokofiev Third Piano Concerto in three weeks.

"No," she said. She had never heard of it.

Everyone stopped smiling, and her teacher threw her a look that could kill.

"I guess so," Young Sun said. Everyone was smiling again. Everyone shook hands.

Young Sun and her teacher took the train back to New York and went straight to the Juilliard library to take the Prokofiev out. "I'll see you at seven," the teacher said as she clicked through the turnstiles at the library exit. "I want the second movement learned." At seven, the second movement was note-perfect. The teacher spoke to Young Sun about taking a month off from school.

PCS granted the leave, and Young Sun practiced like a maniac. The first week, she learned the Prokofiev. The next two, she memorized and refined it.

She performed the Prokofiev at a class meeting. None of the students there knew that she had been engaged to perform the piece with the Philadelphia Orchestra. Young Sun was struck that her teacher had kept it a secret but assumed that she was trying to keep from dividing the class into "the star" and "the rest." Her teacher scheduled a Paul Hall recital for Young Sun to try out the Prokofiev one week before the Philadelphia concert. The Thursday between the Paul Hall recital and Philadelphia concert, she was to play the Prokofiev for the man scheduled to conduct the concert.

Young Sun stood on tiptoes to put some quarters in the phone.

"Hello?"

"Hi, Mom."

"Where are you?"

"I'm at Juilliard. I was wondering if I could stay at Soo Hee's tonight."

It was four on Wednesday afternoon. Young Sun wanted to spend the night with her friend in New York City so she could practice late. (Soo Hee lived two blocks away from Juilliard.) Young Sun had forgotten up until then to tell her mother about the run-through with the conductor. Now that she remembered, she decided not to let on. If her mother knew, she would make her come home for a proper night's sleep and a clean set of clothes.

"All right, you can stay," she said. "Just this once."

"Thanks, Mom."

Soo Hee barged into Young Sun's practice room at nine-thirty and invited her to a party across the street, a reception for a Korean violinist who had just played in Paul Hall. Young Sun was tired and hungry. She stuffed her music into her tote bag and followed Soo Hee out of the room. It was pouring outside. By the time the girls crossed the street they looked like drowned rats. Young Sun's white jeans were splotched with mud from passing cars, her white cotton blouse clung to her skin and her hair was matted to her head.

The door was unlocked, and the party was in full swing. Soo Hee grabbed Young Sun's wrist and pulled her toward the living room to introduce her to Sammy, the host. Young Sun yanked herself away and scurried off to the bathroom. She grabbed a towel and tried to rub her scalp dry, then loitered there, feeling unpresentable. Soo Hee started to jiggle the door. Young Sun opened it. Soo Hee took her by the wrist again and dragged her into the living room.

"Sammy, this is my friend Young Sun," she said.

Young Sun tried to smile at him, but ended up smiling at her feet. She thought he looked like a Korean Marlboro man.

"Hmmmm," he said. "Wet."

He took Young Sun into his bedroom, opened the closet and surveyed a pile of sweaters on the middle shelf.

"What do you think of navy blue?" he asked. The sweater was much too large, but she adored it.

Young Sun knew Sammy only from a distance. He intimidated her. He was a violinist working on his doctorate, ten years older than she and already an assistant to one of the violin teachers. All of a sudden, Young Sun realized that she had a crush on him. She had never felt this way about anyone. In her excitement over him and over the party and over the upcoming concert, she didn't notice that she was drinking more than she could handle. Now she was not only in the throes of an ardent first crush, she was drunk. She passed out. Soo Hee dragged her to Sammy's bedroom and put her to sleep. When she left the party, she carried Young Sun the two blocks home.

The apartment was very still when Young Sun woke up. No one was home. Young Sun couldn't figure out where she was. Her white jeans were a dirty grey, her blouse was splotched with ugly wine stains and she smelled like stale tobacco.

She noticed Sammy's sweater and suddenly realized both where she was and that the run-through with the conductor was fast approaching. She leaped out of bed, slipped back into the sweater and found the bathroom. She splashed water on her face, ran to the sofa to grab her purse, then back to the bathroom to comb her hair. She opened the medicine cabinet, pulled out a half-empty bottle of tea rose perfume, poured a generous puddle into her palm, wiped it across her neck and on her wrists, returned the bottle to the shelf, closed the cabinet, grabbed her tote bag and made a beeline for the door.

The sunlight was brilliant as she headed down Broadway. It seemed even more brilliant than it was, because of the recent rainstorm. Young Sun considered stopping at a pay phone to ask her mother to bring a fresh set of clothes to the Academy stage door, but didn't. The conductor wanted to hear her play, she thought to herself, not see her model.

She spent a frantic hour at Juilliard, running through the Prokofiev, then went to check the clock near the fourth-floor elevators. It was exactly noon, exactly two hours before the run-through. She sped out.

The conductor and her teacher were at the Academy of Music waiting for her. Young Sun walked into the rehearsal room and smiled, trying to look as if nothing was wrong. Her teacher took one look at her stained clothing, and her jaw dropped.

"How *dare* you," she muttered under her breath, loud enough that Young Sun could hear but muted enough that the conductor couldn't.

Young Sun looked away and shrugged. She felt a little self-conscious after that, but she played well. The conductor asked her to be at the hall at least half an hour before the concert to discuss last-minute changes.

Young Sun showed up an hour before the concert, reeling from a fight she had had with her mother the night before. Her mother was obsessed with nylon stockings, especially ultrasheer nylons, and made Young Sun wear them for concerts, whether she wore a long gown or a short one. She thought they looked more professional than the opaque pantyhose Young Sun preferred. Young Sun hated nylon stockings. She had always hated them, but not until that evening did she make those feelings clear. She made them so clear that evening that the argument turned into the most violent fight she and her mother had ever had. Her mother, as usual, prevailed.

The concert went well anyway. Up onstage with the orchestra at her left and more than two thousand people in rapt attention at her right, she felt like a child on the top of a giant parade float, fans lined five men deep up and down Fifth Avenue.

Her teacher assigned her the Beethoven "Emperor Concerto" to learn for a Pre-College competition. The week before the competition, she was to play it in a class meeting. She played the "Emperor" at her lesson the morning of the class meeting. Something felt funny. Young Sun sat and listened to her teacher demonstrate, and she became restless. She suddenly became aware of every key change, melodic detour and inconsistent rhythmic pattern. She got the feeling that she couldn't get through the piece. The feeling came out of nowhere. She had learned the "Emperor" quickly, but it had felt secure.

Her class-meeting performance was nerve-racking. She waited behind when the other students left. Trevor, her accompanist, stood at the door, a hand in his pocket.

She went up to her teacher. "If I do the competition . . ."

Her teacher had sensed that she was going to try to back out. "You have to do it," she said.

"I'm not feeling secure," Young Sun said.

"You're already signed up," the teacher replied.

Young Sun and Trevor left the room. Young Sun, who looked like a scared child, told Trevor she wanted to pull out of the competition.

"It sounds beautiful, it really does," he said sincerely.

Young Sun was silent.

"It's so fresh and new. It's all there. I mean it."

"I don't know," Young Sun said, dropping her head.

"Listen," Trevor said, "I'll be at the fourth-floor elevators at ten next Saturday for a warm-up. I don't want to pressure you. You can spend the week thinking about it."

"O.K.," she said meekly.

"But when you wake up Saturday morning," he said and gave a threatening look, "you better decide to do it."

"Thanks," she said and left.

Young Sun had lost a Pre-College competition the year before. It was the first competition she had ever lost. Her teacher said the decision was political, but the defeat still hit hard. It had hit Young Sun's mother even harder than it did Young Sun. So when Young Sun told her mother she wanted to pull out of the "Emperor," her mother had said, "Fine." Unless Young Sun felt one hundred percent confident, her mother thought, she should stay away.

Young Sun breezed into Juilliard at noon the next Saturday and went straight to the cafeteria for a cup of coffee. She bumped into her teacher, standing at the end of the canteen line.

Young Sun was wearing the lacy lingerie top she liked to wear for practice, a stretchy black skirt and high-heeled shoes she couldn't possibly pedal in.

"I'm not doing the competition," she said.

Her teacher's eyes opened wide. "Oh, no," she said, shaking her head, as if she were berating an ill-behaved dog, and put the tray back on the pile behind her. "You're not getting out of *this* one." She escorted Young Sun to the rear of the cafeteria for a talk.

Young Sun borrowed a pair of low-heeled slingback sandals. They were dressy enough for the competition, but too big. They wobbled when she walked onstage, and wobbled when she played. Twice they made her lose control of the pedals, but she played well and won the competition.

The "Emperor" concert, however, was traumatic. Young Sun had been nervous. From then on, her nerves were unpredictable. She was never again as confident as she had been. She played just as well, but worried about everything she did.

Young Sun graduated from PCS and decided to take a year off to get hold of her nerves. She decided not to do any concerts that year and went through a transition at the piano. She began to consider the questions people had always been asking: How do you trill so evenly? How do you play those double thirds so fast? How do you leap without looking? It was a painful process. Young Sun knew that too much scrutiny would paralyze her. But not understanding these things was paralyzing in its own way.

Young Sun practiced hard. At the same time she had her first boyfriend and started doing things normal girls did. She got her ears pierced, started wearing makeup and went to movies and discos. She emerged from her shell. The girls from her boarding school would not have recognized her. She had started drinking heavily.

She enrolled in the Upper School class of a man her Pre-College teacher had recommended. His students were good, but were not known for dazzling techniques. Young Sun's Pre-College teacher didn't think she needed help with technique. He would teach her how to produce a beautiful tone, how to play a beautiful phrase, how to play "stylistically." Young Sun was the star of the class.

She in fact created a stir when she returned to Juilliard. No one would have believed she had a shred of doubt about her pianism or her future as a concert artist. The students from the Pre-College already knew her as an impressive pianistic force to be reckoned with. Those who didn't came to. For besides her phenomenal pianism, she had developed a formidable personality. She had become the quintessential prima donna. She was the leader of a clique of pianists—mostly gay men and Korean women —who sat on the carpet outside fourth-floor practice rooms and intimidated students. When the halls were empty, they swapped gossip and told dirty jokes. They ranked the students in different categories: who was cute and who was ugly, who was rich and who was poor, who could play and who was spastic. They played poker and ordered up from John's Coffee Shop. When the delivery boys arrived in the Juilliard lobby and announced an order for Room 426, the security guards waved them up. There was a rule that students ordering in had to pick up deliveries in the lobby, but Young Sun refused. The delivery boys all knew where Room 426 was. They knew they would find Young Sun inside or holding court just outside. Young Sun had once again staked out Room 426 as her turf. If someone went near it when she was outside, she said she was on a smoking break. If someone was in it when she wanted it, she went in and said, "This is my room." If she could not bully him or her, she found another room and offered to trade. If none of this worked, she sat outside the room until the person in it took a break, then usurped it.

She marched into the cafeteria on her practice break, and all eyes turned toward her. She banged her fist on the table. "I'm practicing the Tchaikovsky Concerto, and I want my octaves like Bolet!" she announced, referring to the pianist Jorge Bolet. Or she mocked someone who had flirted with her. On the subject of men, she made her desires perfectly

clear. "I want my two-hundred-thousand-dollar-a-year-doctor!" she declared just as intensely as she declared her desire for Bolet-like octaves.

No one would have believed she was falling apart. Pianistically, no one
threatened her. She was practicing eight hours a day and playing as well
as ever. But she was losing confidence. Her fear of failure began to overwhelm her. She was signing up for recitals and canceling them, entering
competitions and withdrawing from them. Her fear of failure had become
her Achilles' heel.

Matthew's life was haphazard. His parents started him on the piano when
he was seven simply because he was hyperactive. They thought piano
lessons might get him to sit still for at least a few minutes at a time.

They found a piano teacher who was possibly the only person in the
world who could make Matthew concentrate. He was like an athletic
coach. His approach to the piano, in fact, was athletic. He devised obstacle
courses for Matthew. He made him practice while sitting on the floor with
rubber bands around his knuckles. Part of Matthew's technique developed
wonderfully. Another part did not develop at all.

Matthew's parents split up, and the piano and his teacher became a
substitute for the family that had fallen apart. Matthew lost himself at the
piano and got attention for his playing. He was not an outcast at school,
but he was different from the other children in his affluent suburban town.
His mother was a German refugee. She disapproved of Matthew's schoolmates, who she thought were rude and spoiled. She tried to keep her sons
from becoming like them.

Matthew was depressed during most of his early teens. He spent endless
hours lying on his back, staring at the ceiling. He thought about girls and
friends and fitting in. He thought about the way he looked (which he
didn't like) and about his clothes (which he didn't like). He was handsome
and sensitive, but full of adolescent misgivings. He came home from
school, went to his room, turned on his radio, buzzed out for an hour or
two, then went downstairs to watch TV. After dinner he watched more

TV. When he didn't come straight home from school, he smoked ciga-rettes with his friends in their family garage.

Matthew was invited to perform the First Mendelssohn Piano Concerto in Carnegie Hall with the New York Youth Symphony. The conductor of the orchestra knew both his father and teacher. Matthew was to be a soloist in a series of concerts that featured three teenagers as budding concert artists.

Matthew didn't think he was up to it. He knew the Mendelssohn, but the prospect of performing it in Carnegie Hall made that seem irrelevant. He had never performed with an orchestra. He adored the Mendelssohn, but that made the prospect of performing it more frightening than if he had cared less about it. He had never heard the piece with orchestra, except on the Serkin recording he had nearly worn out. The last time he had been to Carnegie hall he had heard one of Arthur Rubinstein's fare-well concerts. Matthew's teacher convinced him that despite all this, he could do it.

The concerto was on an all-Mendelssohn program. The Overture to *A Midsummer Night's Dream* was to open the program, and the "Italian Symphony" to close it. The concerto was just before intermission. During the overture, Matthew stood in the Carnegie Hall green room, his muscles tight and his hands freezing. He put them in his pockets, flattened them on the radiator and rubbed them together, but none of that helped. He undid the second and third buttons of his shirt and slid them in his armpits. That warmed them up, but then they started to get sweaty, and that was worse than cold. Matthew paced. His teacher, who appeared out of nowhere, gave him a hand massage that seemed to caress every muscle in his body, but didn't break the cold edge. It didn't make him feel that he would have the piano at his command.

The applause after the overture broke what little calm he had. A stage-hand came into the green room to say that it was time to go downstairs. Halfway down, Matthew ran into the conductor, who smiled and said something about tempos in the concerto. Matthew didn't absorb a word.

Matthew thought he played terribly despite a warm reception. He was nervous from start to finish. His hands had stayed sweaty, and he missed the runs he had worried about. He thought he had played radically under tempo, but when he listened to the tape, he realized that he had sped all the way through.

He decided to switch teachers. It was not just the trauma at Carnegie. Matthew had begun to doubt his teacher's musical ideas and was struggling with technique. He was entering competitions and losing them, listening to other pianists—wonderful players his own age—and realizing something was missing. He wished he had left his teacher earlier.

Matthew's mother called his teacher to say that Matthew would be leaving. The teacher said he was disappointed that Matthew hadn't told him himself. That, he said, would have been the manly thing to do.

Matthew went to his house to talk to him.

"I owe you a lot," Matthew said.

"You owe me nothing," his teacher said.

Matthew said he would be going to a teacher in the Juilliard Pre-College and mentioned the man's name.

"He's a good man," his teacher said, but Matthew got the feeling that he didn't know him.

Matthew was one of the oldest students in the Pre-College but much less fluent than most. The ten-year-olds sounded as if they had learned everything right the first time. Matthew felt like an oaf when he had to play after them. His technique was undergoing a radical transformation, so he sounded even clumsier than he had at his audition.

He had to make a decision about the future. His Pre-College teacher advised him to apply to the Upper School. His playing had improved considerably and he was thought of as a talented pianist with tremendous potential. Matthew didn't think he would stand out among the Upper School pianists, but he felt that he would have nothing to be ashamed of. He doubted that he could make a solo career—he doubted that he had the facility or the temperament—but he loved music more than anything in the world.

The Upper School admitted him, and he enrolled.

Matthew hated the Upper School. It was completely different from Pre-College. Maybe it was the steady diet of music. Maybe it was the difference in people. (Most of the Pre-College students Matthew knew had gone on to liberal arts colleges, not conservatories.) But he didn't just find his schoolmates narrow, he hated them. They intimidated him, pianistically and personally. He had never seen so many prima donnas. They did nothing but practice and talk about music. The pianists he met sat around the cafeteria and fourth-floor corridors for hours, eating junk food and smoking and wailing at one another. They complained about everyone and everything. Matthew didn't think he could trust any of them. He had always been quiet but had always had a niche. Now he was one of the herd, a solid pianist, but less good than even the average in the bunch.

Matthew was living in a two-room apartment on Fifty-seventh Street. He had spent his whole life at home with one or the other parent. Now he lived alone in the middle of the most unfriendly city in the world. He felt strange and stranded.

Matthew studied with the same man as Young Sun. He was not happy with him. He thought of him as an intelligent man, a spectacular pianist and a genuine artist, but inarticulate. Or simply unable to convey his ideas. Matthew was not developed enough just to watch and absorb. He went to his lessons and played. "Sounds good," his teacher always said, then sat down and played what Matthew had played. It always sounded like a different piece. His teacher touched the keys, and a creamy golden sound oozed out of the piano.

Matthew tried an experiment once. His teacher demonstrated something that sounded extra beautiful.

"Would it be all right," Matthew asked, "if I tried that on your piano?"

They switched pianos. Matthew sounded the way he always did, and the teacher sounded the way he always did. Matthew became more and more frustrated. He sat down in his practice room and didn't know where to start. So he stopped practicing. He kept coming to school, kept checking into a practice room, but then spent the day walking the fourth-floor corridors, seeking out friends. That is where he got to know Young Sun.

Matthew had not heard her play, but he had heard the rumors. Everyone said she was a fabulous pianist but in the next breath always said to watch out for her. A girl who had once been her best friend called her a witch. Matthew thought of her as evil, someone to avoid at all costs.

But he got to know her a little and decided she was not a witch, just the ultimate prima donna. She had opinions on everyone and everything. She talked nonstop about the pieces she played and the competitions she had won. With a little prodding—very little—she talked about the Philadelphia concert. She made no secret of her prowess.

And Matthew could see she was a stellar pianist. Her fingers, unlike his, were fast and clean, possibly the fastest and cleanest in the school. She had tiny little solid accurate fingers. She would play a Mozart sonata so cleanly it sounded almost silly. Her pianism gave her credibility. Matthew was young and impressionable. The fact that she had strong opinions made him think he should. So he adopted hers. They talked for hours, everywhere, about practicing and students, teachers and concert pianists. Matthew found Young Sun straightforward, unlike the other pianists at school. He never felt that he got honest answers from them. It was different with Young Sun. She knew the ropes and had nothing to hide.

One evening Young Sun told Matthew she was falling in love with him. Matthew didn't know what to make of the declaration. He had had a girlfriend in high school but nothing serious. And his friendship with Young Sun had not been tinged with romance. They had spent time together strictly as friends. He liked that. He had trouble with strong emotions.

He actually had once realized that he had romantic feelings for Young Sun, but he had suppressed them. He thought they might be just part of a passing fascination with Korean women. He knew, anyway, that Young Sun would be trouble in a relationship. She had a strong personality. She was flirtatious and wild. He was detached and reserved. Her charisma attracted him, but he knew that the qualities that attracted him could undo him.

The relationship began. Matthew tried to be careful. He had told himself he would never let his heart rule his head, but he felt himself slipping into something he could not control. It was like quicksand.

But at the same time he felt safe. His world narrowed in scope, and his focus intensified, as if a lens were being adjusted. Priorities were easy to order. Matthew didn't want to do anything but see Young Sun and practice. He felt the euphoria, the quiet intense high, that comes from feeling purposeful. He started to forget appointments. The phone calls he used to ache for became intrusions. He grew numb to things that had riled him, and smiled at people who had left him cold.

Matthew couldn't sleep one night in bed with Young Sun. He lay staring at a crack in the ceiling while his insides swirled around and seemed to swell until he felt as if he were going to burst. Young Sun had begun to doze off. Matthew rubbed her arm lightly and told her he was scared of what was happening. She opened her eyes a crack and turned toward him.

"Do you feel alone in the world?" he asked.

She asked what he meant.

He said that he had always felt alone in the world, but that he had a coping system. His feeling for her, he said, was starting to threaten it.

"I guess I always have my family," she said and drifted back to sleep.

Matthew looked over at her and felt pangs of love, then looked again and thought, Who is this person in my bed?

The room was cold when they woke up. "I'll only be three seconds," Young Sun said and got out of bed to turn on the heat. The moment she left, Matthew felt abandoned.

The relationship was something of a flirting game by day. Matthew liked Young Sun but was guarded in expressing his affection. She seemed most interested in him when he ignored her. He sometimes wondered whether she cared more about him or about the attention.

The relationship seemed solid nonetheless. They spent most of the time together talking about music. They gave each other an education. Young

Sun taught Matthew about the piano, and Matthew taught her about music literature. Young Sun's life had revolved exclusively around the piano. She knew almost no literature for any other instrument. Matthew, who had grown up listening to symphonies and chamber music and opera, couldn't believe how little she knew. She went to orchestra concerts, heard the piano concerto and left. So Matthew played records for her. They listened to chamber music and symphonies, but Young Sun liked the concertos the best, especially the Mendelssohn Violin Concerto. She constantly asked Matthew to put it on. "Jesus, don't you ever get sick of that piece?" he would ask. Young Sun didn't like singers, so they never listened to lieder or opera, but her introduction to other works was wonderful for both of them. Teaching them, Matthew got to love them all over again.

Young Sun didn't like to do things with Matthew outside the apartment or school. When they had plans to go to a movie, she always canceled at the last minute, saying she was tired or had to practice.

This upset Matthew, but he never showed it. He had some friends at the start of the relationship, but he kept them away from her, afraid she would usurp them. As he and Young Sun spent more and more time together he lost touch with them. He saw only Young Sun and her friends, a clique of Korean girls. Matthew found them ghastly, at least as a group. He thought they were insensitive, spoiled, selfish and ill-mannered. All of them were wealthy. Their fathers were film directors and doctors and high-ranking executives in big businesses, and the girls lived in luxurious high-rise apartments around Lincoln Center, dressed in designer clothes and owned expensive instruments and all the latest electronic gadgets. They gave their teachers gifts of silk and gold and exotic flowers from the Orient. Juilliard was a finishing school for some of them. They all played piano—and some played incredibly well—but their primary goal was to catch a husband. Their parents thought the Juilliard name would attract a successful Korean man. They were all fluent in English, but when Matthew was around, they spoke only Korean. Not to irk or exclude him, only because it was convenient. But what bothered him most was that when they were around, he felt himself on the fringe of Young Sun's life.

Matthew was afraid to let his insecurity show, afraid that Young Sun would lose respect for him. He became lost as a person. He became lost as a pianist, too. Young Sun's pianism undermined the mere shred of confidence he had in his. He watched her play, went back to his practice room, tried to imitate her and failed. She started to teach him on practice breaks. She barged into his room, and he said he was having trouble with a passage. "Oh, that's not so hard," she said, and sat down and tossed it off. Now she was not only his best friend and lover, she was his teacher, too. And competitor. They tried to pretend they weren't competitors, but the reality loomed over them. When Young Sun talked about pianists, Matthew thought, My God, what must she think of me? He never asked, but he imagined the worst. He eventually stopped playing in front of her.

He was, however, prepared to stay with her at any cost. The mere idea of separation was painful. He was prepared to sacrifice anything to prevent it, including his work and self-esteem.

Young Sun had always been ambivalent about Matthew. She didn't go out with other men, but she kept doors open. Making a commitment would have meant putting herself on the line. Besides, Matthew was not the kind of man she planned to marry. She wanted someone stronger than she—a better pianist or at least her $200,000-a-year doctor. Matthew sensed this. It made him push harder for her attention. He became so possessive he wouldn't let her out of his sight. When Young Sun went out with her friends, he tagged along. The girls often took Young Sun dancing. "Dancing" meant drinking and picking up guys. The girls preferred the evenings when Matthew stayed home. He did too, in a way. When he went, Young Sun acted as if she barely knew him. Matthew couldn't bear it, but keeping an eye on her had become an obsession.

The relationship became destructive all the way around. Young Sun stopped practicing. Neither she nor Matthew was the least bit productive. They spent weeks watching late-night movies and eating Doritos until four in the morning, then sleeping until two in the afternoon. Young Sun canceled lesson after lesson. Matthew went to his but faked his way through.

And Young Sun was drinking. She started with a beer at four in the afternoon and finished with a shot of brandy at four in the morning. When she and Matthew spent the night at home, she drank an entire bottle of wine. When they went out, she drank five Scotches. Drinking was an escape. Her parents were fighting, and she worried about her playing. She was obsessed with things she didn't talk about. She couldn't understand, for one thing, why she wasn't getting the breaks she got as a child.

Drinking also made her angry. When she was drunk, she lashed out at anything and everything. Matthew criticized her drinking, but did so cautiously. "You drink an awful lot, and I don't think it's good for you."

Young Sun got defensive. If he continued, there was a fight. Matthew was scared of fights, afraid that Young Sun would walk away forever.

Matthew went to his mother's house to throw a party for her fiftieth birthday. That night back in New York, Young Sun had a one-night stand with another pianist.

She confessed to Matthew the next night over double espressos at the Saloon. Matthew decided this was the perfect time to bail out.

"O.K. That's it," he said. "Good-bye."

It seemed easy. He lifted his bomber jacket off the back of his chair, feeling both sick and relieved. For two hours he circled the area between Lincoln Center and Seventy-second Street, West End Avenue and Central Park West. He kept tracing and retracing his steps. He felt liberated. He could walk away blamelessly now. If he were to have second thoughts, he would remember her affair and feel revolted all over again. He knew he would be all right. At two-fifteen in the morning he opened the door to his apartment. Young Sun was there.

He wanted to ask her what the hell she thought she was doing, but instead he was very nice to her. They talked about the affair. Matthew believed that for the first time ever Young Sun was genuinely sorry for something she had done. She cried. That was something she generally did only when she was drunk.

"Look, I forgive you," Matthew said. They talked until dawn, then went to sleep.

The next day they went to Central Park. Matthew felt what he thought was real love from her. It scared him, especially considering that hours earlier he had been prepared to put her behind him forever. And he knew that would have been the right thing to do. But he had never before seen the emotion she exhibited that day in the park.

It lasted only a day. The next morning, something reminded him of the affair, and they fell back into the old destructive groove. The first year of the relationship had been rocky, but there had been pleasant times. From then on, Young Sun's infidelity loomed over the relationship. They stopped listening to records. Young Sun spent more and more time with her parents, and Matthew felt best when he was alone. There was nothing left to the relationship but the comfort of something familiar.

The relationship lasted another year. When it finally ended, Matthew felt liberated. He decided he needed a clean slate: a new teacher, a new girlfriend and a new outlook.

George, Matthew's best friend, was throwing a party the week after Matthew and Young Sun broke up. He invited fifty people, mostly Juilliard pianists. Had the party been two weeks earlier, Young Sun would no doubt have been invited.

Young Sun didn't like being left off guest lists. She discovered, a week before the party, that she had not been invited.

Kurt and Soo Hee were on the guest list. But they were closer to Young Sun than to George and decided to spend the evening with her. Soo Hee and Kurt cooked an elaborate feast of *dak gui,* marinated and broiled at the dinner table, and *jat juk,* spiced with ginger sauce, and invited her sister-in-law and two girls who lived downstairs. The evening began at eight with a bottle of wine. Young Sun asked for Scotch and barely said a word after that, but in the middle of dinner she burst out crying.

They all went to Chipps Pub for after-dinner drinks. Young Sun grew more and more upset about George's party and decided to crash it. She asked who would go with her. Kurt raised a finger.

Young Sun arrived at the party all smiles. Matthew spotted her across the room. Here comes trouble, he thought. She cornered him and asked how he had been.

"Can we talk?" she asked.

Matthew was silent.

"I just want to talk, I'm really upset."

Young Sun was irrational when she was drunk. Matthew, who had been feeling good, didn't say anything.

"We can go upstairs," Young Sun said. Upstairs meant Matthew's apartment.

Matthew thought to himself, Matt, don't go upstairs. Then they went upstairs.

They talked. There was really nothing to say. Young Sun never came right out and said she wanted Matthew back, but she acted as if she did. Matthew knew she didn't really want him. She missed him, and her pride had been hurt.

George came upstairs to see if everything was all right.

"Get out of here," Young Sun said.

"You have no right to talk to me that way," he said. "This is Matthew's apartment, and I'm Matthew's friend. I'm staying unless *he* asks me to leave."

Matthew acted as the referee between the two. George protected Matthew. Matthew protected Young Sun. Young Sun protected her pride.

George said something nasty to Young Sun.

"You're just trying to steal Matthew away," she said. "I see what you're doing. You're trying to make him gay." She hit him. He hit her back. She went crashing into the piano.

Then she went crazy. With one broad sweep of her arm, she shoved all the music off the back of the piano. She whipped a decorative bugle off the wall and threw it at George. He grabbed her by the fists and held them together. She wriggled until she realized that she had been overpowered. Matthew suggested that George return to his party.

Matthew had seen Young Sun violent from alcohol before. He once had to carry her home from a party. She screamed "I hate you, I hate you" all the way down Broadway. A policeman in a marked car pulled up to the curb. Young Sun simmered down long enough to tell him everything was all right, but when he drove away, she started to scream again. A beat-up Chevy pulled over, and a man rolled down the window and yelled, "Leave that woman alone." People on the street were giving Matthew dirty looks. Young Sun screamed "I hate you" all the way home and until she fell asleep. The next morning she didn't remember any of the scene. When Matthew told her what had happened, she didn't seem sorry at all. She only half believed him anyway.

George left Matthew's apartment, but minutes later, Young Sun stormed into his. George had not recovered from the tussle upstairs when Young Sun appeared before him like a warrior ready for battle.

"Look," he said, lowering his voice so it was barely audible, "you're not invited. I really wish you would leave."

"I'm not leaving," Young Sun said. She grabbed an empty beer bottle from the table, bent her arm back and threw the bottle at George with all her might, aiming straight for his head. George ducked. The bottle hit the wall and broke. A hush fell over the crowd. Young Sun made a grand exit and returned to Matthew's.

The screaming upstairs started all over again.

The Young Sun incident put an end to festivities downstairs. Kurt went upstairs to collect her but, hearing the screaming, decided not to interfere and went home.

The scene went on all night. "What's the point of relationships," Young Sun howled over and over. "They just end in pain." At one point Matthew made a move for the door.

"Am I so terrible you won't even talk to me?" she asked.

"I don't want this anymore," Matthew said. "It's over."

Young Sun was hurt by Matthew's unwillingness to budge. "My God, you're so cold," she cried. "You don't even care."

Matthew sat on the sofa flicking his nail against the tip of a corkscrew.

"How could you not be upset by this?" She tried manipulating him every way possible. When all else failed, she went for the jugular. "If your parents died, you probably wouldn't be upset."

Matthew dropped the corkscrew and slapped her. He had never before hit anyone in his life.

They were screaming at the top of their lungs. Matthew enumerated all the hurtful things Young Sun had done in two years. His neighbor called the doorman to say that someone in the next apartment might be getting killed. The doorman came upstairs and knocked on the door. Matthew answered it. "Don't worry," he said, "everything is under control."

The battle went on until eight in the morning, when Young Sun passed out. Matthew called her sister to come pick her up. When the doorman buzzed up from the lobby to say she was there, Young Sun was sound asleep. Her sister and Matthew carried her down to the lobby. A doorman who had just come on for the morning shift took a look at them and ran to the street to hail a cab. One stopped, within seconds. The doorman offered Matthew directions to Roosevelt Hospital.

Young Sun's sister took her home and tucked her in bed. She pulled the goose-down comforter over her shoulders so that only her smudged face and knotted hair were visible.

Matthew had gone back upstairs. He tripped on the doormat on the way into his apartment, but he regained his footing and floated straight into the bedroom. He was asleep before his head even hit the pillow.

Matthew and Young Sun did not speak again until that day they met at the Japanese restaurant. Young Sun had often wanted to call him but resisted the temptation, finally convinced that obsessing over the relationship kept her from moving ahead. Matthew avoided Young Sun too, but in time began to think fondly about his life with her. For all the cuts and bruises to his heart, he had come to know himself.

10   GETTING OUT

A strange thing happens at commencement. All of a sudden, every-thing looks different. The competition, the forbidding teachers and the tiresome rehearsals are part of the past. But there is a new beast to contend with: the void. Hardly anyone is warned about the void.

Emerging from the Juilliard womb is difficult—artistically, pro-fessionally and personally.

Concerns don't really change. Days still revolve around practic-ing. But somehow, without the structure, everything feels different. There is no base. There is nothing to identify with. Existence had been easy to define, practicing easy to justify. When one was a Juilliard student, no further questions were asked. Now out in the cold world, one realizes what a rarefied atmosphere Juilliard is. The classmates who had been rivals seem like allies. No one out there speaks the old language. No one seems to care whether one is playing well or poorly. Or playing at all.

One thought that one had conquered the world by rising to the top at Juilliard. Now there is an entire new world to conquer, a world that cares more about money than music. Now one is one of thousands of musicians living between West Fifty-seventh and West 110th streets, trying to get by.

Hardly anyone ends up with a solo career. Some earn spots in orchestras, some in principal seats. Some teach, some free-lance and some do both. Some leave music entirely. Some reach the top and are disenchanted. Some drift into new careers and find contentment. But at least at first, there are questions. Nagging questions without clear answers. And while they nag, one sits and practices, counting on the roulette wheel eventually stopping at the right number.

Half the battle is perseverance. It's a hell of a fight existing on faith alone. Some say that if one can exist and be at all content as something other than a musician, one should. The musician who wants a solo career must make a new commitment once out in the real world. The rest of life will be ruled by excessive discipline. The commitment must be seen as something one has chosen. The musician who sees the commitment as a sacrifice will always be bitter.

The ominous words of an eminent impresario echo in the memory:

The worst thing you can do is to kid yourself that you're going to have a career when underneath you know you probably will not. . . . Don't play that game with yourself. . . . I do not respond to a tape, a photo, a bio or a letter from an artist. That sounds pretty mean, but I don't. I respond if a major teacher, a major conductor, or another major artist talks to me about a young artist. If no one is willing to speak on behalf of that artist after four years at Juilliard, why should I take my time away from the artists that I have? Somewhere in this process of your becoming a musician, there must be someone who believes in you well enough to recommend you to a major management. Somewhere along the line, the news gets out. There's a continual flow of information. Talent is not hidden. You can't hide a major talent.

Some see the broad picture and drop out. Some hang in there, remembering that Albrechtsberger once said about his student Beethoven, "He has learned nothing and will never do anything properly." Some give themselves deadlines before they drop out. Some hold out as long as the money does. If one is not fully committed to a solo career, the playing will show it.

One sits and practices and enters competitions and rents halls to play debuts to sparse crowds. One runs to the mailbox at noon every day, praying that between the circulars and the bills there is an offer of management or a letter of apology from the chairman of the last lost competition saying, "Please forgive us, there was a terrible miscalculation in scoring. . . ."

One tries to figure out how to crack the Catch-22's to breaking into the business. To win competitions, one must have experience playing concerts, but to play concerts, one must win competitions. To get a record contract, one must be famous, but to become famous, one must have cut a record. To solo with a major orchestra, one must have soloed with another.

One takes the subway uptown and glances at *The New York Times* the lady in the next seat is reading. Charging across the top of the page is a four-column headline announcing, "For Many, Music Careers Ask Too Much," and one looks down at the floor, sorry for the visual trespass.

One tries to figure out how to meet the rent on a Manhattan apartment. One refuses to sell books or wait on tables. One considers moving to another city but hesitates to leave New York. The sheep that climbs up the steep mountain must stay there. If he takes a step down, he will fall and break his neck.

One wonders what happened to the American Dream, the belief that if one works hard enough, one can have anything.

One tries to contend with the vicious cycle that undoes performance. One leaves school, and the chances to perform dwindle. The less one performs, the more nervous one gets. The more nervous one gets, the worse one plays. The worse one plays, the more competitions one loses. The more competitions one loses, the fewer concerts one gets. The busy performers get busier, and the dormant ones atrophy.

One wonders about the point of it all: whether there is anything left to do in performance, what one has to say that has not been said, and whether anyone would want to hear it anyway.

Artistically things are often rough at first. One must adjust to making decisions alone. But this is often a period of exploration and discovery. One can delight in fanciful flights that go unchecked. After having been force-fed from the start one can think for the first time about how to play the instrument. One discovers a voice and taps the literature bypassed for the stuff that was easy to put over.

One has time to explore life, too. Without constant lessons and deadlines, one can take a vacation from practicing, crack a 300-page spy thriller, try out new recipes, go to the San Gennaro festival or opening day at Shea Stadium. Some come to realize that this is necessary. It feeds art. Art can't be taught in a classroom or learned in a practice room. Art expresses how the world looks to the artist. Experience awakens the artist. One need not leave a room to experience life, but one must somehow connect with and respond to the world. The connected person sounds alive. The unconnected sounds dead.

Some come to realize, finally, that music does not begin and end with technical mastery. They come to understand why it doesn't matter that some people miss notes. They come to understand that they need to master the basics, but more than that they need to sit back and listen and say, God, this is really beautiful—it's really hitting me, really grabbing my heart.

The personal trials are perhaps the most difficult. Identity was bound up with life onstage. The link between the person and the performer—the constant high when one is performing—depresses when one is not performing. One had been a mass of promise. Now is the time to deliver. One musician avoids his family. They greet his brother, "How are you?" and him, "So . . . how's the career?" His father says, "Time to get out of the pool and into the ocean." Everyone wants to know the score: the number of concerts, the size of the audiences and the size of the fee.

Some are forced to think about why they play. The answer, for some, is clear. Music, for them, is like a religious calling. In others, there is an ambivalence. Some play because it's all they know, something they happened to be good at, something that put them on a treadmill of preordained steps. Some approach their instrument like athletes, as if they had a job to do, a game to win, an obstacle to overcome. Some play only for the attention. Some play because only when they play do they feel worthy of love. Some get the Heifetz Syndrome and quit: if they can't be Heifetz, they would rather not play. Some only want to be famous.

Things are hardest for the ex-child prodigy. The prodigy gives up childhood to master an instrument. Things get rolling, and the prodigy gives up adolescence. Then the dam breaks: the big life issues come crashing.

There was a prodigy at Juilliard with a dream career. He was plucked from the Pre-College and sent abroad to study. He returned to the United States for a debut with the New York Philharmonic, then enrolled in the Upper School. He had concerts all over the world. Before long he had performed with virtually every great orchestra and great conductor in every important city of the world. A recital he played at the White House was televised worldwide. His professional life accelerated to the point where he was tumbling, unable to catch his breath. But something was not right.

He was depressed and exhausted. His responsibility was overwhelming, especially for someone his age. His head was on the chopping block at every performance. The critics were always there, and the public was always demanding. I haven't lived, he said to himself. I don't know a lot of things. He became very bitter. I'm doing all this work, he thought, and for what? I'm sick of this. I'm going to cancel all my concerts. I don't care.

He sat at the piano and practiced, depressed. He didn't want to play the piano, but he was engaged to do concerts. So he practiced and performed, but the music was produced without any joy.

He cut himself off from everyone. His parents had just separated. That upset him, so he didn't talk to them. He was sick of his friends. They talked about nothing but their concerts and reviews.

All his senses went numb, as if someone had thrown the "off" switch.

He used to like to read. Now when he took books to bed with him, he never got past the second page. He tried going to the movies but always walked out in the middle. He didn't feel like eating. He cooked only to pass the time.

He slipped deeper and deeper down the spiral. He started to walk from midnight until four in the morning. Once he walked from Lincoln Center to Greenwich Village and back, then to Chinatown and back. Once he spent fifteen dollars to go into the Ritz nightclub and spent four hours standing against the wall watching a heavy-metal crowd scream the night away in a bacchanalian frenzy. He was living like a fugitive.

He felt sad and lonely, angry and frustrated. He had never been angry or depressed for more than minutes at a time. He felt as if he were losing his center.

His playing was note-perfect. Nothing was out of place. But it was boring. He wasn't saying anything. He was so afraid of making mistakes, he couldn't do anything memorable. He was so self-conscious, he was losing his confidence. And he was getting more and more clogged up. He was practicing but going nowhere. His playing got more and more pushed and tight and compressed.

There was something else. It was very hard for him to admit, but he said to himself, I've never been in love, really. The only thing I have ever really loved was my music. That's sick. There's something wrong with me.

There was nothing in his life but music, he realized. He clung to his music because he had nothing else. And the more he clung to it, the more he resented it. In his despair he was choking the music. He hit rock bottom.

Then everything turned around. He was playing a Mozart concerto on the other side of the world. He loves Mozart so much, he says, the feeling defies description. He loves Mozart as if Mozart were a living person. During the concert, he felt as if something—as if Mozart himself—were leading him by the hand. The force overcame him. He went with it, as if he were on automatic pilot. He had never felt anything like it. It was liberating.

He realized then that it was all worth it. He realized that the joy music gives him nothing else could. He could find joy in a person, but not the kind he finds in music.

It has been a clear road since then. He used to be terrified before concerts. Now he can't wait for them. He doesn't care what people think. He plays for himself and for the music. He used to sit onstage and say to himself, Oh my God, the hard part's coming. Now he says, Please let me do something to fill me, to make me feel good.

He talked to his manager about the difficult time. "You know," his manager said, "you probably never had your adolescence. You had all this adult responsibility and adolescent emotion rolled up in one package. You had so much responsibility, you couldn't let the emotions out."

He thinks he had to go through that period. He's very passionate. He seems mild-mannered, but he's volatile. He feels things very strongly.

He knows there will always be obstacles, but now, he says, he will never lose his pride or dignity or strength. Now he knows what he wants. He knows what he can and can't do. He knows what he can give. He knows who he is, and why he does what he does.

He decides to use a Juilliard practice room one day. He has not been a Juilliard student for years. He has not even been in the building. He remembers he needs special permission to use a practice room, but decides to sneak up. He has an audition at Avery Fisher Hall in two hours. He needs to warm up.

He walks past the guards. He is careful not to break his stride, not to smile too hard, not to look at them too long, not to betray that he is without an I.D. (At least he's in a suit.) They remember him. His is one of the faces that passed by for years, day in and day out. They lose track of time with all the faces they see come and go. They can't tell the people they saw two days ago from the people they saw two years ago. Or maybe they know and don't care.

He crowds into an elevator. The doors shut. He is cushioned between a twelve-year-old dancer, a crusty librarian, the cafeteria cashier and a fiberglass cello case covered with STP stickers. He stares straight ahead. He suspects he knows someone in there. The way things go, even if he knows only two people in a building with hundreds in it, he's going to run into them. That always happens when he's trying to avoid people.

He has been avoiding Juilliard. He has skipped recitals of friends he wanted to hear. He has agreed to meet old friends anywhere but at school. He asked the registrar to mail him his transcript, even though it took two weeks longer to get it that way. He has been avoiding Juilliard the way one might avoid an ex-lover one is trying to get over. He is coming to terms with his time there and his time out, getting a footing, a hold on things, regaining his equilibrium. There was a period when he thought he had done all that, but then he bumped into his teacher at the Carnegie Hall box office, and the old feelings flooded back. His breath fell short, his hands started to sweat, and his stomach started to tremble. It was as if the tape of that part of his life had been rewound and played on fast forward. But more time has passed now, time for the wounds to heal, for the euphoria to dissipate, for the anxiety to level out.

He gets a rush of nostalgia in the elevator, a sweet nostalgia. Juilliard seems different. The distances seem shorter. The white walls seem darker. The edges seem duller. The Byzantine structure with the empty walls and square corners and cold open spaces seems to caress him.

He gets off at the fourth floor. The gold carpet looks dirtier than it used to. The hallways are deader. Everything seems smaller. He winds around the labyrinth of corridors to the room he lived in for nearly one fifth of his life. The buzz from the fluorescent lights doesn't prick him under the skin the way it used to. The piano is at a slightly new angle. He laughs to himself over how much, despite this, the room feels exactly the way it always did.

He drops his music on the piano ledge and sits down. He takes off his watch and puts it on top of the pile of music. He has an hour and a half to limber up.

He loses track of time and place. Then he becomes vaguely aware of something like a moving target passing back and forth at the window in the door. He ignores it at first, but then it stops moving. He looks up. There is a face at the door. It is a girl visible only from the chin up. She blinks. The door clicks open.

"Excuse me," she says, "this is my room."

He looks at her and smiles. She backs off and leaves.

ABOUT THE AUTHOR

JUDITH KOGAN was educated at Harvard University, The Juilliard School and the Royal Academy of Music (London). She entered Juilliard when she was eight, left when she was eighteen and returned when she was twenty-three. She is a harpist and a lawyer. She lives in New York City.